Concussion

Jeanne Marie Laskas is the author of six previous non-fiction books, including *Hidden America,* her latest collection of stories, and she is a correspondent at *GQ*. Her writing has appeared in publications including *Esquire, Smithsonian,* the *Washington Post Magazine* and *Best American Magazine Writing*. She is professor and director of the Writing Program at the University of Pittsburgh and lives in Scenery Hill, Pennsylvania, with her husband and two children.

jeannemarielaskas.com
Facebook.com/JeanneMarieLaskas
@jmlaskas

BY JEANNE MARIE LASKAS

CONCUSSION

| | | | | | | | | | |

JEANNE MARIE LASKAS

VIKING
an imprint of
PENGUIN BOOKS

VIKING

UK | USA | Canada | Ireland | Australia
India | New Zealand | South Africa

Viking is part of the Penguin Random House group of companies
whose addresses can be found at global.penguinrandomhouse.com.

First published in the United States of America by Random House,
an imprint and division of Penguin Random House LLC, New York 2015
First published in the United Kingdom by Viking 2016

001

Grateful acknowledgement is made to Cambridge University Press for
permission to reprint an excerpt from 'The Aftermath of Boxing' by J. A. N.
Corsellis, C. J. Bruton and Dorothy Freeman-Browne from *Psychological
Medicine*, vol. 3, issue 3, August 1973, pp. 270–303, copyright ©
Cambridge University Press, 1973. Reprinted by permission.

Portions of this book have appeared, in different form, in *GQ*.

The motion picture *Concussion* is based on the *GQ* article 'Game Brain'
by Jeanne Marie Laskas, published September 2009.

Printed in Great Britain by Clays Ltd, St Ives plc

A CIP catalogue record for this book is available from the British Library

ISBN: 978-0-241-97591-6

www.greenpenguin.co.uk

For Alex

Onye ji onye n'ani ji onwe ya.
"He who will hold another down in the mud
must stay in the mud to keep him down."

—Igbo proverb (translation by Chinua Achebe,
in *The Education of a British-Protected Child*)

CONTENTS

CONCUSSION

CHAPTER 1

| | | | |

OBSCURITY

The prosecutor approaches the witness box. He's all in gray, beautifully tailored, sleek as a dolphin, cuff links, a half Windsor knot. One thing Bennet appreciates about the American legal system is that the attorneys always dress impeccably like this. The same cannot be said, by the way, about scientists. Half of why he couldn't survive academia was because of the sartorial slobbery. Shirttails hanging out, moccasins, saggy-ass jeans. It was too much.

"Good morning, Doctor."

"Good morning, sir."

"Doctor, would you please state your name for the members of the jury?"

"My name is Bennet Omalu, B-E-N-N-E-T, Omalu, O-M-A-L-U."

Already the jurors are exchanging glances. *What did he say?* His accent is thick. He needs to enunciate or something.

"Dr. Omalu, I'm going to ask you to speak into the microphone so all the members of the jury will be able to hear you. If you'll wait for just a moment, I'll give you a bottle of water."

He waits for the water. The whites of his eyes pop like flashbulbs. His face is round, a perfect circle, like a smiley-face button on a teenager's backpack. It might make him appear calmer than he is. Does he appear calm? *Thank you, thank you.* He tries to appear calm. He is almost never calm. He is a man who thinks in double exclamation points. *Excitable!!* Everyone tells him he looks much younger than his thirty-nine years. Maybe because he's short, he'll say. He's short because they didn't have much of anything to feed him during the war, he'll joke. It's not a joke, actually. His sisters think it's funny. Anyway, he likes it when people say he looks young. Also he likes to talk about himself. *I'm a Christian. I'm a humble man. I surrender to God's mercy and love.* There's an inwardness about him, but also a happy-go-lucky veneer of innocence.

He twists the cap off the bottle of water, sips.

Honestly, right now he wouldn't mind a cigarette. He hasn't smoked in years, hasn't even thought about it, but right now a cigarette might be a terrific help. Cigarettes and kola nuts were how he survived the stress of med school. The green nuts, he broke them with his thumbs, plucked the fleshy lobes, and chewed them like taffy. There is no quicker kick of caffeine than the one a man gets from kola nuts. His father and everyone in the village in Nigeria, they thought the nuts were holy. His father in his tall red hat, three feathers standing high as if touching the spirit world, saying the Ibo blessing: *"Ihe di mma onye n'achö, ö ga-afü ya."* *Whatever good he is looking for, he will see it.* The men washing fingers, peanut butter dip, prayers, elders in robes.

Bennet doesn't miss any of that business. Honestly, none of it. He never wanted anything to do with those tedious old-world village rituals. He would be a man of his time. In America. Everything back home in Nigeria was about busting loose from the pettiness, the corruption, the wicked tendencies of man.

Now he's in America, in 2008, stuck in a boiling hot courtroom in Pittsburgh, and it feels like everything is once again about busting loose from the pettiness, the corruption, and the wicked tendencies of man. The irony is not lost on him. *Thank you, God. I'm grateful you got me to America. I am truly grateful. But the irony is not lost on me.*

"Dr. Omalu," the lawyer says, "would you tell the members of the jury, please, how you are currently employed?"

"I'm the chief medical examiner of San Joaquin County in the central wine valley region of California," he says, turning then to the court reporter with that super-straight posture, typing madly. "S-A-N J-O-A-Q-U-I-N," he says.

"How long have you been the chief medical examiner in San Joaquin?"

"My official appointment started September 1, 2007."

"Can you tell us, please, where San Joaquin County is located, give us a sense of where it is on the map?"

"It's about one hour east of San Francisco and about forty-five minutes south of Sacramento, which is the capital of the state of California. It's located in the central wine valley. In San Joaquin. We produce the Zinfandel. Zinfandel red wine . . . Zinfandel grapes. You find wine in San Joaquin—"

Oh my God, shut up about the wine! What are you, the Chamber of Commerce? That was so stupid. He's nervous. He's so angry. He does not want to be here. He looks down, taps his feet together, reaches down to yank at one sock, then the other, wipes a speck of dust off his shiny new shoe.

He got these shoes for the trial. Black cap-toe oxfords, shiny as tar. He wanted them wider. He told the guy, he said, wider? The guy said no, they'll stretch. But they're not stretching. Tight, like a band across the cuneiform bones, the cuboid bone, the navicular bone. *Everything feels so tight, oh my gosh!* His collar. The span of pin-striped wool across his back. Everything should not feel so tight. He's testified in court hundreds of times; he's gotten guys off death row, for God's sake. A courtroom is not unfamiliar territory—and this courtroom specifically, in Pittsburgh, this is the one he knows best. This is where he used to live. This is where he made his mark. He needs to just calm himself down and remember he is here because he has to be, not because he wants to be. *Bennet, you are a child of God doing your imperfect best in an imperfect world.*

"Dr. Omalu," the prosecutor says, "how long have you been living in the United States, sir, either as a student or working as a professional?"

"I came to the United States in October 1994."

"Are you married, sir?"

"Yes."

"Do you have any children?"

"I have a five-month-old daughter."

"Is that your only child?"

"Yes, sir."

"In what country were you born, Doctor?"

"I was born in Nigeria, West Africa."

The prosecutor glances at his notes, as if planning to move on past the introductions. He has fat eyebrows. A turnip nose. The heat in the courtroom is cranked way too high, an old boiler system, so the windows are cracked and you can hear the February wind whistle.

The prosecutor is not done with the introductions. "Can you outline very briefly for the members of the jury," he says, "what your educational background was prior to coming to the United States?"

"I attended medical school in Nigeria," Bennet says. He explains how it works there, six years, then a clinical internship, then mandated paramilitary service—three years doctoring in a rural village in the mountains. "I was the only physician," he says, leaning into the microphone. "My primary responsibility was to stop people from dying."

He reaches inside his collar, pulls where it pinches. He toggles his tie. This is a full Windsor knot. Many American presidents throughout history wore a full Windsor knot. Bennet thinks Barack Obama should at least try it. But instead Obama goes for the relaxed four-in-hand knot, a much less commanding statement. Bennet keeps all his ties already tied, loosened, in his closet, ready for action. That is the secret to always having a perfect, presidential full Windsor knot.

"Dr. Omalu, correct me if I'm wrong, you're board certified in four separate areas of pathology, is that correct?"

"Yes, sir."

"Those are anatomic, clinical, forensic, and neuropathology."

"Yes, sir."

Dutifully, he explains how all that happened, coming to America, the research scholarship, the second medical degree at Columbia University.

Two medical degrees?

"Yes, sir." He chose forensic pathology as his specialty. "A specialist in death, why and how death occurs."

Becoming an expert in death would seem to be a counterintuitive move for a physician, a person committed to saving lives. He would need an entire afternoon to explain to the jury how he ended up doing autopsies for a living; none of this had been in his plan for his life. *None of this.*

"Just to round out the academic picture here," the prosecutor says, "you are also currently finishing up one other degree?"

Two more, actually, for a total of seven. "I have a master's in public health in epidemiology. I did that at the University of Pittsburgh. I'm also completing in May, thankfully, May of this year, a master's in business administration at Carnegie Mellon University, which I'm happy about completing. That is it."

"You are not going to get any more degrees?"

"No. My father said, Bennet, you should retire as a professional student when you turn forty, and I'm turning forty this year."

Heh. A little levity. He looks over at the jury—two rows of blank faces. Do they even understand him? He knows people sometimes have a hard time.

There is one person in the courtroom who understands him. The defendant, his former boss, Dr. Cyril Wecht. He's over there at the table, a ghost in Bennet's peripheral vision. Bennet hasn't even been able to look at Wecht. *That is so juvenile. Come on, Bennet, just look at him.*

He summons the courage, turns toward him, is disappointed to find that Wecht looks like a raisin. Tiny and shriveled. Sitting there with his head hanging low, dangling, like a grape shriveling off a vine. *It hurts. It hurts my heart to see him like this.* Cyril Wecht used to rule the courtroom. Like the pope walking in. And now look. In 2008, he is a seventy-six-year-old man facing a jury that could send him to prison for the rest of his life. It's like seeing your father go crazy and lose his bowels.

Wecht won't make eye contact, won't even look at Bennet. *That is so juvenile. Please, Dr. Wecht. I'm sorry, Dr. Wecht. You have to know I'm sorry.*

Bennet told the FBI no, a thousand times no, he would not testify against his former boss. He said please, no, please don't make me testify. And now he's here in this stupid witness box in a shiny new pair of cap-toe oxfords and a ready-made presidential full Windsor knot. *I'm sorry, Dr. Wecht. They said they would deport me, Dr. Wecht.*

In the autopsy business, Wecht was a rock star. Early in his career, Wecht keyed in to the fact that America's love for murder mysteries, especially real ones, could mean a bonanza for the guy with access to the dead body. He was Pittsburgh's medical examiner, but his private practice was where the action was in his forty years as a medical-legal and forensic pathology consultant. Wecht had performed tens of thousands of autopsies, testified in criminal cases throughout the United States and abroad. In 1972 he discovered that John F. Kennedy's brain was missing from the evidence at the National Archives, and that's what first put him on the national stage. He got placed on a nine-member forensic pathology panel reexamining the assassination of JFK. Everyone on the panel concurred with the Warren Commission and the single bullet theory—except Wecht. Kennedy was struck by two bullets, Wecht maintained, and would continue to maintain, to the delight of conspiracy theorists around the world. "Two shooters were involved!" He loved saying that, especially on TV. He became the media's go-to forensic pathologist, and his own kind of crime fighter. He busted the coroner responsible for Elvis Presley's autopsy. No, Elvis did not die of a heart attack, as the original report said; he died of a lethal drug cocktail, and Wecht exposed the cover-up. He got interested in Marilyn Monroe, raising suspicion that she was murdered. He inserted himself in virtually every famous case of his day: Sharon Tate and the Manson family, Brian Jones of the Rolling Stones, the Symbionese Liberation Army, the mystery behind Legionnaires' disease, the Scarsdale diet guru, the Branch Davidians, Vincent Foster, Laci Peterson, Anna Nicole Smith, O.J. (he did it, Wecht said, but not alone), and JonBenet Ramsey, who, he claimed, died at the hands of her father while engaged in a sex game.

To Bennet, a young forensic pathologist on the threshold of his career, Wecht embodied a particularly glamorous American dream, and that's who Bennet wanted to study with and that's who he wanted to work for and that's how he ended up coming to Pittsburgh.

Seven years he worked for Wecht. Seven transformative years. Wecht taught him things. How to stop being meek. How to project self-confidence like an American. How to be ruthless when it came to local politics. How to curse bombastically, slamming down the phone, *motherfucking cocksucking ass-kissing bastard*. That was simply incredible! Bennet would have had to stop and think like a kid reciting Homer to put a string of curse words together like that. Bennet copied Wecht like a kid copies a hero. He bought the same suits, followed Wecht to the finest tailor in town.

"You're a black guy," Wecht would tell him. "It's a lot to overcome. You have to give it that extra edge."

Wecht would talk frankly about race, prejudice, being a black guy, being a Jewish guy, or one of those gays. He was brash, arrogant, would throw a glass of water in your face if you didn't get the point. He started to involve Bennet in his private-practice work, a little at first, then more. He would slap a file on Bennet's desk, say, "Here, I need you to do this independent autopsy," and Bennet would do it, whenever Wecht demanded it. Bennet did not do those private autopsies on county time. *For the record, never on county time.* He would do those autopsies on Sundays, after church, after brunch with his wife, Prema, the two of them then heading off to some godforsaken morgue in some godforsaken Rust Belt town. Then Bennet would hand in the report and Wecht would put his own name on it, collect the substantial consulting fee, and then throw Bennet a few hundred bucks. Bennet did not complain. *For the record, I never complained.* He was building a career. He was paying his dues. They had a good gig going. Wecht got what he needed out of the arrangement, lots of cheap labor from Bennet, and Bennet got what he needed, too: the freedom to do his own private research. Wecht gave him room, the opportunity to follow scientific hunches—explore statistical patterns of suicide, study the impact of viruses on the brain. Bennet's mind was brimming with ideas for scientific investigation, and he loved not having to answer to any big university or government-grant-type windbag who would tell you yes or no, what to research. He had certain things he wanted to study and he couldn't stand having people looking over his shoulder. Wecht gave him room.

It's the individual that matters. That was probably the biggest thing Wecht taught Bennet. Wecht taught him lessons about the harsh reality of American individualism. "Save yourself. Promote yourself. It's all about *you.*" This is a paradigm shift Bennet has come to understand intellectually but even now struggles to internalize. Agreeing to testify against Wecht certainly feels like movement in that regard.

. . .

In the courtroom, the prosecutor wants gory details. This is for shock value. Bennet gets that.

"Now, I'd like you to describe for the members of the jury," he says, "a little bit about the autopsy process. By that I mean, from when the body is brought into the autopsy suite, who works on the body, what are their responsibilities, and how long does the process typically take?"

"An autopsy can take from sixty minutes to five hours," Bennet says, expressionless, like a soldier. "Depending on how complicated it is. The sixty minutes is for the straightforward drug case. An individual who is shot thirty times by the cops could take eight hours. So, um, it varies. An autopsy is essentially a systematic and comprehensive examination of a dead body from the head to the toe, using every tool of technology that is available to you to document findings, to identify findings, and to complete the forensic value of those findings."

Well, that was pretty succinct. He feels good about that. He does not feel good about anything else. Tight. Can't wiggle his damn toes. Wecht sitting there, hating him. Wecht's wife, Sigrid, not even here, not even able to watch this appalling act of betrayal. *I'm sorry, Mrs. Wecht. I had to do it.* If it's the truth, you have to tell it, even if it's painful, even if it means laying bare a guy who gave you everything.

"The body has three major cavities, the cavity of the head, the cavity of the chest, and the cavity of the abdomen," he continues. "We open up the cavities of the body, we examine. We examine each organ. We take each part of the body for microscopic examinations and for other specialized types of tissue analysis. We also take some blood, the eye fluid, bowel, do toxicology analysis for the presence of toxins and drugs. We take it to any dimension of science. We can take the tissue to very sophisticated analysis, but our objective is to devise a cause of death within a reasonable degree of certainty that can be supported with prevailing medical knowledge."

How many, the prosecutor wants to know. "Doctor, could you just give the jury some idea of how many autopsies you would do in a given time period?"

"The Allegheny County coroner's office was a remarkably busy office," Bennet says. "I did generally maybe three hundred, three hundred fifty, three hundred sixty, three hundred seventy. The last year before I left, I think I did four hundred seventy, some ridiculous number."

The jury stirs, everybody shifting weight as if on one collective pair of buttocks. It's unsettling to think about all those dead bodies. Bennet gets that.

"During the course of your forensic training, Dr. Omalu," the prosecutor asks, "did you develop an interest in matters that have to do with the brain?"

"Yes," Bennet says. "I realized that most deaths are actually caused by trauma to your brain, and I wanted to study the brain."

He looks over at Wecht again. Nothing.

It's largely because of Wecht's confidence in him that Bennet became a brain expert in the first place. The field of forensic neuropathology—the study of the brain to determine cause of death—was still in its infancy, and Bennet proved himself something of a savant in this area. Wecht recognized it, encouraged Bennet to pursue a fellowship at the University of Pittsburgh.

"I would examine brains once a week," Bennet tells the court. "Either Tuesday, Wednesday, Thursday, or Friday, but usually once a week, I would examine brains and sign out those brains. An example is, okay, Mike Webster, the NFL player who died? We suspected he may have an underlying brain disease. We saved his brain."

Bennet considers explaining to the court that Mike Webster was a famous Pittsburgh Steelers football player who played that game in the 1970s and 1980s and won many awards, including four large gold rings for U.S. football championships. But people in America, and especially in Pittsburgh, seem to have a handle on the basic biography and some will laugh at Bennet when he begins to offer it, so he has learned not to do it.

Bennet had no idea what a Steeler was until he encountered Mike Webster's body in the morgue in 2002. That was the beginning of a beautiful friendship, truthfully. Bennet grew to love Mike Webster. His spirit. *Like, his soul.* It is difficult for some Americans to understand that. He gets that. But meeting Mike Webster changed Bennet's life. Bennet made a discovery in Mike Webster's brain that would help people forgive Webster for turning into a madman the way he did—and would go on to rattle America in ways Bennet certainly never intended.

Bennet gives Wecht a lot of credit for making the discovery possible, for giving him permission to study Mike Webster's brain in the first place. That was when everything was going great, business as usual at the morgue. Three hundred, four hundred dead bodies a year moving through the place, Wecht and Bennet running around doing Wecht's private cases, Bennet studying brains. Then one cold Friday morning in 2005, FBI agents showed up at the coroner's office and started ripping through boxes, logbooks, hard drives. It had nothing to do with Bennet or his brains. It was the culmination of a decades-long political fight with local Republican Party leaders who wanted Wecht out of the coroner's office.

They had found a vulnerability and they pounced hard on it. Wecht was indicted on eighty-four federal counts, including mail fraud, wire fraud, and related offenses arising from his alleged use of government resources to benefit his private practice. Sending personal faxes, mileage vouchers, misusing office stationery. *Piddly shit!* Honestly, half the city says it's piddly shit and a waste of taxpayer money to pursue this. Let the old man go. But it's piddly shit that Wecht's political enemies, who are numerous, can hang him on, so they're going after him, depleting his life savings in legal fees and dangling the very real possibility that the famous Cyril Wecht could live out his last years in prison.

I can't believe I'm a part of this. It's like joining the villagers flogging your own father. I'm sorry, Dr. Wecht.

Seven years. Seven years Bennet worked for Wecht. Seven of the most productive years a scientist could ever dream of, and Bennet can't, at this moment, pinpoint how it all unraveled so completely. He can only say for sure that it did. *And I'm collateral damage.* He wonders if his former boss has any idea how Bennet's own life got tangled up and derailed in the wake of his sorry mess. No, Wecht has no idea. That's always been part of the problem. Bennet was run out of Pittsburgh, kicked into obscurity, kicked off to some grape field south of Sacramento—and his groundbreaking research was all but stolen from him. Now he's back to testify against his former boss, and he feels like a traitor, like the lowest of God's creatures, and so, yeah, he wants a cigarette, he wants to kick off these cap-toe oxfords and flee, run the hell out of there, go home to Prema.

If there's one reason why he chose to spend his life with dead people, it's captured here in this trial in Pittsburgh in 2008. Living people mess you up. Living people are messy.

Dead people are clean. There is no politics with dead people. With dead people what you see is what you get and you can keep looking and looking and get more, and once you look inside the brain you find the story is beautiful in the way all things infinite are beautiful. Holy. Every dead person is a controlled story, a distinct narrative revealing itself on the edge of a scalpel and through the lens of a microscope. It's honest. It's linear. It's all right there for you, solid, still, not a single moving part.

It became an escape, a place to run to. *Save yourself. Put yourself first. Run!* He does not fully understand *save yourself* or *put yourself first,* but he understands *run.* In Nigeria, there was no self to put first. In Nigeria, you were part of a unit. You didn't move without the unit. It would be like a spider leg crawling without the rest of the legs and the body attached. In Nigeria, the family, not the individual, was the unit that moved in relation to the rest of the world. Collective finances, collaborative meals, communal decisions behind walls that protected you. You stayed with your family inside the walls of the compound. A solid steel gate, tall concrete barricades, loops of barbed wire on top, until your family told you okay, everything is set, it is time to go.

CHAPTER 2

RUNNING

Bennet never stood up to Oba, his father, and never disobeyed him, and neither did his brothers or his sisters or his mother. To do so would be to spit on Oba's legendary history of survival, a kind of sacred family allegory. Bennet himself appeared as an angel in the story, and so for him, the pressure to believe and obey was particularly acute.

In Igbo, the name of his boyhood village in southern Nigeria, Enugwu-Ukwu, means "on top of a hill." The terrain was all up and down, round, low mountains glowing lime green in the hot sun, the earth a bright, dusty red. There were seven children in the Omalu family and Bennet was second from the youngest. All of the Omalu kids were smart, but Bennet and his baby sister, Mie-Mie, were said to be especially gifted. Bennet did not challenge the notion, but he kept his doubts private. Mie-Mie was a genius, unquestionably. But Bennet believed himself to be merely studious. *Let them think I'm a genius. I will work hard, and harder still, so they will think it!* Early on he figured out that if you got labeled "genius" you could get out of doing work around the house. You could open a book and furrow your brow as if processing important information and someone else would sweep the floor. Rake. Do the dishes. "Oh, Mommy, I have to study," he would say when she would assign him household tasks. She would relent, send him back to his books. "How are you ever going to make it in the world if you don't learn how to do chores?" she would say. "There will be machines," he'd say. "Where I am going to live there will be machines to do everything for me. Don't worry about it."

No one did. He became known as the kid who simply could not abide physical exertion. The other kids picked up the slack, especially Chizoba, the brother Bennet was closest to, just two years older. Chizoba was freakishly normal, Bennet thought, as they reached school age. Bennet would watch him outside the window playing in the dirt. He would watch him kick a soccer ball around the compound with his friends. Kick? A ball? Friends? Bennet had none of these things and none of these aspirations. He hated the outdoors. He could not be bothered with friends. He loved his mom and whenever he imagined God he pictured her square dark face.

As for Bennet's father, he was in and out, doing highly impressive father things. Government matters. Village chief matters. When he was home he would receive visitors in the *obu*, the reception room in which he alone was allowed to sit in the velvet chair and break open the kola nuts, the green ones, breaking them with his thumbs, plucking the fleshy lobes as he prayed the Igbo blessing: *"Ihe dï mma onye n'achö, ö ga-afü ya."*

He was said to be defender of the widow, voice of the underdog, protector of the fatherless and the orphan, helper of the helpless, and these matters occupied him. He was a learned man who expounded generously about the value of education coupled with a radical and absolute surrender to the love and mercy of God.

Because of his reputation in the village as a wise leader,

Bennet's father earned the Igbo title of Oba, or "ruler," and when villagers would come to the compound to partake of his wisdom he would greet them in his tall red hat adorned with three white feathers. This was the highest level of distinction. When you become an Oba, people no longer refer to you by your given name; they call you simply Oba. Bennet's oldest brother, Theodore, aspired to become an Oba one day, and so did Ikem, the middle son, and so did Chizoba. Bennet had no interest in that whatsoever. Much of the tribal mysticism associated with his Igbo ancestry was lost on him. So much silliness. But he would come to recognize that the culture he came from was distinct, the values particular, the violent history inescapable, and that these things were a part of him.

Oba's legendary history of survival began when he was orphaned at age three. Onyemalukwube, his surname, means "If you know, come forth and speak"; the shortened form is Omalu. He was born in 1923, not quite a decade after the country of Nigeria was formally established during Britain's imperial expansion into West Africa. Britain chose boundaries that made economic sense to Britain, not to the indigenous people. The oil-rich lands of the Niger River basin were some of the most densely populated of Africa, representing hundreds of distinct ethnic nationalities and countless cultural and religious traditions. The three most prominent groups were the Hausa in the north, the Yoruba in the southwest, and the Igbo in the southeast. None of these people ever agreed to get together and form one country.

In 1927, Oba's father drowned in the village river, and the suspicion that he had been murdered would haunt the Omalu family for generations. Oba's mother found another man to marry and she left Oba behind. A church elder took him in and put him to work as house help. Oba was smart so the church elder sent him to school. Education equaled freedom; Oba caught on to that equation early and put his teeth into it. He got a job as a trainee in a government office where they dealt with mining and engineering. He worked hard to impress his superiors, and because of his outstanding performance he was offered a scholarship to study engineering in England. He came back five years later with a job as a mining engineer for the Nigerian government—the orphan boy who made good.

Oba married Bennet's mother well after he had established his career. As teenagers, the two had been paired by villagers for an arranged marriage, but her father had rejected the union on the grounds that Oba was penniless. Now he was back, a civil servant, and she was unmarried and poor, a seamstress with no schooling. Charity as much as love drove him to her. Catholic doctrine demanded that you serve the meek and he felt the calling intensely. He took her in. He bought her clothes and gifts. In time he would search for his own mother, the woman who had abandoned him, and he took her in, too. He built a home just up the road from the house in Enugwu-Ukwu where he was born. He assigned his wife the role of taking care of his mom and he put a concrete barricade around the house to protect them, as many villagers were doing. He added rolls of silver barbed wire with razor-blade teeth on top of the barricade, and he would add rooms and more walls and buildings to the compound as his family grew. If there was talk of war back then it was still just a rumble.

Oba rose quickly in the ranks to become Nigeria's assistant director of mineral resources, and so the family enjoyed many privileges of the country's elites: cars, drivers, housing, cooks, butlers. They relocated around southern and eastern Nigeria according to Oba's postings, but their compound in the village would remain home base, the place to return to for holidays and vacations.

Eventually, Oba moved north, to the city of Jos. Political tensions were mounting in the region. It was the 1960s; the great wave of nationalism and demand for self-governance was sweeping across West Africa. Nigeria had declared independence from Britain. After a half century of trying to figure out how to coexist as one country, the Hausa, Yoruba, and Igbo tribes were now jostling for supremacy. The cultural and political differences between them were sharp. Christian missionaries and the Western education and culture that came with them had been excluded from the conservative Muslim north—the most underdeveloped region in all of Nigeria, with a literacy rate of just 2 percent by the time the British left.

The opposite had happened in the south. The Yoruba were the first to adopt Western forms of education, and they provided the country with its first Nigerian doctors, lawyers, and professionals. They remained mostly Islamic, with only a portion of the population converting to Christianity.

The Igbo went full-on Christian, full-on education, full-on Westernization. The Igbo people were always said to be freethinkers, with an individualistic ethic—completely at odds with their Muslim countrymen in the north. By the 1960s they had become the country's literate elite. They moved to other parts of Nigeria in search of opportunity, thousands of Igbo emigrating north, opening businesses and small companies. They thought of themselves as the engine of Nigeria's advancement onto the world stage—but northerners regarded them as a threat. The Hausa and some of the Yoruba derided the Igbo, called them the Jews of Africa. Economic and social modernization—the very goals of the Igbo—were considered sacrilegious and intolerable to the Hausa.

These tensions boiled, and then, in 1966, after a military coup led by the Igbo to take control of the government and a countercoup led by the Hausa and Yoruba to regain it, the lid blew.

The genocide against the Igbo began in the north when Oba was working in Jos. Tens of thousands of Christian Igbo were slaughtered by the Muslim Nigerian army, their bodies left disemboweled and savaged on roadsides.

An eyewitness quoted in the October 14, 1966, issue of *Time* magazine remembered his visit to the northern city of Kano this way:

> The Hausa troops turned the airport into a shambles . . . hauling Ibo passengers off the plane to be . . . shot. . . . The troops fanned out through downtown Kano, hunting down Ibos in bars, hotels. . . . They were soon joined by thousands of Hausa civilians . . . looting and burning Ibo homes. . . . All night long . . . the massacre went on. . . . Municipal garbage trucks were sent out to collect the dead.

More than a million Igbo fled south. They declared independence from the rest of Nigeria in 1967 and tried to carve out their own country in the south. They would call their new nation the Republic of Biafra, taking the name from the Bight of Biafra, the vast blue bay where the Niger opens like freedom to the Gulf of Guinea.

The Nigerian army would have none of the secession; the

resulting bloody civil war between the Nigerian army and the Igbo would rage on for more than two and a half years.

Oba was stuck hiding in Jos during the massacre of the Igbo in the north. Friends in his office, British engineers of no political allegiance to the north or the south, wrapped him in blankets and shoved him onto the floor of a truck. They hid him in basements and on train cars on a weeklong journey from Jos to Enugwu-Ukwu. The family back in the compound did not hear from him for more than a month, because communication had been cut to the south; they presumed him dead.

When he came staggering down the hill toward the compound, starving, emaciated, and filthy, the children and their mother ran in tears to greet him. They led him limping inside the gates.

Bennet wasn't born yet. Winny, his older sister, was six:

He came down this hill. It was more than a month. Everybody yelled like he'd come from the dead. Broken. Stories to tell. Horrifying stories. There was no time to plan. We have to run, he said. You only listened to the radio to know where the soldiers are. Or people tell you, they tell you, fifteen miles away, you start to run. Daddy! Mommy! Don't ask me questions, just go get this and that. One car. Luggage. We packed some clothes and then food and water. Just one car. Packed in the night. Where are we going? They say don't ask questions, just pray.

"We have to leave here," Oba said to his family. "We have to flee."

The soldiers were making their way south. On July 6, 1967, the federal government in the then capital city of Lagos had launched a full-scale invasion into Biafra. The Nigerian army came in tanks and bombarded the area with artillery. The air force sent bombers and the navy sent missiles and established a sea blockade that denied Biafra food and supplies. The strategy was to slaughter all the Igbo they could and starve the rest. They claimed rivers and roads and bridges, and the flow of food to Igboland stopped altogether.

Oba and his family loaded the car with yams and water and ran from town to town as the Nigerian army came closer.

We went thirty miles to my grandmother's town, but the soldiers were already there. Rationing food, parents yelling. We moved again. There was nowhere else to move to. We settled there in that town, Nnokwa, where we were for almost two years. Wartime. The teachers had left. We were going to some school, I don't know what it was or who paid. Food had changed. Now we're dependent on food supplies dropping from the sky. Egg yolk, corned beef, powdered milk from airplanes, but sometimes the aircraft dropped bombs, one, then the other, you had to tell the difference. You see them. They stick out their heads with their guns and then they bomb residential areas. That was horrible. You don't wear colorful dress. You don't wear colorful clothes. You learn where to run and hide. Horrible horrible. We were seeing these men. They come so low! You see them and they drop bombs.

The Igbo were vastly outnumbered and they had no army and they had few weapons and now they were starving—as many as five thousand people a day dying from starvation.

The world took notice, but not, at first, because of the genocide. Because of oil. By claiming an independent Biafra, the Igbo were also claiming the vast oil reserves pooled beneath the ground in the south of the country. British companies had claims on that oil. So the British helped the Nigerian army fight the Igbo; they sent more airplanes and guns, and then the Russians sent arms, and then the United States did—although the United States officially declared itself neutral. Israel, France, Portugal, Rhodesia, and South Africa helped Biafra.

The Nigerian-Biafran War became famous around the world because of what the Igbo did as their last resort and only fighting chance. Outgunned, outmaneuvered, facing starvation, they waged a public relations war. They sent photos of dying babies to international newspapers: pictures of starving children, their bellies distended and their faces covered with flies. This was something new. Forty percent of the casualties of World War I were civilians, fifty percent in World War II. But now here was a war of one hundred percent civilian casualties, an outright genocide with pictures to personalize it, and soon the world responded. The French charity Doctors Without Borders was created in response to Biafra's appeal. The Red Cross and churches around the world raised money for Biafran relief. American children took boxes distributed by UNICEF on collection drives sponsored by schools. "Trick or treat for UNICEF!" became a cry in suburban America, the images of the Biafra babies now a symbol of a humanitarian crisis to which citizens of the world would respond if individual governments would not. Joan Baez and Arlo Guthrie took up the cause, John Lennon gave back his Member of the Order of the British Empire medal to the Queen of England in symbolic support, Kurt Vonnegut wrote screeds, Martin Luther King Jr. gave speeches, as more and more planes flew over the Igbo people delivering dried milk and rice and blocks of dried fish. Food was the main issue. As many as two million Igbo lost their lives, fewer than ten percent of them killed by military gunfire. The rest starved to death.

And so it was in the midst of this that Bennet came. My daddy was gone for food. We were all waiting. We knew a baby was coming. Exciting. A baby! And we were all waiting for Daddy to come with our food. The air raid came about 2 P.M. These aircraft. So my father was coming out of the town building where they were distributing food, he was running and he fell. He was blown up, explosions everywhere, and while he was lying down there, he couldn't move, he didn't realize why he couldn't move. He looked up and saw his car—that car. That car was everything. Next thing he saw he was in hospital. Somebody rescued him and drove him in that car. My mom didn't believe.

Bennet was born in September 1968 in Nnokwa. One child among the seven million Igbo refugees boxed into the Biafran enclave.

Oba's body was filled with shrapnel and he was patched up in the same hospital where Bennet had just been born. The doctor who had delivered Bennet tended to Oba. His name was Ifeakandu, which means "life is the greatest gift of all." He brought the baby to Oba. "Ifeakandu," Oba said. "That will be his name." This middle name would memorialize Oba's miraculous survival from the air raids. Bennet was said to be the angel who bore the miracle. Bennet, meaning "blessed," would be the child's first name.

In its entirety, then, the newborn's full name carried a specific and ominous weight:

Blessed.

Life is the greatest gift of all.

If you know, come forth and speak.

Biafra surrendered in 1970. The food falling from the sky had only prolonged the inevitable. Oba was reabsorbed into the Nigerian Department of Mineral Resources but at a much lower rank; the family's privileged economic and social status was no longer. They came back to reclaim the compound in Enugwu-Ukwu, but it had been destroyed in the war, all their belongings gone. So they began rebuilding.

Nobody said "Biafra" anymore. Igbo graveyards were bulldozed by a Nigerian army that was trying to erase physical reminders of the war. The Bight of Biafra was renamed the Bight of Bonny. Biafra Light, the oil pumped from Igboland, got renamed Bonny Light.

When Bennet grew up they didn't mention Biafra in schools and they didn't teach the war. It was something that sat in your history, like the shrapnel still in Oba's body. Your people had been persecuted. It was a wound that was supposed to heal.

Bennet started school at age three instead of five like most kids. It had nothing to do with being smart. It was because of the anxiety that overtook him when his brother Chizoba started school.

All of the Omalu children were protected behind the gates of the compound after the war—they were not permitted to leave unless it was in a car and with an adult escort—but Bennet, with his delicate constitution and aversion to physical exertion, was especially pampered. At that time his big brother was his world. His mother was occupied with infant Mie-Mie, and the older siblings were big kids concerned with big-kid matters. Without Chizoba in the house, Bennet was overcome with sorrow. Inconsolable. So they packed him a lunch and sent him to school with Chizoba. And if they were surprised that a boy so much younger could keep up academically with his older peers, they explained it by declaring him a genius. In truth Bennet was simply desperate to be with his brother. If he made himself as smart as the older kids he could remain by Chizoba's side. Intelligence, he came to understand, was a matter of will.

The plan backfired when it was time to go to secondary school, the equivalent of high school in Nigeria, and Bennet earned entrance into the boarding school for super-smart kids, Federal Government College. That was special. That brought honor to the whole family. It would be a place for Bennet's mind to grow and soar.

But Chizoba didn't get into the smart-kid school. He was sent to the regular school across town.

So now Bennet was alone. Twelve years old, starting high school, living in a dorm with thirty strange, loud boys.

The first months did not go well. His mom came every other weekend with home-cooked yam porridge, ogbonu soup, and other delicacies for him, hoping to ease the transition. One Saturday, when she didn't come, Bennet paced in the bathroom like a prisoner. He panicked. He needed Chizoba. He needed his mom. There was a window overlooking the avocado trees and he plotted his escape. He rationalized his decision to bust loose by saying, hey, the cool kids are always sneaking out, hitching rides into town, smoking cigarettes, or doing other crazy things. He was sneaking out more as a lifesaving mission.

Still in his uniform shirt and tie, he climbed out the first-floor window, scooted out the school gates, and ran toward the main road. A car was approaching and so he dived at once into the culvert, the deep, dank gutter. It was horrifying and exhilarating all at the same time, a secret, forbidden adventure. He kept running and when he got to town he stopped to catch his breath and walked. He realized, in that moment, that he had never walked down a street by himself. Twelve years old and this was the first time.

Fear overcame him with a thunderous clap on his chest and up his spine. He was not allowed to do this. There must have been a reason he was not allowed to do this. Surely something bad was going to happen.

He began to sweat and he did not like the wet feeling. He began to pant, his chest heaving. He felt he was discovering the real world for the first time that day and he did not like it. There was . . . *trash*. It was disgusting. People were loud, yelling about the price of milk. There were cows curled up in the beds of pickup trucks, legs tied to horns, live cows curled up for sale and transport. The goats bleated vomit sounds and were smelly and people stepped in the excrement of those goats. People without shoes. *Where were their shoes?* In his family everyone wore shoes. Girls carrying plates of kola nuts on their heads came after him begging for money. Well, this was a horrible place! He ran, and he ran; he ran five miles home, and when he arrived at the gate his mother saw him and dropped her bag of onions. She scooped him up. "What is wrong? What happened? What have you *done*?"

He was dirty, sweating, crying about those horrible streets and all those strangers and one man picking his teeth. He sobbed in her arms about the horribleness of the real world. She stripped him naked and put him in the tub to scrub the filth of Nigeria off him. "I'm sorry, my baby boy. My precious baby boy."

. . .

"He can't take the real world," Bennet's mother said to Winny one day, recalling the events of Bennet's terrifying journey out on the streets alone. Two years had passed and studious Bennet seemed emotionally equipped for little beyond his life of books. "He is too fragile," his mom said to Winny. A pampered angel. What happens to the angel when he grows up?

"We will take care of him," Winny said. "We will find him a place where he will never know sorrow or ugliness." Winny was already in college when Bennet was off trying to survive secondary school. Like everyone else in the family, she adored her baby brother. "But right now we have to support him, Mommy. We have to go watch."

"I don't think I can," her mother said.

It was spring, Bennet was fourteen, and word had come back from the headmaster at school that he had joined the track team.

"Track," her mother said. "That is . . . *running*."

"I know, Mommy," Winny said.

"But why would he volunteer for something that involves perspiration? He hates sweat."

"I don't know," Winny said. The important thing was that today was his first track meet and they would need to go support him, she said.

They drove through town and worried together if Bennet had the constitution to do an athletic event. Perhaps the fresh air would make him keel over, they joked. They sat on the bleachers and popped open an umbrella to shield the sun. Bennet came out in his running shorts and Winny reached for her mother's hand as if to say, "Do not laugh." He was tiny compared to the other kids. Square, and short. Holding his hands on his hips, studying the posture of the tall boys and trying to assume it, kicking at the dirt like the tall boys.

They watched Bennet stretching his skinny chicken legs and prepared themselves for his humiliation. Why in the world was he running track? Perhaps this represented some newfound courage or maturity. They worked on optimism but mustered little. Bennet was running the 4 x 100-meter relay, and he was positioned to be the last runner on his team to pick up the baton and run with it to the finish line.

"Oh, Mommy—" Winny said.

"Oh, Winny—" her mom said, and she wrapped her arm around her.

The gun goes off. The ground beneath his thin track shoes is soft. It's kind of bouncy, he thinks. He would like sunglasses but it seems kids here don't wear sunglasses. He can see that his mom and his big sister Winny have come to watch. They probably think he actually wants to run track. They probably think this is a sign of something good.

The reason Bennet has decided to run track has nothing to do with running. Mainly he wants to look at Christy's thighs. He has discovered one good thing about school and it is Christy. He goes to bed each night thinking about her. He would like to speak to her someday. But that is a long way off. People who run track wear shorts and when he heard Christy saying she was going to run track he knew he would get to see her in shorts. He had been imagining her thighs for some time. The first time he saw them, firm, arching like palm trees, he felt so much excitement it was like a drug and he wanted more. After he runs this relay he will get to watch

Christy run, watch her thighs move through the air like missiles.

Four runners, four more waiting for the baton. It's kind of boring waiting. He has figured out what he wants to do with his life when he grows up and a lot of it has to do with Christy. He loves girls. He loves girls so much. Nobody prepared him for this feeling of loving girls and it has come on with such a wallop. What he wants to do with his life is talk to girls. Some day he will do it. He has not once spoken to a girl who isn't a relative. When he grows up he will talk to so many girls, girls in every city of the world. He will be an airline pilot and he will have girls in every city he flies into, and he will talk to them and hold them. He will buy them condominiums and they will wait for him in the condominiums, wait for him to fly in. Then he will fly to the next one. And then the next. It will be his own airplane and he will have to keep it running on time. He will treat the girls with respect and he will never be late and he will buy them presents.

The third runner has the baton and soon it will be Bennet's turn. His team is keeping up. Where is Christy? He can't see her in the crowd but she will be here, he knows it, as soon as he finishes running this race it will be her turn. He's thinking about speeding up the plane to get to Paris because he will not be a man who makes a girl in Paris wait. It will take a lot of determination. If he isn't on time he could lose the girl in Paris and then the girl in Rome and the girl in Dubai. He will send them flowers and jewelry but that won't be enough. He has to hurry, has to put his foot on the gas or whatever a pilot does to an airplane to make it go supersonic. His future depends on it and he will just have to do it.

The third runner on his team is approaching, his face tight

with resolve, mouth stretched and cheeks bouncing and eyes like coyote eyes. But then, with no warning, that boy trips. Down on the ground, a roll and then a scramble. Bennet can see his mother and Winny standing up as if saying, "Oh, no!" because now Bennet won't even get a chance with the baton and his team will lose. Right now losing is not an option. "Get up! Get up! Get up!" Bennet screams to the boy on the ground. And Bennet runs, runs back to the boy who fell, runs like a crazy child for the baton when it is clearly so hopeless and then he grabs it, and like fire turns toward the finish line and he knows what he has to do.

Doing what he has to do! He is violating some important international airspace law, and a few principles of physics probably. And he can go faster still. Rocket scientists will turn to their calculators to come up with new laws of orbital mechanics because of how fast he can go.

Winny has both her arms wrapped tight around her mom's waist as she watches Bennet run toward the finish line that day. *Oh, Bennet, run!* And it isn't that Bennet begins to sprint so fast, legs a blur of circles inside circles, running toward the finish faster, faster, from so far behind overtaking the other kids, one, then the next, then the next, in the most uncharacteristic burst of athleticism—that is not the most remarkable part. The most remarkable part is the sound coming out of Bennet's mouth, a guttural explosion, *agghghgh!* as he runs, *AGGHGHGH!* loud like a full-throttle fighter jet blasting over the hills of Enugu.

Impossibly, Bennet wins the race that day, despite the boy on his team who fell; Bennet grabbed that baton and carried it triumphantly over the finish line, and Winny and her mother flopped back on the bench with exhaustion and wonderment.

What was that noise coming out of him? Who *was* this boy?

After family brunch in the village compound on a warm Sunday when Bennet was fifteen, his father called him into the obu, the receiving room with the big velvet chair, to talk to him about what he would do with his life. His mother sat in the corner, stitching a hem.

"I will become an airline pilot and travel around the world," Bennet said. He was excited about the plan, had been dreaming about it all year.

Oba grinned, picked up a bottle of cognac, popped out the cork, and poured. "Oh, Bennet," he said. His voice was a deep baritone, and he was a very large, fleshy man; the overall effect was of a tuba. "My silly boy."

One thing about being the angel who represented everything good that ever happened to your family is you didn't have a lot of movement in terms of identity. That was pretty much already solidified the day you were born. From that point on, your main job was to fulfill expectations.

Bennet felt stupid for saying he wanted to be an airline pilot and he reached for the drawer on the long table and he opened it. He was relieved to see that his bottle caps were still there. The Fanta team, the Sprite team, the Ginger Ale team, and the Heineken team. Table soccer, his private game, just him and his bottle caps all those summers when Chizoba was out in the compound, playing real soccer with real people. Each team comprised ten players and a goalkeeper, and in the off-season they lived in paper boxes that fit neatly inside the drawer and kept everyone organized. The boxes doubled as goals. The thick caps of brandy were the coaches and the wine corks were refs. He used the caps of BIC pens to move the players. The balls were pellets of squished aluminum foil. He loved those teams. He loved that game. He built Ginger Ale a big trophy from the foils of cigarette packets—a bigger trophy than he ever built for Coke. Just because it was truly remarkable the way Ginger Ale pulled out that victory and he wanted to do something special for them.

He held Ginger Ale's trophy between his fingers and rolled it back and forth. He tried to think of a way to tell his dad the reason why he wanted to become an airline pilot, but just saying the words "airline pilot" out loud had already made the dream seem ridiculous. His father was not, anyway, interested in hearing what he had to say. He cast a long and dark shadow. If Oba sometimes behaved like a bully, if he drank too much, if he was sometimes mean to Bennet's mom, well, everyone forgave him. What he'd been through. All he'd been through! What he'd made of himself. What he'd done for everyone! He instilled God in his children, a backbone of Catholicism from which none of them would ever stray, and he instilled in them the value of education that was somehow light-years beyond most other kids in the village. The boys, the girls, everyone would get the best education money could buy and go as far as they wanted, even if it meant traveling abroad for school, which many of them did.

"So I should be an engineer?" Bennet said to his father that day. Perhaps he should choose his father's line of work? None of the others had done so. All of the Omalu children would go on to succeed mightily in their professions. Theodore, the oldest, studied industrial mathematics; he would become partner in a land reclamation company in Nigeria and live part-time in the United States. Winny, the second oldest, would become a nurse practitioner and live in London. Uche, the next, would become a physician and a professor of pediatrics in Nigeria and live part-time in the United States. Ikem studied economics and would go on to own a chemical marketing company in Nigeria. Chizoba studied marketing and would go on to own a farm. Mie-Mie, the baby, the genius, would become a lawyer, with a PhD in international energy law, and would become general counsel of a multinational petroleum company in Nigeria. All of them would marry and produce children, and that fact alone would translate to an even higher standing in the village for Oba.

Bennet hoped his father wouldn't say yes to engineering that Sunday after brunch, because he imagined it a very boring career. Certainly nothing compared to flying jumbo jets around the world and all that went with that life. Bennet's father poured himself another glass of cognac and Bennet sat on his hands and he tried to think about how to go another round on this pilot idea. Perhaps he could present an argument? No one in even his distant family had chosen such a career. Bennet had never been on a plane ride. He was not, now that he thought about it, even a tiny bit interested in aviation. That wasn't what the dream was about at all. If it was about fleeing Nigeria and not just about women in condos, he was not aware of it then. Flying away from this broken country: Coup after countercoup in the wake of a war no one dared talk about. A government so corrupt nothing worked. Water mysteriously shutting off. Electricity on one hour, then off the next. If you wanted to make sure the lights would stay on for a funeral or a wedding or some important occasion you had to bribe some shady government man who would make it happen. Random checkpoints on roads, soldiers demanding cash.

"It would be exciting to be an airline pilot," Bennet said.

"Why do you keep saying such foolish things?" his father said.

There was no way he could admit to his father all that the dream represented. He did not know how to talk to his father about these matters. He certainly did not know how to talk to him about girls and the thunder awakening inside him. He still had not had a girlfriend, still longed to be touched and to be held. He did talk to Christy one time when she dropped her pencil. He picked it up and handed it to her and said, "Here is your pencil."

"You will die in a plane crash," Bennet's mother added.

Bennet reached for the comfort of his bottle caps. Fanta and Ginger Ale and the trophy. Then he slammed the drawer shut. He was fifteen years old, too old for games.

Bennet's father reminded him of the Catholic doctrine that said life was about serving the Lord and the way you did that was by serving your fellow man. How would he choose to serve? "What matters is how much you make yourself an instrument of God's peace, love, and joy," he said. "And how much difference you have made in the lives of people around you."

"Yes, Daddy," Bennet said. "Of course, Daddy." He thought of what his father had done for people as an engineer, the erosion control and the paved roads and the efforts to restore postwar Enugwu-Ukwu. "Then I should become an engineer?" he said.

"Engineers work in dirt," his mother said. "My Bennet cannot handle dirt."

Bennet let out a sigh of relief; engineering sounded so dreadful. His father held the brandy to his lips and it seemed he had known the answer all along, and mostly at this point

Bennet just wanted to get it over with, to find out what his future held.

"The smartest boy in a family studies medicine," his father said, as if this were some sort of biblical law, which Bennet knew it was not. "You will become a doctor."

"*Ka anyï kpe ekpere,*" his father said. *Let us pray.*

CHAPTER 3

| | | | |

SPIRAL

*Theodore, my oldest brother, accompanied me to medical
school, since that was my first time ever stepping so far out
into the world on my own. It was September 1984 and I had
just turned sixteen years old. I was not prepared for what I
saw.*

The University of Nigeria's Enugu campus was fifty miles
and a lifetime away from the family compound in Enugwu-
Ukwu. Here was eastern Nigeria's fourth-largest city, nearly a
million people pushing and laughing, buses, traffic, sirens
blaring, power lines zigzagging the sky. During the war, Enugu
had been declared the capital of the short-lived Republic of
Biafra; for this reason the city was known as "the capital of
Igboland." Perhaps Bennet should have felt welcomed in a
community of people who shared his family's history. Here
was the generation of Biafra babies who hadn't starved, a
generation of refugees all grown up and preparing to take on
the world. Perhaps he should have felt comfortable.

He did not feel comfortable.

His brother Theodore was big, like Oba, and he had that
same deep, booming voice, and in those first few days Bennet
marched obediently in his shadow and paid attention. Theodore got Bennet's new life organized, textbooks, keys, a din-

ing card; he would bark orders at strangers, wave his hand, shout, "Go!" He threw money at people, handed out naira as if they were edicts. Just flashing those bills got you service. Theodore made urban life and manhood look so easy.

"You sure you understand everything?" Theodore said, after days of manhood lessons in Enugu. He was standing outside the dormitory building, and he had his luggage by his feet, and Bennet was holding a campus map.

"Thank you, yes," Bennet said. "Thank you for everything, Theodore." It was a hot morning and Bennet was wearing starched chino trousers and a starched white shirt, just like his secondary school uniform. Was this what a medical school student should wear? He had a feeling it wasn't. He felt short. It didn't help that he had a round face like a bowling ball. He looked like a ten-year-old boy and he knew it.

"Now you go make Daddy proud," Theodore said, handing Bennet a thick roll of naira for his own use, a starter pack, and patting him on the shoulder.

"Okay, Theodore. Okay, bye-bye." Bennet waved as the taxi scooped his brother up and slowly disappeared from view. "Bye-bye." He stuffed the money into his pocket. He looked at the campus map and took a few steps, then turned the map this way and that. A putter and a roar came from behind him, a motorcycle whizzing, nearly clipping him, and then another right behind. Girls on motorcycles, bare feet, bright skirts. They sounded like monsters growling, so loud and scary, this whole city, so loud and scary. Urban life, like manhood, was a confounding, impenetrable adventure. He was not ready. He was not even a tiny bit ready. He folded his map and went back into the dormitory and stayed there, locked himself away, locked away the real Bennet—whoever that was—and came out pretending.

· · ·

He was a boy on the inside, suffering, choking, and yet to the outside world he was a fun guy, quirky, happy-go-lucky. He made friends easily, went to soccer games and parties and church. He was the smiley-face kid with the super-neat attire and the cleanest lab coat—starched, everything starched. He was the neurotically organized guy with the spotless room who swayed and belted out Lionel Richie songs while he shaved. He was that guy with the strange cackle-laugh, a rhythmic *ack-ack-ack* that you might expect out of a cartoon hyena. When he made that noise he would hold his shoulders up, and sometimes actually slap his knee. *Ack-ack-ack!*

"Bennet is here!" people would say, at bars or coffee shops, hearing that distinctive sound. He had a certain charm, and women were drawn to him. But not in the way he wanted them to be drawn to him. He wanted so much more. He learned to cook to get women to like him. He bought fancy candleholders and candles and little twinkle lights to hang. He bought a white tablecloth made of linen and matching napkins. He practiced before he asked a woman over, practiced stewing the tomatoes and searing the steak and lighting the candles. Then he started asking women over, one by one. They would come because it was so adorable. A teenage kid in starched chinos staging candlelight dinners! Oh, Bennet, you are so adorable!

He didn't want to be adorable. He wanted to be a man with a woman on a date. He wanted to throw naira at people and bark orders. He found himself falling far short of these basic matters of adulthood and in his mind he called himself a failure, a loser, a pathetic excuse for a man.

Depression starts like a membrane, a shield you can't pierce, the internal world so vivid and nagging, the external world right *there,* right in front of you. He felt angry at the world for being so difficult to enter. He felt angry at manhood for eluding him. He did not want to be a doctor, he did not belong in this stupid town. He did not want to go to medical school, he wanted to be a pilot, *a beautiful girlfriend in each city with whom I could spend blissful nights in condominiums.* His dad had stolen his dream from him; he would never forgive him for that.

Adolescence is by definition a state of nonbelonging. You're supposed to be fearful. You're supposed to be angry at your parents. So maybe this would pass.

It did not pass.

The problem, he believed, was his dad, was Enugu, was Nigeria, was outside him. He was a sixteen-year-old boy growing angrier by the day.

I had led a very shielded and protected life. I was not prepared. I had a pristine sense of idealism in my naive and virginal mind.

In medical school he encountered political strife. That was a remarkably new concept. As a child growing up in postwar Nigeria, he understood the world in terms of good guys and bad guys. Persecuted people over here, and soldiers who had tried to kill them and starve them over there. You fit into one category or another.

But now he was in the real world and it turned out the situation was considerably more complicated. A military coup had just swept away the reelected president of Nigeria, ending civilian rule. The military was in power. Bennet saw classmates on the streets chanting in protest. The televisions in the med school cafeteria showed chaos and mobs fighting, and Bennet sat alone and watched and tried to understand the complexities and the nuances.

There was one emerging leader who seemed like the most obvious person to calm the chaos, to fix all of Nigeria's problems—and, by proxy, Bennet's own. Moshood Abiola—they called him M.K.O. Abiola. He was always on the TV in the cafeteria making speeches. He was a philanthropist and activist who had worked his way out of poverty, and his story symbolized the aspirations of so many downtrodden Nigerians. "On the face of every Nigerian today, there are bold expressions of despondency and disillusionment," Abiola said on the TV, with the smooth intensity that made you feel he was speaking just to you. "I know that together we can replace cynicism with confidence; we can replace disillusionment with optimism; we can replace apathy with mass involvement."

Yes! Bennet thought. *Yes! This is what Nigeria needs!* He was echoing his classmates. He was getting swept up in the rhetoric of a political party, the first one ever pitched to him, and he adopted it wholeheartedly.

"I want your support to banish the thinking that our beloved country cannot know real development in our lifetime. . . . Our people today are united by one cry, the cry for a new source of hope."

Yes!

It seemed so obvious. There was talk of Abiola rising up and becoming president one day. Bennet listened to the speeches and wondered why all of Nigeria didn't just stop with the chaos and start doing whatever this man said. Nigeria was a mess and here was a guy who said he could fix it, so why didn't everybody just hand over the reins to him? He did not understand the nuances. He had no patience for disagreement or argument. What he saw on TV and on the streets was a broken country and it exhausted him and fueled his depression.

I began to notice deficiencies in the society I grew up in. My youthful idealism was strongly inconsistent with what I was observing. People accepted the status quo and somewhat embraced and encouraged mediocrity as a way of life. It really got me very upset and impatient. I began to think that I did not belong to this society, with these people, with this system. I became more unsettled and angry.

You could flip the channels on the cafeteria TV, and when Bennet did that he saw worlds that were so much calmer, cleaner, happier. Satellite television was new to Nigeria, and the channels were windows into other cultures, places he had read about in books, but now here they were live, far more enticing worlds than the mishmash streets of Enugu, or the mobs fighting in Abuja on the Nigerian news.

It was the Reagan era, and on the TV, Bennet saw that life in America was beautiful. Life in America was about dancing in cosmopolitan nightclubs, playing high-tech videogames, and wearing fashionable clothing with shoulder pads. The streets in America were paved and manicured. Reagan spoke eloquently and exuded a clean charm. In Brat Pack movies Bennet saw that kids his same age were capable of achieving perfection and happiness. Nothing like that was happening in Nigeria. Also from America came MTV. Bennet watched Michael Jackson singing "Thriller" and Whitney Houston singing "Saving All My Love for You," and he became mesmerized by their performances. Every note: perfect. Every movement: perfect. Every outfit and every hair on their heads: perfect.

Why couldn't people in Nigeria be perfect like Michael Jackson and Whitney Houston?

Watching those videos, I had an awakening intuition. I thought I should strive to be perfect in whatever I do. If every person in my country would be perfect in whatever they did, one person at a time, in whatever calling, my society and my country would be like the USA. In that moment it seemed like a good and viable plan. I was not sophisticated in my thinking. My mind was a child's mind.

Later that night after watching the music videos, while lying in bed, I realized that most other people in my country were not thinking like I did. Very many people did not strive for perfection. This was one more reason to become angry at the world around me. The lackadaisical way we led our lives. Especially the government, the filthy corruption that permeated every fabric of our society, from the housekeeper to the chancellor of the university.

Extreme corruption steals our dignity from us as human beings and degrades us to the level of animals, and not the children of God that we rightfully are.

Around the world, young men from oppressed societies see rich, shiny America on TV and grow angry and become easily seduced by fellow angry men. They stew and lash out. What saved Bennet from lashing out was an insight, the stark, frank realization that his problem was only incidentally Nigeria, his dad, Enugu, women. His problem started from the inside, not the outside. Depression is like a virus festering in your mind, and the discovery of it can cripple before it cures.

By the time I was eighteen, in my third year of medical school, I could not wake up in the mornings. I just wanted to be left alone in my dark room. One Sunday after mass I went and had lunch in the cafeteria, then walked back to my room. I just could not do anything. I grabbed my medical biochemistry book to go to a reading room somewhere, and while I was walking up the hill I realized that I simply did not have any energy to walk. I stopped and sat on a rock by the roadside and just gazed into the air. I was extremely tired. I just could not move on. I spent hours sitting on this rock. While sitting on this rock, I decided to go to my sister Uche and tell her about the insight I was having. Something was wrong inside me, very very wrong.

Uche had attended the same medical school as Bennet; she was now doing her residency at the Enugu university hospital and she had an apartment across town.

Bennet went to her and told her what was happening to him. He felt so terrible for bothering her. He thought he saw embarrassment on her face. In Nigeria, in those days, people did not acknowledge psychiatric illness, or any such disgraceful matters. And now here was her little brother suffering from something terrible in his head.

Uche did not judge him. She listened and showed compassion and love. She scooped Bennet up, found him a doctor. The doctor diagnosed him with developmental crisis in an adolescent and prescribed group therapy. Bennet went to a few sessions. The people sat in circles and the doctor instructed them to breathe and stretch. A guy next to him was unshaven and muttering, a girl across the room was rocking and weeping. These people scared him and he felt he did not belong and he did not go back. He decided to run away instead. He hopped on a bus, went to an uncle's house, then another relative's, and then another's. He told them, "Hello!" and, "Hi! I'm on vacation!" and he kept running.

Uche called her big sister, Winny, at her home in Lagos. "Bennet is broken," she said. "I took him to a doctor. His mind is broken. And now I can't find him."

"He's here!" Winny said. "He's standing here in my yard watching the sky."

"He's *there*?"

"He told me he's on vacation," Winny said.

"There is no vacation," Uche said.

"He's outside looking into the sky."

Winny lived near the Murtala Muhammed International Airport in Lagos, and her backyard was as close as he could get to the airplanes. He liked to watch them at night because those were the planes headed overseas. If only he could be on one of those airplanes. He no longer wanted to fly them. He wanted to be in them. He wanted them to carry him away, to America.

Winny and Uche wondered together what was the problem with the Omalu men. Theodore had started carousing like a teenager, would fall off the map for days. Ikem was getting into serious mischief. Chizoba had dropped out of school. And now Bennet, the angel representing hope, resurrection, and new life—he had perhaps the hardest distance to fall, and he had fallen with a thud.

Winny watched her broken baby brother standing there staring at airplanes, and she sought counsel from Uche and their youngest sister, Mie-Mie, and together the sisters hatched plans to save the Omalu men, because that's what the Omalu women did.

Uche yanked Bennet back to Enugu. She called in favors, so many favors. She knew some of his professors and explained his absences. She arranged for make-up tests, allowances, extra-credit assignments. Bennet imagined himself a zombie doing what she said to do to get through medical school. There would be freedom on the other side of medical school, she said. He could use his degree as a ticket to leave Nigeria, secure a fellowship or scholarship overseas. He should use whatever he could to survive, she said. Like the way he figured out a way to get out of household chores. Like the way he powered through and won the relay race in high school. Use your charm, use the gifts you don't even know you have, use what you can and get through. He was too depressed to argue. He was too depressed to attend class; he could not get out of bed; he could not bear the light of day. He reached out to a friend who signed the attendance sheets, another friend who would give him notes; he devised a system of friends and favors and he studied through the night while they slept and he passed the tests.

I became a physician in 1990 at twenty-one years old. Instead of rejoicing and partying, I went back to Uche's house all alone away from everyone. I sat down and wept. Diseases of the mind are difficult to heal.

He had to move north, to Plateau State, to fulfill his duty for paramilitary service. Tin mining was the economic driver of the region known for its dramatic scenery: the plateau went on for hundreds of miles, a craggy flat-topped mountain range of red and golden brown granite. The mines had drawn people from all over Nigeria, so the region was a melting pot of Hausa and Yoruba and Igbo. Despite that history, or maybe because of it, it was a hotbed of violent clashes between the Christian and Muslim populations.

Bennet's job as the village doctor was to stop people from dying. He couldn't stop all the people from dying. The futile urgency of that mission, day after day, made his psychological problems seem petty and indulgent. That turned out to be the opposite of helpful; hating yourself for having stupid problems is a surefire way of exacerbating them. He became acquainted with all sorts of suffering, all kinds of trauma, infections and amputations, strokes and heart attacks, but what he couldn't shake were the suicides. He saw suicide victims, guys his age, old guys, young guys, and he would look at their ash-gray bodies, their faces frozen in that same perpetual expressionless gaze, and each time he would think: Why? Why did this person choose to end his life, but he had not? What was the difference between him and them? It was a question that would challenge him for the rest of his life.

Death, death, and more death. I saw so much death. I attended to terminally ill patients and patients who were dying from all types of trauma. I realized that there were different categories of death. There are those who die peacefully, having fully embraced death. There are those who die with so much trepidation and fear, actually fighting death and wanting to stop it, and there are those who die with so much sadness and melancholy. I promised myself that I will die peacefully, and I needed to figure out what would make me die at peace.

Political strife was now nothing so new or tantalizing; it was the air you learned to breathe in the north, the thick, horrible air. In 1993 Bennet's political hero, the leader he still believed in, M.K.O. Abiola, ran for president. He was now a man of enormous wealth, and yet a man of the people, and had proved himself in word and deed. His philanthropy resulted in the construction of more than fifty schools, more than a hundred mosques and churches, libraries, water projects, bookstores—development all over Nigeria, across the multifarious ethnic and religious divides.

Abiola represented hope for Bennet and so many Nigerians, and when election day came, people stood in lines for hours to vote.

He won by overwhelming margins, an unprecedented feat for a leader to emerge from the south. Northern Muslims had dominated Nigeria's political landscape ever since the British left in 1960. Abiola was a southern Muslim. The fact that he was able to secure a national mandate freely and fairly was the miracle people needed. He won in the nation's capital, Abuja, at military polling stations, and in two thirds of Nigerian states. It was declared Nigeria's freest and fairest presidential election by people around the world.

But in the end no official winner was declared.

The miracle was aborted. Nigeria's military rulers refused to accept Abiola's victory.

The corrupt junta who were ruling us then, who had come to power through a military coup many years prior, annulled the election because their candidate did not win. Annulled it! And the reason they gave was "for the interest of the country."

Riots erupted in the streets and lasted for two days, tens of thousands of people screaming, clubbing police officers, stoning them, looting stores, overturning buses and cars and setting fires.

In June 1994, Abiola was arrested for treason and thrown in prison—behind bars in solitary confinement with a Bible, a Koran, and fourteen guards as companions.

People around the world called for his release. Pope John Paul II and Archbishop Desmond Tutu lobbied unsuccessfully. The pope came to Nigeria for three days, urging leaders to build a new reality by respecting human rights. "Respect for every human person, for his dignity and rights, must ever be the inspiration behind your efforts to increase democracy and strengthen the social fabric of your country," he said, his voice rumbling through speakers like thunder over the gathering of more than ten thousand Catholic worshippers in Abuja. He called for the release of sixty political prisoners, including Abiola—he said, *Let him be free!* And the people in the streets hollered and cheered at those words, howled in solidarity until the police came to silence them, brandishing whips made of electrical wire, flailing the people, saying, *Get back, damn you, get back!*

For Bennet, the mounting political tension combined with his deepening depression was a pressure cooker. He began searching for scholarship opportunities in the United States. It hardly mattered what subject; he began searching and applying.

I had to leave. I had to leave as soon as I could, otherwise I may end up badly, either committing suicide or getting swept up in a violent struggle against the government. And guess what, I would leave. I would come to the USA. The land of perfection and excellence. A land where mankind is at its best. The land of milk and honey.

I assumed that the moment I arrived in the United States, my mental disease would be cured.

CHAPTER 4

AMERICA

Oba granted permission for Bennet to travel to America; as soon as he gave his blessing, that was the signal for the rest of the family to open the coffers. Uche and her husband, Sam, donated six thousand dollars to the cause. Winny and her husband, Chuma, gave two thousand, and an uncle gave another thousand. That was the Omalu system: collective giving based on what you had to offer and whose life transition happened to be teed up, and this was Bennet's turn.

Chizoba helped by counseling Bennet on matters of sex. This was an important life skill, he said. *So I asked Chizoba, I said, can I borrow your apartment to have sex in?* Bennet hired a prostitute and brought her there. She was small and delicate, and Bennet looked in her eyes and saw they were vacant as a goat's. No one home. A lost soul. Bennet feared her, and pitied her, and he called Chizoba, said, "Help! I don't know what to do!" Chizoba came home and rescued him, and took her away. Later, Chizoba called a neighbor, a friendly woman in her twenties. "Do you want to learn?" she said to Bennet, slipping off her dress. And Bennet said, "Yes," and so she showed him.

The scholarship Bennet received was in epidemiology at the University of Washington in Seattle. He had little interest in epidemiology and had never heard of Seattle. His medical degree earned him the scholarship, the scholarship triggered a J-1 visa, and he would figure out the rest when he got there.

The night before the flight, in October 1994, Ikem and Uche came to Winny's house in Lagos to pray over Bennet. Ikem had abandoned his troublemaker past and had turned to preaching, and he wanted to lay hands on his brother. He called upon the Holy Spirit to accompany Bennet to the United States, to guide him and protect him, and Winny and Uche were in the prayer circle leaning their heads back toward the sky, and tears came tumbling down Winny's cheeks. Bennet's own prayer was not for help but for thanks and also to discharge God of his duties. He told God he didn't need him anymore because now he was going to America, God's own country, where there would no longer be pain.

"You can go help someone else now, God," he said in his prayer-mind, as if God were Jiminy Cricket and he were Pinocchio and now he was not just a real boy, but a man.

In the morning they drove in silence to the airport and Bennet watched the clog of a stagnant Nigeria outside his window, motionless women selling peanuts, boys with nowhere to go splashing in the muddy puddles of yesterday's rain. He tried to summon feelings of nostalgia but found none. He felt: flat. He felt: nothing. Ikem was driving and cursing the traffic as the car inched along, and Winny couldn't take it anymore, so she pushed open the door with her shoulder and stepped out into the street. "Hey!" she hollered, at oncoming traffic, hailing a motorbike taxi. "Go!" she said to Bennet, commanding him to get in. "Turn around!" she said to the driver, and in one swift motion she grabbed Bennet's suitcase, climbed into the open-air taxi, and hoisted that suitcase on top of her head.

· · ·

It was funny to think about all that, in 1999, five years after moving to America, reviewing all of this in his mind. When you drive you have a chance to review things in your mind. When he left Nigeria, things back home had gone from bad to worse.

Abiola had languished for four years in prison, refusing to surrender his claim that he was the lawful president of Nigeria. During that time his wife was shot dead by an unknown gunman on the street. On July 7, 1998, the day Abiola was finally due to be released, he died in his prison cell. The official autopsy said it was a heart attack. Eyewitnesses said he had been beaten to death.

More riots broke out, a nation exploding again and again in rage.

Bennet tried to muster heartache for his country, but he found himself unable to feel it. He was numb to it.

That was all behind him now. That was no longer part of his life or his concern. Now, in July 1999, he was five thousand miles away, on the Pennsylvania Turnpike, where the air smelled sweet and strongly of cows and the landscape was emerald green and smooth. The Pennsylvania Turnpike was supposed to be the crappiest highway in America and that part puzzled him. *What more do you want?* The road was solid and they had signs to show you where to go and they even had lights above so you could see at night. He was headed west in an Avis rental car and driving was *oh my gosh such fun!*

He never drove anywhere in Nigeria. That was always Theodore or Ikem's job. Everybody said it was too dangerous, too complicated for Bennet, and so on road trips he was always the guy sitting in the back, reading. A Nigerian police officer would be up front, holding his rifle, so they could get through the checkpoints without paying. The checkpoints could be anywhere the police felt like putting them and they slowed you down, so on a trip of any distance, one of the brothers rented the cop for the day to sit up front and look menacing.

No checkpoints here in America! Remarkable. And you could just walk up to a counter and pay for a car and take it wherever you wanted to go. These were some of the wonderful things Bennet had not anticipated about life in America. He appreciated the absence of garbage on roadsides. He appreciated the fact that shopkeepers didn't post DO NOT URINATE HERE signs everywhere; people in America seemed to know intuitively not to pee in public.

Also, in America everyone stayed on his or her side of the road. That was a noteworthy feature right there. The people going west stayed in the westbound lane and the people going east stayed in the eastbound lane. *That is so organized!* In Nigeria, with the way the roads were, sometimes flooded, sometimes just . . . missing, cars and trucks moved over to whichever surface was better and there were many head-on collisions. In Nigeria coming and going anywhere was perilous and chaotic and filled you with anxiety. But here, at least on the Pennsylvania Turnpike, it was so calm he could fall asleep.

He thought about Winny with his suitcase on her head riding that motorbike taxi on the way to the Lagos airport. Nobody here in America carried anything on their head. That seemed like a shame, frankly. *It frees up your hands!* In Nigeria that was so normal. But from that point forward, Winny with that suitcase on her head weaving through traffic, nothing would ever be normal.

On the airplane to America, Bennet could not figure out how to use the seat belt and he was too embarrassed to ask for help. When the airplane took off he was afraid to look outside because he could feel the height inside his pressure-filled head and he was so glad at that moment that he was not the guy flying the plane. He was headed to Seattle but had a layover in LAX and when he got there he wanted to use the toilet. He couldn't find any toilets anywhere so he became frantic and held his crotch and hopped. A woman pushing a cleaning cart showed him to the restroom. He did not know the term "restroom" and to this day can't make sense of it. The other thing that happened in LAX was that he saw two men kissing passionately, his first time ever seeing something like that. That same day he saw a woman with legs so smooth and glistening, *oh my gosh,* he had never seen such lovely legs. How could a human being's legs be so smooth and lovely? In the coming weeks, on the campus in Seattle, he began to notice many women had such beautiful legs.

In Seattle he made a friend in the hospital, a guy studying oceanography who had come from Nigeria a year earlier and already had so much American sophistication. His name was Jimmy. He explained the American version of manhood. He explained dating. In America, he said, you didn't have to worry about asking girls out because plenty of girls just came right after you. In America a woman could even initiate sex with you at a party or nightclub, take you to her car, and do it right there. *I had never heard of anything like that in my entire life!*

Also in Seattle he met Edith, an Igbo woman who had been in America for many years. She was a nurse, twelve years older, and he could tell she felt sorry for him the way you do for a lost pet. She had a car. She picked him up, showed

him around town, and took him to her apartment. She cooked
for him and asked him to spend the night and his heart flew
and tumbled into a happiness spasm. They were sitting on the
couch and her legs, oh my gosh, they looked so smooth and
shiny and beautiful—how did a Nigerian girl get those beautiful American legs? He closed his eyes and reached as if over a
century and across the globe to touch her thigh.

"Wait, what?" he said.

That startled her. "What's wrong?"

"*What is this?*" he said.

"My leg—" she said.

"It's fabric?" he said.

"What?"

"Your legs have fabric?"

He didn't know about pantyhose. She explained and took
them off and he held the lifeless nylon legs in his hands in
disbelief. So many things about America would turn out like
this, beautiful treasures just beyond your grasp that pop like
balloons when you touch them, shrivel into rags.

Edith took care of him for the eight months he lived in
Seattle. She was like a mother to him, but at the same time,
she was his girlfriend. She got him a job as an aide at a nursing home. He spent weekends at her apartment and she
cooked for him and showed him around and gave him sex.
He gave her companionship. She was in so much need of
companionship. She explained to him that in America people
suffer a specific kind of loneliness that the Igbo language did
not have a word for. America was not a communal society
like Nigeria. Bennet was not aware that he had come from a
communal society until Edith pointed it out and showed him
the difference.

"In America," she said, "your neighbor may not even care

whether or not you get out of bed in the morning, may not even know."

Most weekends I slept at Edith's apartment. I paid an elderly woman and her blind son about $250 a month to rent an attic room where I lived during the week. I used all the facilities in that lady's house, including cooking utensils. She was such a lovely bent-over woman. Her son was in his fifties. He owned a dog that guided him. He was a very angry man who drank all day. He was a divorced man. That was the first divorced person I ever met. It was a very white neighborhood. At this time I first began to sense racism. I did not know the word for it yet, but I began to observe that some white folks treated me differently. For example, there was a small grocery store about two blocks from the house I lived in. Some days after school, around 7:00 P.M., I would stop by to purchase groceries, I may be the only black person in the store, and I noticed that whenever I walked in, someone would be following me. I could not understand why. Sometimes, while walking home late at night, around 9:00 P.M., I may not be the only student walking on the streets, but the cops will pull over in front of me and ask me who I was and where I was going. Luckily I had been told at the school to always carry my ID card on me. I would show them my ID card, they will inspect it and leave me alone. But I always wondered why I was the only person that was always pulled over. I would be walking down the street like every other person, but some white folks, when they saw me coming toward them on the street, would quickly walk across the street to avoid me. I wondered why. What did I do wrong? I wondered if I smelled or if something was wrong with me. I looked at myself in the mirror and did not see anything that was wrong with me. As a child in Nigeria, *we were not taught about racism. As a man from Nigeria, until I began to experience these behavioral patterns, I was not mentally aware of the concept of racism.*

In the rearview mirror the rising sun filled the sky with orange and he imagined it pushing him, propelling him forward like rocket fuel. Nothing could stop him now. The dawn of a new century, him in an Avis rental headed west on the Pennsylvania Turnpike.

The thing he realized while he was driving was that he had figured everything out. *Everything!* He gripped the steering wheel tight and thought about all that he had figured out. He was a man now, no denying it, thirty-one years old. He was a highly educated and sophisticated man in America where the currency is education and work. He excelled at both of these things and so he would keep getting educated and he would *work*. He would work and work and work. He would not bother with women or other distractions of the flesh.

He pushed the buttons on the radio but he couldn't get any music. In the middle of Pennsylvania most of the radio was people talking, and what they talked about was God. He didn't mind the God talk, but he wanted music. There were billboards on the roadside demanding time for Jesus, images of giant praying hands beneath halos. That made him homesick. In Nigeria every bus had Jesus on it somewhere, every car had some reminder to give praise.

How arrogant he had been, telling God goodbye like that when he left Nigeria. Honestly, he didn't see it as arrogance at the time, but more as a generous offer to let God take care of needier people. But in America he once again found himself needy. He had spent less than a year in Seattle, his transition to America cushioned by the friendship of Jimmy and Edith.

Then in the summer of 1995 he left Seattle for New York, where he joined Columbia University's Harlem Hospital Center for a residency training program in anatomic and clinical pathology. America was supposed to heal him but he found out in New York that it hadn't. He wasn't, in fact, a new person. He was the same Bennet, only more so. He was a doctor who had never wanted to be a doctor and he had to find something to do with his education and skills. Patient care was out of the question; he believed he was not good at dealing with people, even though people around him said he was so great at dealing with people. So cheerful! That happy-faced man with the cackle-laugh!

The discrepancy between his inside experience and outside experience was getting big and out of control.

Depression isn't a thing that lifts or disappears just because of a change of scenery. The voice follows you no matter where you go, reminding you that you are worthless.

Working behind the scenes of patient care was the only option, he thought. He simply could not deal with patients. And so that meant: the lab. That meant: pathology. He would be the guy with the microscope who looked at blood and tissue samples and told the doctors on the front line what the problem was.

The work suited him. He was comforted by the regularity of the slides, just like the bottle caps in his drawer back home; he liked the way they all fit so neatly in boxes and you could pick them up systematically, one after the next, and explore, deepening your understanding and forgetting about everything else. He would lose himself in the slides and the stories they told, the way a musician or any other artist loses himself in the art. That was liberating, and it was there in New York that he first felt a glimmer of what it might be like to feel free of the weight of his depression. He felt a sense of accomplishment. He felt like Bill Gates. He felt he was making it in America. He went clubbing, met girls, slept with them, became intoxicated by the noise and rhythm of urban life. He found it soothing. Loud noise outside you that overpowered the static of sorrow inside you. Standing close to nightclub speakers pounding, beating so loud at his brain, breaking through.

As the winter months passed, he began to feel frightened by a persistent sore throat. He felt an exhaustion so deep. Partly his training in epidemiology, the study of the spread of disease, partly the culture of New York in the nineties, partly fear and partly guilt for his promiscuous behavior—add it all up and he was convinced he had AIDS. He took the test on a Friday, went home and drank, drank all weekend, promising himself that he would kill himself if he had AIDS. He called Winny and told her he was going to kill himself if he had AIDS. She told him not to be afraid, that the good Lord who had led him thus far would not desert him. She told him that if the test came back positive, please, he should come home immediately and not do anything foolish. She told him God was a healer. On Monday he found out the test was negative, and he got on his knees and wept, held his hands together in prayer and begged for forgiveness. On Easter Sunday he went to church, sang "Hosanna in the Highest," thanking God for not abandoning him despite his many sins of the flesh. When he got to the front of the communion line, he saw that the woman giving out the body of Christ was one of his former sexual partners. She held the host to his tongue and winked at him.

He felt so conflicted he wanted to run home and wash all the sin off his body.

* * *

But the thing that really complicated everything now was racism, which I still did not understand. At this time in my life, I had not read a lot about slavery and the history of racism in the United States. When I got here, I started reading the books. If I had known all that before I came to the United States, honestly, I may not have come. I would have been so disgusted that I may have simply decided to remain in Nigeria. And the ironic thing was that America was a Christian nation founded upon Christian principles! How can a Christian nation perpetuate such evil over centuries? I could not understand it.

I could not understand why so many blacks in America did not become educated. I learned that over half the immigrants coming from Nigeria had bachelor's degrees—and yet here in America most blacks did not even finish high school. There was something wrong with America.

He read about the Igbo and American slavery. His own people trapped like dogs, coming here on ships. The Igbo had earned a reputation in the American south for being fiercely independent and unwilling to tolerate enslavement. They were considered high maintenance, and so they were sold cheap. In May 1803 a shipload of seized West Africans were brought to Savannah, Georgia, to be auctioned off at the local market. Seventy-five were Igbo men and they went for $100 each. The cheap Igbo were chained under the deck of a schooner named *York* to be delivered to a plantation on nearby St. Simons Island. During this voyage the Igbo men rose up in rebellion, taking control of the ship. They drowned their captors, causing the grounding of the *York* in Dunbar Creek—a site now locally known as Igbo Landing.

Under the direction of the Igbo chief, the men marched in unison into the creek singing *"Orimili Omambala bu anyi bia, Orimili Omambala ka anyi ga eji na,"* the Water Spirit *brought us here, the Water Spirit will take us home,* accepting the protection of God over slavery. They walked into the water in a collective suicide.

When Bennet was walking home that Easter Sunday in New York, the woman who winked at him while she gave him communion was there in a taxi. She called out his name from the taxi, opened the door for him, and said, "Get in, Bennet." He got in and she took him to lunch and he felt he was falling under her spell. They went back to her apartment and this time she taught him things he never knew people did. He discovered new dimensions of pleasure and perhaps it was too much, or perhaps it was evil, or perhaps something else, but he would mark that day as the day he became impotent, a problem that would vex him for years. He went to doctors, who said nothing was wrong with him. The problem was all in his head. *But I am broken and my body no longer works the way a man's body is supposed to work.* He went to a psychiatrist who told him what was wrong with him. Depression isn't something you just pack up and move away from. It can manifest itself in so many physical ways. He had not left the depression back in Nigeria. It had followed him to America like a virus inside him and now it was causing devastating symptoms. He pleaded to the doctor to fix it and the doctor said the only way to fix it is to understand it, get underneath it, and Bennet tried and tried but nothing worked.

He gave up on himself and his body and he got back to work. If you didn't have to talk to people, if you could spend your days looking at slides, moving them in and out of boxes, handling them gingerly, studying them lovingly, well, you could survive just fine. That was all he needed, slides in boxes.

Anyone studying pathology eventually has to rotate through autopsy training. He was not surprised by how disagreeable, how smelly and gruesome he found that work to be. What surprised him was how intriguing—and oddly comforting—he found it to be, once he got past the physical unpleasantness. He would put his scalpel to a chest and he couldn't tell if he was cutting into a banker or a bum, a CEO or a hooker, and it didn't matter. In death, he thought, everyone was equal. Death was one thing we all had in common. No matter the race or the nationality or the age or the gender or the wealth or the education, every dead person was equal to the next, and that was the part that comforted him. That was the part that reminded him of his own humanity. *I am just like this guy and he is just like me. We return to the earth, and we return to God, all of us the same.*

He performed autopsies of murdered men like his grandfather. Drownings, gunshot wounds, stabbings, asphyxiation. He performed autopsies on babies and toddlers and old ladies and teenagers who had committed suicide. He easily imagined himself as one of those teenagers. *So what happened to you?* he began to ask of the bodies of the people who had been murdered, or who had died suddenly, or without obvious reason. He would find clues. A corpse held a story, told in tissue, patterns of trauma, and secrets in cells. He wanted to unravel the mysteries. Here was a place he felt he could help. *I'll tell your story,* he would say to the bodies. *I'll set the record straight.*

Forensic pathology is the science of determining the cause of death by examining a corpse. He made up his mind to study forensic pathology in his third year of residency in New York, and when he looked around to find the best person to study under, the best forensic pathologist in America, that's when he found out about Pittsburgh.

The turnpike tunnel burrowing through the Allegheny Mountains was a square tube of light, and when he emerged on the other side the landscape changed into hills and steep valleys with evergreen trees like the ones you see on Christmas cards. If he was on the move again, running away from his problems, well, so what? Maybe that's what life is. Maybe people just get good at running. They find ways to forget, using pacifiers like money and power, and if they can't forget they commit suicide. Violence against a whole people isn't over after the violence. Its aftermath afflicts the next generation and then the next, an inescapable haunting. Maybe depression is in the blood, passed on, a past that's inside you like shrapnel and over which you're powerless.

It would help, anyway, not to have to take responsibility for it.

He thought about the bodies and all the times he had to write "suicide" on the autopsy reports. Why do some depressed people commit suicide, and some, like him, do not? What was the difference between him and them? It couldn't be random; he was a man of science now and there was no room for random. Perhaps there was something in the chemistry of the brain that worked like a switch, on or off, suicide yes or suicide no. He thought about his depression and he thought of all the Igbo people of his father's generation who were killed in war, and the slaves who walked to their death at Igbo Landing, and when you thought like that it was easy to hate yourself for the indulgence of your own petty problems. Set in relief, this is how violence against a whole people lives on, one generation after the next.

Bennet did not have a job in Pittsburgh. He had a scheme. He'd arranged for an appointment at the Allegheny County coroner's office to inquire about a one-year forensic pathology fellowship. It was a highly competitive job, and he wanted it so badly he needed to do something different from other applicants. He needed to command notice. So instead of filling out the application, he decided to drive to Pittsburgh with a suitcase and a plan. He would offer to work for free, a trial basis, an internship. He would make it sound as if Columbia University was paying for it, or some such official thing. He would leave that part vague. It would seem more enticing if the internship he was offering to do was sponsored by an institutional-sounding something. In fact, Winny and Uche were paying for this scheme. Winny and Uche sent Bennet money to pay for him to live in Pittsburgh to work at the Allegheny County coroner's office for free while he convinced the people there he was worthy. He would live in a hotel, do a month's worth of beautiful autopsies, and they would see. They would have no choice but to give him the fellowship once they saw with their own eyes.

He thought this was a bold move for a man suffering debilitating depression, and so perhaps he didn't have depression after all. Would a depressed man be able to scheme like this? That gave him hope. Did a depressed man have hope?

He had been dazzled from the moment he realized who ran the Allegheny County coroner's office. Cyril Wecht. *That guy!* That guy he saw on television back in Nigeria, in between the American music videos and the Abiola speeches on the TV in the cafeteria in med school. Again and again they would play a CNN documentary about JFK's assassination and the forensic pathologist debunking the single bullet theory. That guy was so fast-talking and slick and sharp. Cyril Wecht worked in Pittsburgh?

Who Killed JonBenet Ramsey? That was Wecht's most recent book, still featured on the "New Titles" stand in bookstores. Bennet did his research. Before that Wecht had written *Grave Secrets: A Leading Forensic Expert Reveals the Startling Truth About O. J. Simpson, David Koresh, Vincent Foster, and Other Sensational Cases.* He wrote *Cause of Death: A Leading Forensic Expert Sets the Record Straight on JFK, RFK, Jean Harris, Mary Jo Kopechne, Sunny von Bulow, Dr. Jeffrey MacDonald, and Other Controversial Cases.* "Wecht is lord of the morgue," one of the book jackets said. "Outspoken, provocative, persuasively argued: a full platter for true-crime fans who won't mind—or may even enjoy—looking over Wecht's shoulder as he takes scalpel and buzz-saw to yet another corpus delicti."

Big time, Bennet thought. Nothing could stop him now. He would study with Cyril Wecht, the most famous forensic pathologist in the world. He would learn from the master. He had found what he wanted to do with his life, and he would become the best at it. Right up there with Cyril Wecht. He pushed the buttons on the radio and now he was close to Pittsburgh and that was when all the good songs came on.

CHAPTER 5

FANCY

I worked my butt off for Dr. Wecht. While other doctors at the office worked at their leisure, I worked with a mission, to make it big and buy myself a Mercedes-Benz. My dream car since I was four years old. Lo and behold, within one year of completing fellowship training and working for Dr. Wecht, I purchased my very first new Mercedes, an E350! The day I drove that car was one of the most exhilarating experiences I have had in my life. In my mind, a Mercedes-Benz car epito- mized my resolve to overcome my odds in life. Driving home in that car, I kept on telling myself, Bennet, you have to be like a Mercedes-Benz car! I felt so much potency and power. To make a confession, it improved my self-esteem. I felt like I had accomplished something. For the first time in my life I was able to reach out and touch something I desired from the bottom of my heart.

The thing about Cyril Wecht was he looked at your chest when he talked to you, or your hair. It seemed difficult for him to fully lock in. He was sixty-eight when Bennet entered his world. It was like getting sucked into a vortex. Wecht was brash, outspoken, and full of enthusiasm about the business of dead people. "Murder, accidents, suicide, people killing, people being killed!" he once said to a reporter about why he loved his job. "My God, there's nothing that comes near it on a steady basis!"

He was stylish, dressed in designer suits; he flaunted an intellectual's vocabulary, said "vis-à-vis" and "ergo," as if to clearly delineate himself as a man who had risen well beyond his roots as the child of Eastern European immigrants in the poorest section of shot-and-a-beer Pittsburgh. Brilliant, athletic, a violin virtuoso, he had put himself through med school, then law school, then was elected county coroner, then said, Hell, I'll just go be a goddamned senator. He won the Democratic Party nomination to oppose Senator John Heinz in his bid for a second term in 1982. He lost, then decided to run for county CEO, but lost to another goddamned Republican. All along, ever since 1962, he ran a private practice, Cyril H. Wecht and Pathology Associates, and that's where the money was, and that's where the power was, and that's where he flourished.

Wecht had an outsized personality the national media loved, even if the local press regarded him as a bit of a head scratcher. He was *Pittsburgh's* coroner—why was he on TV all the time talking about high-profile cases that had nothing to do with his day job here at home? By the time Bennet met him, Wecht had performed more than fourteen thousand autopsies and consulted on thirty thousand others; he had seemingly inexhaustible energy, delivering half a dozen speeches in one day, teaching and consulting worldwide, publishing books and papers, piling up awards, railing about everything from police brutality to anti-Semitism. He enjoyed arguing and toying with the press: "Malicious editorial pimps and reporter prostitutes," he once said in a letter to the editor of the *Pittsburgh Post-Gazette,* accusing the editorial board of "paranoid hatred of me." Then he sent a follow-up apology—to the "honest, hard-working panderers and prostitutes for having analogously referred to them in such a pejorative fashion."

All that gall, all that education, the refugee background, a misfit—Bennet saw much of his own story in Wecht's, and Wecht saw it, too. Bennet's meticulous work habits easily earned him the fellowship, then a staff position at the coroner's office—and in time the two formed a friendship, albeit a lopsided one.

"You know, I never even wanted to go to med school," Bennet confessed to Wecht one day.

"Yeah, I didn't, either," Wecht said. He was a short guy, compact, always tan, bald as a cantaloupe. "That was my dad's bullshit idea."

"Mine too!" Bennet said.

"Because you were smart," Wecht said.

"If you say so."

"And you worked hard," Wecht said. "So what? Good for you. I took four violin lessons a week and practiced four hours every day."

"Oh—"

"Six hours on weekends. So don't give me any goddamned father bullshit."

"Okay."

"Eat some pastries," Wecht said.

"No, thank you."

"*Why not? Have some pastries.*" He pushed the plate closer to Bennet's, then reached for the pepper, turned the knob on the grinder over his eggs, again and again. He could never seem to get enough pepper. They were in the kitchen in Wecht's stately old brick home in Squirrel Hill, a tony neighborhood in Pittsburgh's east end where fat, towering sycamores provided dense shade for rolling blankets of English ivy. Wecht invited Bennet to his home often on weekends, usually to discuss work.

Sigrid, his wife, came in, wiping her hands on a dish towel. "You got enough to eat, Bennet?" she said. She was dainty, with bright blue designer glasses, silky white hair.

"He won't eat any pastries," Wecht told her.

"Maybe he doesn't want any," Sigrid said.

"Those are some good pastries," Wecht said.

"So *you* eat them," Sigrid said.

Bennet bounced his head back and forth, listening. He was by now used to Wecht-style constant bickering. Sigrid was badass. She and Wecht had raised four kids, had sent all four to Ivy League schools, had produced a neurosurgeon, an ad exec, an attorney, and an ob-gyn. Here, too, Bennet saw his own family, his brothers and sisters with their big careers. And like his family, the Wecht kids were close; their parents encouraged weekly phone calls to them and to one another.

Now they practically treated Bennet as one of their own. It made him tear up sometimes, just the feeling of being treated like a son, and Sigrid and Wecht would roll their eyes with exhaustion when he got emotional. "Whatever." "Let's move on."

Sigrid, an attorney, was helping Bennet with his immigration papers; he was still on a student visa and until he got a green card she advised him to stay in school somewhere, anywhere. Bennet heeded her advice and started moonlighting at the University of Pittsburgh medical school as a neuropathology fellow. He had discovered a new passion—*dead brains!*—and Wecht encouraged him to indulge his every curiosity. "Get board certified in that shit if you want," he told him. "Get a PhD, an MBA, a goddamned law degree if you want."

"Okay, sir."

The more degrees Bennet acquired, the more useful he became to Wecht in his burgeoning private practice. Wecht would bring Bennet file after file of crazy cases to work on. *Crazy.* An eight-year-old girl strangled by her parents' pet python. *Awful.* A woman who had committed suicide after bariatric surgery; there was another who did the same thing, and another. "Who knew?" There was a guy who tried to smuggle cocaine by inserting it into his rectum, only to OD when the bag ripped. Then there was the curious series of chain saw accidents. "Death by Chainsaw: Fatal Kickback Injuries to the Neck." That was one of the published papers Wecht let Bennet put his name on. Also, "Diagnosis of Alzheimer's Disease in an Exhumed Decomposed Brain After Twenty Months of Burial in a Deep Grave."

But mostly Wecht didn't offer to let Bennet put his name on things. Bennet's work for Wecht was usually without credit, and for minimal compensation, and Bennet convinced himself that was okay. He felt rich, anyway. The coroner's office paid him enough to repay his family, and he even had begun sending money home to Chizoba, who was trying to buy a farm.

Moreover, he was gaining Wecht's approval. He was acquiring self-respect. He had found a new father. He had a chance to be the son a father could recognize not just as some inert angel that had fallen from the sky, but as someone reputable, admirable—a real man.

"You know, there's an Igbo idiom," Bennet said to Wecht that day in the kitchen with Sigrid.

"Oh, Jesus, here we go—" Wecht said.

"*Madu bu chi onye,*" Bennet said. "It means, 'Your fellow human being is the God in your life, the God you have, and

the God you see.' " Wecht shot a glance at Sigrid. *Here we go.*
"Interpreted," Bennet went on, "it means that God will not
come down on earth to help you. Instead, he answers our
prayers and blesses us through our fellow human beings. This
was why I call you my angel, Dr. Wecht. God blessed me
through you. You are the God I see and know."

"You are so fucking weird," Wecht said.

"I don't get it, either," Sigrid said.

"It's a *compliment*," Bennet said.

"Cyril, say *thank you*," Sigrid said.

"Jesus fucking Christ," Wecht said.

Bennet and Wecht didn't indulge each other's eccentrici-
ties, but they allowed for the fact of them. *Abnormal* was the
characteristic they had in common; the specific brand of it
hardly mattered. "Junior Wecht," some of the people at the
morgue had started calling Bennet. It wasn't a compliment.
Wecht was a weird and bombastic boss, and now he had a
weird and eccentric sidekick.

In the kitchen, Bennet pushed away his plate and flipped
open a file. Here was the reason he had been summoned to
Wecht's house that day.

"What is it?" Bennet said.

"You can't read?" Wecht said.

Sigrid held up a bowl of miniature muffins, and Bennet
popped one into his mouth as he read.

In the summer of 1994, in a red-roofed mobile home in
northwestern Pennsylvania's Shenango River Valley, a woman
was fatally stabbed twenty-eight times in her kitchen. Her
two small children and a niece were slashed down to the spine
and nearly beheaded in the bathroom. A neighbor, Thomas
Kimbell, who had a history of psychiatric problems and was
said to be mentally retarded, was convicted of the crime and

sentenced to death. He languished in prison for six years, awaiting lethal injection, and then the Pennsylvania Supreme Court granted his appeal for a retrial. The new defense team had reached out to super-pathologist Cyril Wecht to help get Kimbell off death row.

"What do you want me to do, sir?" Bennet asked.

"Get him off death row," Wecht said.

"He's innocent?"

"How the hell should I know?" Wecht said.

Bennet had never gone solo on such a high-profile case. He felt overwhelmed and thrilled. He would adopt Wecht's confidence and swagger. He bought new suits and shirts made by Wecht's tailor. Dress like Wecht. Act like Wecht. The transformation was deliberate, methodical, and precise.

The morning after Bennet got the death row case from Wecht, he went to church. Every morning, 7 A.M., he showed up for mass up at the convent on Bedford Avenue, a handsome red-brick building left over from a fancier time in Pittsburgh's Hill District, once a vibrant community. Now most of the houses in the neighborhood were bent, leaning, boarded up. Even the Garden of Hope had gone to weeds.

Inside the convent was a small chapel, a twelve-seater. Most mornings at mass it was just the six resident nuns—and Bennet. Bennet in his natty suit, dressed for success on the way to work at the morgue, the nuns all smiles and shy waves. So much to be thankful for, Bennet was thinking. Thank God for Dr. Wecht. *Thank God for the peace today in my heart.* And thank God he found a church he loved in Pittsburgh. Literally, *thank God.*

Thank you, he was saying, in his prayer voice, eyes closed, crouched in the tiny pew. He had been coming to daily morning mass for well over a year, ever since he met and became friends with Father Carmen D'Amico, the pastor of St. Benedict the Moor. The main church where he went on Sundays was down the hill on Crawford Street; the convent with daily mass was up here by the school.

"The Lord be with you," Father Carmen said, standing up, spreading his arms in welcome. He was a young guy, not much older than Bennet, with thick features, a wide smile that took up most of his face. To Bennet he was kind of the anti-Wecht. Humble instead of brash, a person who wasn't about personal glory, or wealth, or ambition. Wecht would throw a glass of water in your face if you didn't get the point fast enough; Father Carmen would offer you a blanket and a hot meal.

"And also with you," Bennet said, in time with the quiet voices of the nuns.

Thank you, God, for Dr. Wecht, and thank you for Father Carmen, who provides balance.

He thought about how funny it was the way Father Carmen had misread his intentions in the early days when Bennet first started showing up at St. Benedict's. *That church was such a find! A church for black Catholics!* Bennet loved it. St. Benedict the Moor had been serving Pittsburgh's African American community for well over a century. In 1889 the first National Black Catholic Congress had convened in Washington, D.C., to cry out for greater recognition in the church, and the Roman Catholic Diocese of Pittsburgh's answer was a golden brick cathedral, topped by a massive statue of St. Benedict, the patron saint of African Americans, his arms outstretched to the sky. Benedict was a sixteenth-century Italian Franciscan friar in Sicily, born to African slaves, who was freed at birth and became known for his charity and the monastic community he established. He was said to be incorruptible.

Father Carmen had been serving at St. Benedict's for nearly a decade, and recently he had begun encouraging his congregation to open its doors to the small influx of Africans who were just starting to immigrate to Pittsburgh—a whole new concept for a city with so few ties to Africa. Now here came people from Nigeria, Kenya, Sudan, Liberia, Congo, Uganda. A trickle at first, then more, and then more. Father Carmen reached out. "Africans, meet the African Americans!" he all but said. He was a white guy, from a solidly white Pittsburgh neighborhood, with no history in either culture, a deficiency to which he would loudly and brazenly confess, *so please, everybody, please be patient with me,* and his honesty endeared him. Bennet was one of the African immigrants Father Carmen reached out to. The timing couldn't have been better. Bennet needed a family. The Africans in the parish needed leaders. Bennet stepped in and got to work, joined the choir, joined Bible study, volunteered at bake sales; it seemed he was always there. Who was this guy? He dressed so well, so much fancier than everyone else. He didn't appear to have any family, was always solo. He never said what he did for a living. And then he started showing up at daily mass up at the convent, hanging out afterward; the nuns would charge off to school, and so it would be just Bennet and Father Carmen sharing coffee in the kitchen convent, making sure to turn off the pot before they left. And then that one day Sister Josephine left them a plate of Danish to share, and a note: "Enjoy!"

Bennet poured the coffee; Father Carmen passed the cream; at this point they were about a month into the ritual.

Their spoons clinked. Something weird. This day was different.

"Bennet, I'm just going to say it," Father Carmen said.

"Say what?"

"You know, I was thinking, maybe I could just give you literature—"

"Literature?"

"Just to, you know, read," Father Carmen said. "We don't have to talk about it. But just if you want information, and how to go about—"

Bennet was deep into the middle of his cheese Danish, chewing eagerly.

"We can talk about this another time," Father Carmen said, retreating.

"What are we talking about?" Bennet said. "I have no idea what we're talking about."

Father Carmen wrapped his hands around his coffee mug, blew. "It's okay," he said. "I'm sorry. In your own time, of course."

"Father?"

Father Carmen put his mug down, waited a beat, leaned in. "Vocations, Bennet?" he said.

"Huh?"

"You mean, you haven't been trying to ask me how to—"

"Vocations?" Bennet said, his eyes popping wide. *"Like, being a priest?"*

"No?"

"No!"

"I thought that's where you were headed with all this, why you were doing all this—"

"Me, a *priest*? Oh, wait till I tell Chizoba! Bennet becomes a priest!" He fell into laughter. Leaned back. His high-pitched cackle. No, Bennet Omalu does *not* want to become a priest. Oh my gosh, no.

Father Carmen had his eyebrows up. Oops. It had just seemed so obvious. Bennet seemed so . . . holy. "So devout!" Father Carmen said. "I mean, Bennet, *you really love God.*" He was laughing now, too, as you do after tension lifts, mysteries are solved.

"All the Omalus love God," Bennet said. "That's like the family business."

"But your singing, Bennet," Father Carmen said. "The *volume*!" And the way he led Saturday morning prayer group, the depths he would reach. "That about knocked my socks off. You are a very good pray-er!"

"You should hear my brother Ikem," Bennet said.

Father Carmen apologized for his mistake, but added that he wasn't the only one. The nuns thought Bennet was trying to pop the priest question, too. This mysterious man, no family, so devout.

"I'm a forensic pathologist," Bennet said. "I work with dead people."

"Dead people—"

"It's more interesting than it sounds."

And so they compared notes that day, asked each other questions, confessed more confusion. "You're a *white* guy," Bennet said.

"Right."

"Running the city's only black Catholic church?"

"I know—"

"I thought that was very strange from the beginning."

"It is," Father Carmen allowed.

They laughed. They talked about race. So much of what

they would go on to talk about day after day in their morning chats after mass would be about race relations in America. Bennet needed help understanding: "Why do so many white people hate black people?" Father Carmen needed help understanding: "Why do so many African Americans feel threatened by Africans?" Father Carmen felt he was in way over his head with that question alone. "I will help you as best I can," Bennet told him. "And I will help you," Father Carmen said, and that was how their friendship began.

How do you get a guy off death row?

Bennet gathered boxes of material on the Kimbell case, the police and autopsy reports, toxicology and histology reports, photos, medical records, transcripts from the first trial. He loaded them into his Mercedes and drove through town, feeling awesome. How he loved that car. That car meant success, meant manhood, meant *achievement*. The files could have been gold, a treasure, a shelf of trophies so long. He unloaded everything into his condo in Churchill, a suburb of Pittsburgh. He organized it all on his dining room table, and there he worked, rising before dawn each morning, poring over the documents. In the first trial the prosecution had claimed that Kimbell killed the family in a "cocaine-induced psychosis"; this was a drug deal gone bad, they said. Testimony had shown that Kimbell was violent toward his own family and had been diagnosed with "intermittent explosive disorder." As far as even circumstantial evidence went, they didn't have much else. The murder weapon had not been found, and Kimbell's clothes had no blood on them. The prosecution claimed Kimbell had stashed both the murder weapon and his clothes.

Bennet studied cocaine-induced psychosis. A person in

such a state would not, he reasoned, be calm or clever enough to successfully get rid of evidence after brutally slashing four people. He studied the gruesome photographs, the patterns of wounds. So many complex wounds, so many unnecessary to killing someone. It was a case of overkill. Driven by rage, or some exploding emotion. Nothing in the police reports suggested that Kimbell knew the victims at all, let alone well enough to want to slaughter them. The woman weighed 250 pounds and measured 5 feet 4 inches and had obviously fought gallantly for her life. She had at least twelve defensive wounds on her left palm and fingers. She was fighting! And Kimbell was a puny guy, 5 feet 3 inches, 120 pounds. He brutally stabbed this woman—and three children—without sustaining any wounds himself?

The doctor's report said, Nope. No wounds on Kimbell.

Bennet kept reading. *This guy did not do it,* he thought. But how could he prove it? He kept looking at the pictures. Night after night, poring over the documents.

His obsessive fixation on a problem, the inability to let go, was the strength that enabled him to discover what others had missed. It was a muscle he had been exercising since childhood, and it was growing strong.

He kept reading. Every page of the trial transcripts and police report, over and over. Maybe he missed something. Maybe there was a clue.

One sentence in the box full of files, one sentence in the papers and books strewn all over his dining room table, kept sticking out. The physician who examined Kimbell a day after the murders stated that he was "a bleeder," that members of his family tended to bleed a lot and the last time his tooth was pulled he bled for almost two days. A hemophiliac? No, there was no such diagnosis provided.

Bennet asked the defense team to take him to meet Kimbell at the prison. He was excited. Surely the guy would be happy to know Bennet believed he was innocent. They would work together. He would provide clues. They brought Kimbell into the anteroom. He was skinny, scruffy, and pale. He did not take a seat as the attorney suggested. He stood there in his orange jumpsuit and the chains on his wrists and he pursed his lips like he was forming spit. He looked at the attorney.

You brought me a black guy? Bennet imagined him saying.

Bennet looked at him, then turned away. The room was hot and the sun was pouring in rays through a high window so you could see dust particles floating.

"I need a blood sample," Bennet said.

The attorney told Kimbell to sit down and hold out his arm.

"I need you to explain this phenomenon of American Negro racism to me," Bennet said to Father Carmen one morning in the convent kitchen after morning mass.

"In twenty-five words or less," Father Carmen said.

"I'm serious."

"I know—"

"People don't like me," Bennet said. "Or they're afraid of me."

"I don't think that's true at all," Father Carmen said. "Or if they act like that it's not personal."

"That's the whole point," Bennet said.

"I see."

"I'm trying to save a guy's life," Bennet said. "And it was like he wanted to spit at me. Like he would rather die from lethal injection than have a black guy help him."

"I can't imagine what that was like for you," Father Carmen said. "I cannot imagine."

"Well, I'm going to win the case," Bennet said. He leaned back, folded his arms behind his head, gazed out the window at the maple tree just forming buds.

Kimbell had tested positive for hemophilia A. People with hemophilia bruise easily, have massive bruises following trivial blunt force impact or other trauma. And Kimbell had had not one mark on him in the photographs.

"That guy sitting in jail for six years had nothing to do with those murders," Bennet said. "He couldn't have. I'm going to prove it."

"Why didn't they know about his hemophilia in the first trial?" Father Carmen asked.

Bennet shrugged. "They also never questioned the victim's husband," he said. "That guy had cuts all over his hands. I found a picture."

The Kimbell trial began in April 2002. In a pretrial hearing the prosecutor argued that Bennet should not be allowed to testify. The prosecutor had his own expert forensic pathologist, a dapper guy in wire-rimmed glasses and a bow tie. The team made the point that there was no scientific way that a forensic pathologist could offer, all these years later, any evidence to refute a guilty verdict.

"Yeah, there is," Bennet said, in so many words. "I'm the way."

He enjoyed practicing Wecht-style arrogance on the wire-rimmed-glasses man, whom he thought appeared visibly agitated. He enjoyed the showmanship in the courtroom the next day. Kimbell had hemophilia A, he told the court; there was no way he committed these murders. He would have had open wounds and he would have bled out.

So if Kimbell didn't do it, who did? Bennet was ready with the answer. He revealed the picture he found. He had had it blown up poster-sized.

"Show me whose hands those are, and I will show you who the killer is!" How he loved delivering that line. "These are not the hands of Thomas Kimbell!"

The hands were those of the victim's husband. At the first trial, that photo had escaped notice, and now here it was, larger than life—and so was Bennet.

That picture was so powerful. And I remember I said it again: "Show me whose hands those are, and I will show you who the killer is!" I had learnt well from Dr. Wecht that it was as much about the showmanship as it was the content of what you had to say. On the stand I was like a miniature Dr. Wecht. At some point it seemed like a spectator sport. The audience in the courthouse said uncountable "oohs" and "aahs." The judge reminded people about the etiquette of the courtroom. The DA was upset and exasperated. He was visibly angry. My direct examination ended just before noon. By now, the media were waiting outside itching to get hold of me. As I walked by Mr. Kimbell, he was in tears, he stood up, opened up his arms, and gave me a very big and tight hug. He was sobbing. He kept on whispering in my ears, in between his sobs, "Thank you so much, I am so, so sorry." I was sneaked out through the back door of the courthouse to avoid the media. I drove back to Pittsburgh with so much peace in my heart. I believed I gave it my very best. The next day, the attorney called me on the phone just before noon, and what came out of his mouth was: "Congratulations! You did it, you did it! He is free! He is free! The jury believed everything you said."

Later that day, Dr. Wecht called me to tell me that the attorney called him to thank him for recommending me to them. Guess what, Dr. Wecht had forgotten about the case entirely. He asked me to come to his office to tell him what the case was about. I looked so brilliant in his office that afternoon. I was proud of myself. That was the very first time in my life I felt so proud.

"I heard the news," Father Carmen said to Bennet when he showed up for mass at the convent after the trial. "Congratulations. I heard you won!"

"Show me whose hands those are, and I will show you who the killer is," Bennet said, explaining his strategy. "You have to admit that was a good line."

"That was *Johnnie Cochran,*" Father Carmen said.

"Wecht," Bennet said. "Pure Wecht."

"Is he going to pay you this time?"

Bennet sighed. That was a buzz-kill question. "I don't know," he said. "He didn't really remember what case I was even talking about when I told him I won."

"He didn't remember?"

"He's a busy man. He has many cases."

"Bennet."

"I know—"

"I think he uses you, Bennet."

They sat in silence for a moment. The radiator made a clunking sound and Father Carmen put his hand on it to see if it was putting out any heat at all.

"Hey, did Yinka tell you about the group she's starting?" Father Carmen asked.

"The group?" Bennet said. "She said you were starting it."

Yinka was maybe fifty, from Nigeria, another powerhouse parishioner. Father Carmen had an idea to create a nonprofit, to expand his outreach to new African immigrants in a more formal way, not just as a way of getting people to join the church, but as a way of helping them with the transition to America. Specifically, an influx of refugees from southern Sudan who were being resettled through Catholic Charities of the Diocese of Pittsburgh. "They have no idea how to shop for food, use the bank, let alone how to find jobs," Father Carmen said. "We'll be the welcome wagon. We're going to call it 'Ajapo.' Yinka said it means 'linkage.'"

"That's not Igbo," Bennet said.

"Yoruba," Father Carmen said.

"Okay."

"Will you help?"

"Of course, of course," Bennet said. "It's more like what I expected to find when I came to America, honestly."

"It's complicated," Father Carmen said.

"Everything is so complicated," Bennet said. He stood up, poured more coffee. "Did Yinka tell you about the woman she introduced me to?"

"A woman?"

"She didn't tell you?"

"Who is it?"

"No one."

THE MORGUE

There was an autopsy I did on a forty-four-year-old woman. Her name was Felicia. She had suffered traumatic brain injury from an assault by her husband and went into a chronic persistent vegetative state and died four years later. I did the autopsy and examined her brain. Surprisingly, I saw Alzheimer's disease (AD) changes in her brain—at the age of forty-four years old! By then I had read that brain trauma could result in AD changes in the brain, but seeing it personally in a case of mine was an eye-opener. I spent so much time with the slides, just studying them at home. I would say that case prepared me for what was to come.

It was weird the way people in Pittsburgh loved their morgue. Everyone you met had some childhood memory of it. Their brother had been to the morgue, or their cousin, or they themselves. "My dad took me to the morgue!" "Our baseball team went to the morgue." "She dared me to go to the morgue!" "I went to the morgue on my sixteenth birthday." "After prom we all went to the morgue."

For years it was open to the public, an imposing structure—a three-story jagged granite fortress sitting there like something out of *The Flintstones*. There was a theater on the first floor, behind glass, where they displayed the bodies so you could come in and identify your loved one. Anyone off the street could come in and look at the bodies before they were autopsied. Then there was a chapel on the top floor with stained glass windows and a barrel vault ceiling and pews where you could sit and cry after you identified your loved one. A full-service morgue, state of the art when it was built in 1902.

Probably the most exciting thing that ever happened at the morgue happened in 1929. City planners decided that they had put it in the wrong place. They decided to move the morgue, the whole thing, a hundred yards down the street to make way for a county office building. People from everywhere came to watch "the men from the Balkan tribe," as they came to be known, mysterious men who specialized in heave-hoing and moving huge buildings. They came from overseas to move the morgue. One hundred men with jacks and ropes and cables and horses. They brought in heavy timbers and they built a railway and they had a whistle. They had to lift the six-thousand-ton building, every ounce and inch of it, to the same height at the same moment; every time the boss blew the whistle the men would breathe in giant gulps of air and grit their teeth and give a quarter-turn on their mighty jacks, until the morgue was twenty-seven feet in the air. It took three months for the men and horses to pull the building, inch by inch, and deposit it in its new foundation at 542 Fourth Avenue. During those three months, without missing a beat, work inside the morgue continued, coroners and doctors and corpses, people identifying bodies and praying, everybody in and out of the moving building, as if nothing was happening, as if that morgue were not on a slow journey south.

. . .

They should tear that old morgue down, Bennet thought. He did not like old things. He liked new and modern things. *A lot of Pittsburgh should be torn down,* he thought. Remnants of the heyday of the steel industry were everywhere, red and orange skeletons, massive remains of mills lying along the riversides. *They should clean all that up,* he thought. Like when he feels sad, he dresses up. Puts that suit on. Gets himself physically out of his shell. Come on, Pittsburgh. Perk up.

He was learning to manage his own depression; that's how he had come to regard it, a chronic condition you had to manage, like heart disease. You couldn't wish it away, and getting angry at it was only going to make it worse. The trick was to surrender to the fact of it, and that's what he was working on.

I engaged in deep-seated meditation, psychoanalysis, and so many therapies. I read books and tried to understand. The moment the healing began was when I realized that I could not determine the exact origin of my problems. This was an irrational disease that cannot be rationalized. I had to relearn how to believe in myself without understanding why I was suffering. I let go of understanding, and that was when the healing began.

Now he was in his car, his freshly washed and vacuumed silver E350, on a steel-gray September Saturday in 2002. He was wearing a pin-striped suit and a couple of splashes of Yves Saint Laurent Kouros cologne, and he was pulling into the lot behind the morgue. Most people did not dress up like this to work at the morgue.

He rode up the freight elevator, walked briskly past stray gurneys, wove through the labyrinth of tired, disheveled desks and into his office. The entire place, the entire building, smelled of a hundred years' worth of dead bodies. A couple of window air-conditioning units blew and coughed as if trying to help, and a spider plant exploding with babies wagged in the stale breeze. Bennet took off his suit, hung it up, and put on a clean set of scrubs.

The autopsy room was dingy, yellow tiles, yellow light, four steel tables ready for what might come. A burly morgue tech was smiling when Bennet walked in. That was odd. That guy never smiled. At least not when Bennet was around. He had seemed to dislike Bennet from the get-go, and mostly Bennet tried to ignore him.

"Looks like you're the winner," the tech said, hands on his hips. He did not have a waist. He had a handlebar mustache and looked as if he belonged outdoors, on an oil rig or something.

"What did I get?" Bennet asked, walking past him.

"Mike Webster," the tech said, handing him a file.

"Who?"

"Oh, Jesus Christ."

He laughed so hard at me. He said I was so fucked up. I laughed, too, and said, why? He told me that I could not live in Pittsburgh, Pennsylvania, and not know who Mike Webster was. He was one of the greatest football players in the history of the game. That was the moment it struck a chord in my mind. I asked him if Mike Webster was the guy everyone was talking about on TV. He said yes. Oh my gosh!

I had seen it on the TV that morning. I had woken up relatively late, at about 7:00 A.M.. I was tired. I had gone out the night before to a club. Clubbing was something I did frequently to help me relax. I loved the loud music and the intoxicating environment of a club. So I was relatively tired, since I typically woke up around 5:00 A.M. every day to go to mass. I fixed myself a cup of coffee. I lived alone in the condominium. I sat down on a couch and flipped through the channels. First I went to CNN and the item on the news was the death of this great football player, Mike Webster. They said he was one of the greatest centers who ever played. I did not know what that meant since I knew nothing about football, absolutely nothing. I did not know what a center was. I turned to another channel and it was the same thing: Mike Webster. Everyone was talking about this guy, how well he played on the field, but how badly he lived after football when he retired. He was derogated on TV, demeaned, and made fun of. I heard things like, retired football players do not save their money and they make very poor business decisions. That they ought to be doing better than they were doing.

I was flustered by what I heard. In fact I may have become angry at some point. I thought that the guy, whatever his name was—I did not bother to even remember his name, honestly—was not being treated fairly. I thought he was rather a victim of the game and not of himself. I thought that he had been exploited and dumped. If he had played a game whereby they wore large amounts of protective gear including a helmet, that meant that the game was dangerous. Having seen this game played on satellite TV on a few occasions in Africa, all I knew was the players ran into one another a whole lot and banged their heads repeatedly like guinea pigs running around.

Football. Now, football was one aspect of American life that Bennet had not keyed into particularly. *What an odd and inelegant game,* he thought, to the extent that he ever thought about it at all. Guinea pigs bashing. All that padding. *If it hurts so much that you have to bubble-wrap your body, maybe you should play something different.* That was about the extent of his football analysis. But, okay, football. Pittsburgh sure loved its football. Black and gold, black and gold, signs on cars and on front yards and black and gold cupcakes in bakeries. You would expect bored guys with beer bellies, guys like the morgue tech, to be engaged in watching that sporting event, but in Pittsburgh it was more than that. It was old ladies on stoops, teenagers, infants in Steelers outfits, Father Carmen and Cyril Wecht and Sigrid, too. *The whole town.* Season tickets passed through generations, were listed in people's wills; divorced couples fighting over custody did so not just for children, but for season Steelers tickets, too.

Football, for Pittsburgh, was a self-esteem issue. Football had come to the rescue during the darkest days in the 1970s, when the once mighty steel town sank like a tank from the twelfth-largest city in the nation to the twenty-fourth. Everybody leaving. All those gray mornings, the city smothered in clouds, no sun, no money, no jobs, no more steel, no more smoke pumping out of the Hazelwood stacks, no more hot metal pouring out of the J&L, no more guys rolling out from the night shift at dawn, guys heading down to Jack's for a shot-and-a-beer breakfast. All of that: done. Everything you grew up knowing your daddy did, and your grandpa did, no, it would not be for you. What would you do? Where would you go? How would you feed a family? No answers. Pull the covers over your head because there were no answers.

But then came Sunday, then came one o'clock on Sunday, the black and the gold. Sellout crowds. The black and the gold. Here were the warriors coming out to fight for your vindication. The Steelers clobbered the Minnesota Vikings in the 1975 Super Bowl, the Dallas Cowboys in 1976 and again in 1979, the Los Angeles Rams in 1980. Four championships in six years. Thank God for football. You lived in Steeler Nation now, not some shithole Pittsburgh. And all those people leaving, they were part of Steeler Nation, too. Pockets of black and gold all over the country. Steeler Nation was an identity, dignity you could never lose because no one could take those rings away—and you had *four* of them. *You!*

So Mike Webster dying, that was significant. Iron Mike. Nine-time Pro Bowler. Hall of Famer. Four Super Bowl rings. He had played center for fifteen seasons, a warrior's warrior; he played in more games—two hundred twenty—than any other player in Steelers history. Undersized, tough, a big, burly white guy—a Pittsburgh kind of guy—the heart of the best team in history.

And now here he was in the morgue, dead at fifty.

"Fifty?" Bennet said, scanning the file. "Fifty is young."

"Heart attack," the tech said.

"On TV, they were saying he went crazy," Bennet said. "Why did he go crazy?"

The tech said nothing. How the hell did he know why Webster went crazy?

They wheeled the body in. It had been embalmed so that the family and the city and all of Steeler Nation could come pay their respects at the funeral the day before. Now it was just a gray corpse wearing jeans. No shirt. No shoes. *Such dense tissue,* Bennet thought. Thick. So much wear and tear. His blocky forehead was one massive scar, perhaps from his helmet? Bennet had never seen such scar tissue on a face. Webster's hands were huge as hams, the fingers mangled and twisted like the roots of a willow. His feet were cracked open and bent in places you never knew feet could bend. The skin on the thighs had been seared, over and over again, by the prongs of a Taser.

"They were making fun of him because he went crazy," Bennet said.

"No one made fun of him," the tech said. "This is Iron Mike."

"They were calling him a lunatic," Bennet said.

If football had battered Webster's body this badly, Bennet could only imagine what it might have done to his brain. He was just finishing his neuropathology training at the University of Pittsburgh, and he was loving brains. Every brain like an innocent child, tender as a naked baby nestled inside the protective cradle of the skull. Bennet was looking forward to seeing what Mike Webster's brain looked like.

As it was for Pittsburgh, football for Mike Webster was salvation. He grew up on a potato farm in Tomahawk, Wisconsin, barely survived a childhood of crippling poverty and regular beatings by his dad. He seemed to never outgrow the singular trait of desperation that got him out of that hellhole. A person could not work physically harder or push himself further. He trained maniacally when he played for the University of Wisconsin and became the best center in the Big Ten. He was small for a football player, six foot one, a little over two hundred pounds. He got picked up by the Steelers in the fifth round in 1974, but his stature didn't overly impress trainers, or maybe they were too busy being dazzled by the team's superstar picks that year: Lynn Swann, Jack Lambert, John Stallworth, a once-in-a-lifetime haul of talent.

Webby, they called him in the locker room. He was the goofy prankster who kept the place happy. He had a wife, Pam, and four kids, and he loved being a dad—the kind of dad to volunteer for homeroom duty. He had a fire inside, a well of determination so deep. The Steelers used him as backup center for two years, and he paced the sidelines like a caged bull, needing so much more.

Determination. Sheer will. Whatever it took. He doubled, tripled, quadrupled the already insane training regimen he had developed in college. Even guys on the team thought it was extreme. He'd be out there in his front yard in the snow at dawn, full pads, helmet, doing drills by himself, pushing the blocking sled. He took amphetamines, steroids, supplements, anything anyone said was any good. By 1976 he had increased his body weight by 25 percent, most of it muscle. "The Strongest Man in Football," they said on TV, when during a CBS special he lifted 275 pounds over his head twelve times, then bench-pressed 350 pounds fifteen times. In 1976, he became the Steelers' starting center—and he did not stop. He played in bare arms so no one could grab his sleeves. Five degrees below zero: bare arms. Collision football. Snap the ball back to Bradshaw, then explode into other guys, head first, smashmouth football, the sound of helmets crashing, grunting, howling. War. He was low to the ground so he could get under people with his head. He would get under and then pull up with his head, *uproot* guys. One by one, then the next, play after play—for more than ten years, 177 straight games, never missed a snap—a streak of 5,871 consecutive offensive plays—four Super Bowls, eight consecutive seasons in the Pro Bowl.

Iron Mike. The best center in the NFL.

Then in 1988 the Steelers were done with him and he went off and played two years for Kansas City. He was the last of the guys from the old Steelers Super Bowl days to retire. He was thirty-eight years old. He was in Kansas. *Kansas?* He built a giant house in Kansas City. Pam loved it. The kids loved it. Mike loved it, and then he hated it. Hated it with a passion and without reason. He would fly into rages. Plenty of guys had a hard time after retiring from football—you had to adjust to a new identity and a new schedule, like coming out of the army, like coming home from war. Maybe this was some kind of PTSD? He got lethargic. He forgot to eat. He was getting so weird. One day he peed in the oven. "Why did Daddy pee in the oven?" The kids were becoming frightened. What was happening to Dad? The family started running out of money. He had made over a million dollars in his last three years of football alone.

"Where did all the money go?" Pam cried.

"Money?" he said.

He had no idea what she was talking about. He couldn't remember. Couldn't keep his thoughts straight.

They sold the house at a loss and moved to Wisconsin, where he and Pam had grown up. He disappeared, came back. Months at a time disappeared, wandered back. His youngest son, Garrett, was seven, so happy to see his dad again whenever he showed up. He would take Garrett to the drugstore, sit in the parking lot, tell him to go on in there and talk the pharmacist into giving him some painkillers. "Don't tell him I'm out here." Garrett would obey, and Webster would fly into a rage when he came back to the car empty-handed. "Dad! Dad! I'm sorry!" He'd wander off again. He slept in train stations, went back to Kansas City, took up residence in the storage closet above the weight room at Arrowhead Stadium. Plenty of people tried to help him, but no one could keep track of him. Here one day, gone the next. He went back to Pittsburgh, slept in the Greyhound bus station, fell into the hands of an opportunist who recognized him— Iron Mike!—and in no time figured out how to profit off him.

Selling autographs at bowling alleys. Speeches in parking lots. For three hundred bucks you could have Mike Webster *come to your home* and watch a game with you! He did what he was told. He had pain everywhere. His neck, his hands and feet. *Pain.* He got pills, finally. Apparently, Pam filed for divorce, but he was so out of it he had no idea. People tried to help, Terry Bradshaw sent checks, Steelers owner Dan Rooney put him up in the Pittsburgh Hilton—for three months. Then he wandered off, meandered through Pittsburgh, slept under bridges, in the Amtrak station, then lived in his truck. He drove to Philadelphia. He showed up in the historic Warwick Hotel. Beautiful hotel! Wandering. Somehow he got guns. A SIG SAUER P226 semiautomatic pistol, an AR-15 semiautomatic assault rifle, a .357 Magnum revolver. He would walk up to strangers and rant. "Kill 'em! I'm gonna kill 'em!" He would say that about Steelers execs and other NFL people. "Kill 'em!" And his feet. All cracked up. His teeth started falling out. Stupid teeth. He got Super Glue, squirted each fallen tooth, tried to stick them back in. His fingers were all bent so it was hard to master the dental work. He wrapped his hands with duct tape and stuck a pen in the tape so he could write letters. He wrote thousands of letters.

What Do I do, I am over fucking overwhelmed . . . what to Do . . . Have NO way Be able to Help my Kids Everyone other Family Dependents and Keep Them Healthy Safe. . . . Maybe me worthless piece of crap but can NOT Let That Get to me have to Keep Trying Keep Work at all this but How Do I Do anything Now?

He bought himself a Taser, used it on his stomach or his thigh, *thwack*! He zapped himself into unconsciousness, just to get some sleep.

. . .

In the autopsy room, Bennet put on his rubber apron and his plastic face shield and his headset and turned the music up: Teddy Pendergrass, Bob Marley, Julio Iglesias. He lined up his instruments. He was easily the most meticulous medical examiner in the morgue; this was, after all, his art. He was the Michael Jackson of autopsy. He sterilized the instruments before each autopsy, which seemed ridiculous to the techs. Infection was *not* an issue with dead bodies. But Bennet thought it only right. "Would you want dirty instruments used on your dad's autopsy?"

He snapped on his purple gloves, pulled up his plastic sleeve liners and approached the slab. He noted that Mike Webster's body was sixty-nine inches long and weighed 244 pounds, and he told the tech to please write that down. Then he propped up Mike Webster's head.

"Okay, Mike," he said.

The tech assisting him on the autopsy pursed her lips. *Oh, here he goes.* No other pathologist at the morgue did this. Nobody but Bennet talked to the dead.

I spoke quietly while standing by Mike Webster's body on the table. I reached out and held his forehead and said, "Mike, you have been misjudged. It is not right. They do not understand. We have to prove them wrong. Please help me. Guide me to the truth, let me use my education to establish the truth. Let us vindicate you."

Bennet picked up his scalpel, sliced open the chest, and cracked open Mike Webster's ribs. He took out the heart and found everything he expected of a man who was believed to have died of a heart attack—thickened, way oversized. Then he took out the liver, the stomach, the kidneys. He measured and snapped pictures, rinsed his instruments, went back in, rinsed, kept his area neat and clean as always.

He respected the dead. *There but for the grace of God go I*. It could be Oba on the table. It could be Winny or Uche or Mie-Mie or his mom.

Then he took Mike Webster's head and he made a cut from behind the right ear, across the forehead, to the other ear and around. He peeled the scalp away from the skull in two flaps. With the electric saw he carefully cut a cap out of the skull, pulled off the cap, and gently reached inside for the brain.

How did this big athletic man, only fifty years old, end up so crazy in the head?

He was thinking about football and brain trauma. He was thinking of Mike Webster, the guinea pigs bashing. The leap in logic was hardly extreme. He was thinking, *dementia pugilistica?* "Punch-drunk syndrome," they called it in boxers. The clinical picture was somewhat like Mike Webster's: severe dementia—delusion, paranoia, explosive behavior, loss of memory—caused by repeated blows to the head. Bennet figured if chronic bashing of the head could destroy a boxer's brain, couldn't it also destroy a football player's brain? Could that be what made Mike Webster crazy? It seemed like an obvious question. Had no one ever asked that question? Perhaps someone had. Perhaps there was a whole body of literature investigating dementia pugilistica and football and he had somehow missed it? The thought disappointed him. He had been so scrupulous in his reading ever since he picked pathology—not like when he was in med school, back in Nigeria, when he was such a foolish boy. Now he was a man and he had chosen this specialty and he was the Michael Jackson of autopsy and he had done a fellowship in neuropathology at the University of Pittsburgh. He was a neuropathologist, the kind of scientist who never skipped a chapter. Surely someone in the history of football had thought to look for dementia pugilistica?

Then again, unlike boxers, football players wear helmets, good protection for the skull. So it would be reasonable to think that the brain would be spared damaging impact. But plenty of people knew better. Anybody who knew anything about the anatomy of the head knew better. It was a simple matter of physics. The brain floats, is suspended in a kind of thick jelly inside the skull. If you hit the head hard enough, that brain is going to move, no matter what kind of protection you put around the skull. A helmet protects the skull. A helmet can't keep the brain from sloshing around in that skull. If you hit your head hard enough, the brain goes bashing against the walls of the skull. Bennet had seen plenty of cases of brains destroyed despite helmets. People in motorcycle crashes wore helmets. *On the surface is nothing, but you open the skull and the brain is mush.* Bennet picked up Webster's brain, carried it slowly to the cutting board, and turned it upside down and on its side and then over again. He reached for his camera and snapped pictures of the brain, as he routinely did for organs he removed from the body for further study.

I had my earphones on playing Teddy Pendergrass. I believe it was "Love 4/2." And guess what, I was extremely disappointed when I looked at Mike Webster's brain. Mike Webster's brain looked grossly normal by naked-eye examination. There was mild atrophy, but it was negligible.

It was not at all what he expected Webster's brain to look like. Regular folds of gray matter. No mush. No obvious contusions, like you find in dementia pugilistica. No shrinkage like you would see in Alzheimer's disease. He reviewed the CT and MRI scans. All normal.

Honestly, I was extremely disappointed. I may have said in my heart to Mike, hey Mike, what is going on? Please do not let me down. I examined all the external surfaces, and there was no single significant gross finding on his brain. Not even one contusion. Typically, I would then have cut the brain in the fresh state, taken one or two small 2 x 2 cm sections and saved them, without performing any comprehensive brain examination. That is what you typically do at that point, when you have no evidence of brain damage. I already had a cause of death. The autopsy had shown that Mike died of heart disease. I should not have saved his brain. I had no reason or justification to save his brain. It should have been cut in the fresh state and placed back in the body. In fact I had the brain knife in my hand, about to slice the brain into two, with the brain lying on the tissue chopping board.

The most important moment in the entire quagmire that befell my life was that moment when I did not cut the brain in the fresh state. I decided to save the brain, fix it in formalin, and examine it at a later date. I had to spend time with this brain. Something just did not match. I could not understand it. I even became more flustered. The technician challenged me and asked me why I was fixing the brain, the brain should not be saved. I looked sternly at her, and said in a deep, firm monotone: "Fix that brain for me." While I walked away from Mike's body, I said to him, in my heart: "Thank you, Mike, thank you. I promise, I will not let you down, but you have to help me and guide me." Every fiber of being in me believed that there was something wrong, but I did not understand it.

You don't just go fixing random brains. This wasn't cadavers in school. This was *Mike Webster*.

"You might need to talk to Dr. Wecht," the tech said. "And the family. I'm not sure if you can just take the brain—"

"*Fix the brain,*" Bennet said, and he flipped off his rubber apron and his face mask and snapped off his gloves and went up to his office to call his boss.

There was nothing usual about the request. Another boss might have said, "Stick with the protocol," especially to a rookie like Bennet, who was acting only on a hunch. But Wecht had already made a professional investment in Bennet; he was becoming a valuable asset to Wecht's booming personal business. And Bennet was such a loyal soldier. Junior Wecht on this neuropathology kick. And, wow, this was Mike Webster.

"Okay if I study his brain?" Bennet said.

"Mike Webster," Wecht said. "What are you looking for?"

"Anything."

"Iron Mike," Wecht said. "Yeah, go ahead. Just be sure to make me fucking famous."

It was late, nearly midnight, by the time Bennet finished the other three autopsies on the roster that day and then completed his paperwork and his reports for the week. He liked working after everyone else was gone. Productive time. He picked up Webster's file and thought about how he might talk to the family about studying Mike Webster's brain. He was glad there was a family attorney listed in the file; he would call the guy's office, leave a voicemail, get the conversation started.

"Bob Fitzsimmons," said the voice.

Oh. So late? On a Saturday night?

"Hello?" Bennet said. "Bob Fitzsimmons?"

"Who's calling?"

He introduced himself. "I didn't expect anyone to pick up," Bennet said.

"I work late," Fitzsimmons said.

A kindred spirit.

Fitzsimmons's office was in a renovated firehouse in Wheeling, West Virginia, and he often would come to the office after he got done taking care of his dying mother. It was a rough time. Work helped. He struggled to understand Bennet's accent on the phone, jutted his head forward. "Okay, wait. What do you need?"

The brain. Permission from the Webster family to process Mike Webster's brain for microscopic examination.

Oh, brother, was Fitzsimmons's initial thought. *As if the Webster case wasn't already complicated enough.*

Fitzsimmons knew more about Mike Webster than perhaps any other person in the world did at that point. He had first met him in 1997, when Webster showed up unannounced at his office asking for help untangling his messed-up life. It was confusing. "Wait—*Iron Mike*?" Fitzsimmons said, at first. Webster was a hulk of a man with oak-tree arms, and Fitzsimmons was not sure how or why he had made it out to Wheeling, West Virginia, for help. Fitzsimmons shook his hand and got lost in it, mangled fingers going every which way, hitting his palm in creepy places that made him flinch. Every one of those fingers had been broken many times. Webster sat down and told Fitzsimmons what he could remember about his life. He had been to dozens of lawyers and dozens of doctors, and at that point Fitzsimmons was another stop along the road. Webster really couldn't remember whom he'd seen or when. He couldn't remember if he was married or not. He had a vague memory of divorce court. And Ritalin. Lots of Ritalin.

"With all due respect, you're losing your train of thought, sir," Fitzsimmons said to Webster that first time they met. "You appear to have a serious illness, sir." Not a pleasant thing to tell anyone, and here was a local icon, a famous football player Fitzsimmons once bowed to, as did all young guys in the Ohio Valley worth the Terrible Towels they proudly waved in the 1970s. The black and the gold. It fueled optimism here, too, just like in Pittsburgh, all along this region, up and down the rivers, abandoned mills and crippled mill towns held tight in the folds of the Allegheny Mountains.

As a personal injury lawyer, Fitzsimmons had fought for plenty of people with closed-head injuries—car and motorcycle crash victims, people getting blasted in industrial accidents. Some of his clients had developed severe psychiatric problems, memory loss, personality changes, aggressive behavior as a result of their injuries. It went with the territory. Was this what he was seeing in Webster?

"Please help me," Mike Webster said.

Fitzsimmons tried. He was the closest ally Webster had during the crazy years of his decline. It took him a year and a half to hunt down all of Webster's medical records, scattered in doctors' offices throughout western Pennsylvania, Kansas City, Wisconsin, West Virginia. Hundreds of pages of medical files. He could find just two references to head injuries, which he thought strange, considering Mike's mental condition. He sent Webster to new doctors for new evaluations. Four separate medical evaluations confirmed Fitzsimmons's suspicion: closed-head injury as a result of multiple concussions.

So in 1998 Fitzsimmons filed a disability claim with the NFL's Bert Bell / Pete Rozelle NFL Player Retirement Plan.

Guys would file claims for lasting effects of knee injuries, back problems, and other physical conditions they believed resulted from their playing days. The six-member pension board making the decisions—three player representatives and three team owner representatives—was notoriously stingy in approving claims, and it had virtually no experience in dealing with players coming forward to say they suffered mental problems as a result of playing football. Football might cause bad knees, shoulders, or backs, but football did *not* cause brain damage. That was a given. There was no proof that football did anything to anybody's mind.

Fitzsimmons went after that notion. He argued that Webster's case was a work-related injury, pure and simple. A guy spends fifteen years bashing himself in the head repeatedly with more than sixty g's of force for a living, and then goes insane—well, his workplace owes him something.

Fitzsimmons won the case. It was the first time the NFL had ever made the finding of football-related brain injury. But it was not retroactive. Webster would qualify for payments only as of 1998, the year the claim was filed. There would be nothing dating back to his retirement in 1991. The difference amounted to more than a million dollars, and Fitzsimmons argued in an appeal that Webster was owed it.

Here was a man who Tasered himself, peed in his oven, used Super Glue on his teeth. "Four doctors," Fitzsimmons argued—"all with the same diagnosis, some dating back years!"

The NFL said no. Four doctors were not enough. They wanted Webster seen by their own doctor.

"Bring it on," Fitzsimmons said.

The doctor the NFL hired for the job examined Webster and concurred with the other four: Closed-head injury.

Football-related. And Fitzsimmons gathered affidavits from people across the nation like TV anchors who had tried to employ Webster only to discover that he was demented. The NFL pension board voted unanimously for limited disability payments anyway.

"You have got to be kidding me," Fitzsimmons said. He filed an appeal with the U.S. District Court in Baltimore, where the pension board is headquartered.

In 2005, the judge would ultimately reverse the decision of the NFL pension board to deny Webster back payments—the first time in history any such action had been taken against the NFL.

And yet still the NFL fought. They appealed that verdict in a higher court. They said Mike Webster—who had endured probably twenty-five thousand violent collisions during his career and now was living on Pringles and Little Debbie pecan rolls, who was occasionally catatonic, in a fetal position for days—they said Mike Webster wasn't crazy long enough to qualify for what the courts had said he was owed.

Mike Webster and Bob Fitzsimmons grew close during those days. In fact, Webster clung to Fitzsimmons like a baby to his mama. He took to sleeping in the parking lot outside Fitzsimmons's office, waiting for him to show up for work. He would write him letters. Hundreds and hundreds of letters. "Dear Bob, Thank you for helping me. We've got to keep up the fight. We have to see this thing through." And then he would start talking about wars. And blood splattering. The letters would inevitably trail off into the mutterings of a madman.

And now he was dead.

Fitzsimmons held the phone and took a giant gulp of air as he listened to Bennet, the stranger with the thick accent who was calling from the Allegheny County coroner's office, four days after Webster died of a heart attack, asking to study Webster's brain. Fitzsimmons was, in truth, grieving his client's death deeply; in his increasingly rare lucid moments, Webster had been living for nothing but the case, the appeal, the last victory against a multi-billion-dollar entertainment industry that had used him, had crippled both his body and his mind, and then had thrown him away like a rotten piece of meat.

And now he was dead.

"Yeah," Fitzsimmons said that night to Bennet on the phone. "You should go ahead and study that brain."

CHAPTER 7

DISCOVERY

Mike Webster's brain sat for two weeks in a white plastic bucket of formaldehyde at the morgue, and when it was firm enough, Bennet pulled it out and put it on the cutting board. He took a scalpel to the frontal lobe, sliced it off, then cut a section from it about the width of a stick of gum. He did the same to the parietal, occipital, and temporal lobes. He packed the four slices into plastic cassettes, put them in his briefcase, and took them up to the lab at the University of Pittsburgh, where he had just finished his neuropathology training and knew the technicians and their particular expertise.

Jonette Werley was the grandmother of the place. She was a round woman with a blond bob and a magnanimous way, and when she saw Bennet she stood up and reached out her arms. "Look at you!" she said. Bennet flashed a smile and tilted his head as if inviting further admiration. "We miss you around here, Bennet. It's so boring!"

Say what you would about Bennet, but his idiosyncratic ways could perk a place up—especially an academic department with a lot of ambitious research scientists in sloppy attire yakking about the size of research grants or complaining about the backbiting ways of rival colleagues. Bennet wasn't like them, wasn't in that racket. He cared nothing about academic rank; he was the quirky guy from the morgue who had come to Pitt and studied brains to satisfy an intellectual curiosity. He was a guy from Cyril Wecht's world—the polar opposite of an academic research laboratory. Forensic pathology, at least the Wecht brand, was about showmanship and conviction and razzle-dazzle and Bennet had unapologetically embraced it. *Show me whose hands those are, and I will show you who the killer is!* That kind of stuff had no place in a research facility. People like Jonette found Bennet's theatricality refreshing.

Bennet opened his briefcase and handed Jonette the four cassettes. He said nothing about whose brain it was; a man's brain was holy. It wasn't unusual for Jonette to process tissue for the morgue or other outside contractors. Certain labs across the country specialized in the work, and Jonette had been at it for decades.

"You just want the routine panel?" Jonette asked.

"If you please," Bennet said, indicating which antibodies he wanted her to use in the processing.

She was to shave each block of Mike Webster's brain into microscopic slivers, then mount the slivers onto glass slides and stain them with the antibodies. The stains bring any unusual patterns of cells into view. A neuropathologist could choose between some thirty stains, and Bennet ordered the selection he had come to use routinely when he examined brains for neurodegenerative diseases such as Alzheimer's, Parkinson's, and Lou Gehrig's. He didn't expect to find any of those diseases specifically in Mike Webster's brain, but maybe something with a link?

He knew it was a long shot. He was acting on a guess, like a kid on some sort of treasure hunt. He decided he would be glad enough if no one ever asked him about it. He told Jonette to submit the bill for the tissue processing to him personally, not to the coroner's office; he didn't want any of the techs at the morgue involved in the paperwork, didn't want anyone looking over his shoulder or making fun of him for his indulgence. It would cost a few thousand dollars for just the first batch of slides, and after that there was no telling. He didn't mind paying for it. For the first time in his life he was making real money—a bachelor earning close to six figures in a city where the cost of living was among the lowest in the country. He was giving large sums to St. Benedict's, and sending money home to his parents in Nigeria. He helped Uche and Ikem and the others buy a generator for the compound, a giant, thunderous orange machine that could provide a reliable source of power; Oba's ailing health now required round-the-clock air-conditioning. It felt good to pay for that. It was a way of showing his father that he was a man now.

"I'll need a few weeks for these, okay?" Jonette said.

"Thank you," Bennet said.

Mike Webster's brain was not, at least not at that point, an urgent mission, or even a calling. It was a curiosity and a whisper. It was him talking to Webster on the slab that Saturday morning and him hearing Webster ask for help explaining what had happened to his brain—which, when you held that kind of transaction up to scrutiny, sounded like poppycock and maybe even its own kind of dementia. It wasn't something you could say out loud in America, wasn't something you could say to Wecht, or the academics at Pitt, or even to a religious man like Father Carmen. If he had been home in Nigeria, sipping brandy with his brothers or eating kola nuts with his sisters, he could have discussed that sort of thing long into the night; the Igbo tradition left room for spirits in all forms. He imagined his father with his high hat, and he pictured Chizoba wearing one, and he heard Ikem praying, and he imagined Winny holding her head back, weeping and rejoicing.

Nigeria was emotion, fire and prayer and hunches, and America was reason, ambition, and wealth. He bounced between those two spheres, not quite in one but not quite in the other. And maybe it was the necessity of having to hang there, in the uncertainty of transition, pulling forward and getting pushed backward, that enabled him to see what others had not yet seen.

When the slides came back from Jonette in late October, Bennet put them on a shelf in his office at the morgue and for weeks he didn't bother to look at them. He was not on a timetable. No one was asking for results. This kind of brain research was a personal curiosity. It was like a novel he had started writing; he would get back to it when he had time.

"Wait, you bought Prema a *dress*?" Father Carmen said.

"It's yellow," Bennet said. "It has a fashion designer label on it and it is very elegant."

"A *dress*?"

"She was very surprised when she opened the box," Bennet said. They were in the kitchen convent and the nuns had left them a pile of gingerbread cookies to share.

"I don't know that women like something so . . . personal," Father Carmen said. "She might have interpreted it as your saying she's not stylish or something."

"She's not!" Bennet said. "She is very drab in her appearance!"

"Hoo boy, Bennet." Father Carmen hardly had authority when it came to dating tips, but still. "You should be careful not to insult her." He sat back in his chair, looked away, folded his arms. The maple tree outside the window had exploded into orange, red, and gold, and the autumn dew made it droop.

Bennet had been spending a lot of time with Prema, a nurse from Kenya who had come to the United States to advance her studies and had joined the parish shortly after Bennet did. Yinka had introduced them at a party. Prema had been sitting with a small group of newcomers and she was not flashy or fancy. She had a long face, long hair, a smooth neck; she was like a zinnia plant with neither bloom nor bud; with a little nourishment she would flower, Bennet thought, that first time he saw her.

Bennet had walked up to her and he tried to be booming and powerful like Theodore and his father. An Omalu manly man! He talked at her, told her about his car, as he was holding his shoulders up to make himself look muscular.

"You must be Nigerian," she said, eyeing him up and down. She said she did not like Nigerian men. She said Nigerian men were arrogant. She turned her back on him.

"I think she may have been tired," Bennet explained to Father Carmen when he recounted the incident.

"Uh-huh."

"It was the end of the day."

"Right."

"I was wondering if you knew her?"

Father Carmen did. He told Bennet that Prema was new to America, had been here only a few months, and he suggested that Bennet try again with her, offer to help her with her transition to Pittsburgh. So that's what Bennet did. He reintroduced himself to her after church one day, a few weeks later, handing her a roll of twenties.

"What is this?" she said.

"Father Carmen said you need help?"

She winced.

This was going nowhere. He was rusty with women, so rusty. Eventually he offered to give Prema a lift to the grocery store, then drove her around to do errands, took her to the laundromat, helped her fold. She liked that. The frequency of the favors increased. Bennet did not take Prema on dates and he did not consider himself to be dating her; he was helping, that was all. He felt comfortable doing things *for* her, not with her.

"I was thinking of taking her to a hairdresser," Bennet told Father Carmen that day in the convent kitchen. He'd been "helping" Prema for a few months by now and it was turning into a kind of chase. Gifts and favors, surprises by her door. The dress and hair ideas were just the latest. "She does not take care of her hair like she should."

"Bennet, I don't think—" Father Carmen said. "My recommendation is that you stay away from fashion altogether."

"Her hair will be so beautiful for church on Sunday," Bennet said. "You will see."

"Okay, well, God bless you, Bennet." Father Carmen grabbed a cookie, popped it in his mouth.

"The hair is too much?" Bennet said.

"Bennet, you're fine."

"I'm just trying to help."

"I'm sure she's very grateful."

"I found out she sends money to her mother in Kenya," Bennet said. "*That melts my heart!* That makes me want to help more."

Bennet continued to bombard Prema with this thing he called help. He told her he wanted to start paying her rent, her tuition, how about some spending money? Prema laughed. Who was this odd man bursting with generosity? It seemed that the guy with the cackle-laugh who sang so loudly in church wanted a project, and she was it. She found it amusing, and, in time, adorable.

As for Bennet, he did not experience the giving as generous. He just wanted to be near her. He saw in her the fire of Uche, the compassion of Winny, the softness of his mom. He saw in her a will of iron he knew so well. Going to nursing school all day, working the cleaning crew at a bank at night, then all day at school the next day, sending money home to her mom. The two of them against the world, that's how Bennet saw it. He was working his butt off and so was she. The two of them not like everyone else. Everyone else their age out having fun, enjoying life, but the two of them working so hard, working to catch up with the Americans.

Prema became Bennet's companion on that fabled journey. And if they were falling in love, Bennet was not yet ready to see it.

One day, nearly a month after he put the processed slides of Mike Webster's brain on his office shelf, Bennet decided to look at them. Truthfully, at that point it was arbitrary. He had at least a dozen research projects in development. He had brain samples from people suffering diseases such as West Nile virus, and from suicide victims. He would take the slides home and look at them under the microscope on his dining room table, scan, imagine, and think. People don't tend to associate scientists with a muse, but Bennet trusted that sort of relationship implicitly. *The mind should be allowed to wander!* It was the same as with his drawer and the bottle caps, his books in school, the files in the Kimbell case. The mind, he long ago discovered, was a private playground, a place for random conversations and games, always welcoming and never proscriptive. It was something that could clamp irrationally onto something unknowable like depression. It was a mystery as vast and elusive as God.

He brought the slides of Mike Webster's brain home to his condominium, where he could study them in the darkness before dawn without having to explain. He sat at his dining room table where there was a reading lamp and a microscope and a white plastic box that opened at the top and when you looked inside you saw rows of glass slides all lined up, clear with hues of pink and tan. Paper-thin slices of Mike Webster's brain.

He loaded the first slide and leaned over the microscope and adjusted the light and moved the lens into focus. He didn't see anything but clean tissue, and so he put in a second slide and then a third. He sat back, tapped his fingers on the plastic box a few times, and he heard the clock in the kitchen tick loudly.

He reviewed the photos he had taken of Mike Webster's body and he went back to the death certificate, unwinding the story and restarting from the beginning as he knew it, and as Wecht had taught him to do. Rebuild the story, block by block, and don't add the next until the pieces fit snugly. The hospital report said Webster had died at Allegheny General Hospital from an acute myocardial infarction. He suffered from "depression secondary to post-concussion syndrome," suggesting the syndrome was a contributory factor to his death, thus making it accidental. Every accidental manner of death falls under the jurisdiction of the medical examiner. So that was the only reason Mike Webster's body ended up on the table for autopsy in the first place.

Bennet thought about the term "post-concussion syndrome" and he took a deep breath and he remembered one of the reasons he hated being a doctor. People always wanting a name for something, doctors inventing names, as if naming had anything to do with healing, let alone science. You couldn't come up with a more vague term than "post-concussion syndrome." Basically it meant someone suffering concussion symptoms such as headaches or dizziness for longer than concussion symptoms usually lasted. And how long was that? Who knew? Who decided? Where was the science? What, anyway, was a "concussion"?

People have been grappling with that one for centuries. Hippocrates mentioned *commotio cerebri* in his medical writings from ancient Greece. He described the loss of speech, hearing, and sight that could result from "commotion of the brain," a vigorous shake or blow to the head. After that you have to move all the way up to the tenth century to find further documentation. The Persian physician Abu Bakr Muhammad ibn Zakariya Razi is thought to be the first to make the distinction between the dramatic kind of brain injury—bruising and swelling and bleeding—that outright killed a person, and this other more subtle thing: an injury to the head that could make you dizzy, could even knock you unconscious, but from which you recovered. Razi was the first to use the term "cerebral concussion," and his definition of the condition—"a transient loss of function with no physical damage"—advanced incrementally over hundreds of years.

In the early sixteenth century the Italian physician Jacopo Berengario da Carpi, a pioneer in the science of anatomy, was dissecting hundreds of human cadavers and sketching his findings. He took apart skulls and examined brains and he came up with the idea that perhaps "brain commotion" was caused by the thrust of the soft structure of the brain against the solid case of the skull. The brain, he posited, was essentially bruised inside the skull by banging against the skull walls.

That would turn out to be a prescient theory. But there was little hope of advancing it, even when the microscope was invented at the end of the sixteenth century. Few people died from concussions, and so doctors didn't routinely have concussed brains to autopsy. Without the underlying pathology to describe it, the word "concussion" remained a description, not a diagnosis. It was a description of the state of unconsciousness and other functional problems that resulted from impact to the head, and most of the medical literature of the day pointed out the good news: unlike more severe forms of head injury, like crushing your skull or getting a bullet through your brain, this condition was temporary.

Or was it? Did the brain really always recover from concussions? Could there be a cumulative effect from multiple such injuries to the head? That question wouldn't get serious consideration until the twentieth century. Researchers like Michael Osnato and Vincent Giliberti, a pair of New York neuropsychiatrists, began finding patterns of mental degeneration in patients who had sustained mild head injuries. "It is no longer possible to say that concussion is an essentially transient state which does not comprise any evidence of structural cerebral injury," the authors concluded in a 1927 *Journal of the American Medical Association* article about one hundred such patients. "Not only is there actual cerebral injury in cases of concussion, but in a few instances complete resolution does not occur, and there is a strong likelihood that secondary degenerative changes develop."

That was a significant claim, and it got people like Harrison Martland, a forensic pathologist in Newark, New Jersey, thinking. He was interested in studying boxers, popular athletes of the day, many of whom were exhibiting strange behaviors. Fans called them "cuckoo," "goofy," or "slug nutty" and people enjoyed screaming at them as they staggered around the ring like intoxicated fools. What was going on in their brains?

"Punch Drunk" was the title of Martland's article in the October 13, 1928, issue of *JAMA*. "Punch drunk most often affects fighters of the slugging type," he wrote, "who are usually poor boxers and who take considerable head punishment, seeking only to land a knockout blow. It is also common in second rate fighters used for training purposes, who may be knocked down several times a day."

Martland's paper read as a plea on behalf of punch-drunk boxers everywhere who ended up going crazy and were sent to asylums where they would eventually turn into full-blown lunatics and curl up and die. It was not an unknown path; boxing was so popular it seemed everybody knew somebody who was slug nutty. Boxing was the most popular spectator sport in the United States and England, and anyone could put up their dukes and do it. The boxing booths would come to town for fairs and shows and the boxers would invite anyone to take them on and people would place bets and drink and holler. The punch-drunk boxers were the showstoppers.

"As far as I know this condition has practically not been described in medical literature," Martland wrote. "I am of the opinion that in punch drunk there is a very definite brain injury due to single or repeated blows on the head or jaw which cause multiple concussion hemorrhages in the deeper portions of the cerebrum."

But he didn't have any proof. He hadn't autopsied any boxers' brains.

"I realize that this theory, while alluring, is quite insusceptible of proof at the present time," he wrote. "But I am so convinced from my former studies on post-traumatic encephalitis that this is the logical deduction that I feel it my duty to report this condition." Martland posited that a boxer's brain was bruised, and that the bruises formed scars and caused the brain to atrophy. He said he believed that nearly one half of fighters who stayed in the ring long enough would develop the condition.

"The condition can no longer be ignored by the medical profession or the public," he wrote.

And yet it was. People loved boxing.

Prema had taken to visiting Bennet and watching his TV because she didn't have one. Then, as long as she was visiting, she figured she may as well cook, and so the two of them began sharing meals regularly. No candlelight dinners; none of that. This was just eat, get back to work. Prema's own studies kept her up late and she enjoyed the companionship. On the days she had hospital rotations outside the city where the buses didn't reach, Bennet would drive her, and if she had an early morning rotation she would stay at his apartment the night before. It was convenient, they both agreed. Nothing more to it.

"I know I don't live here and I have no right to complain, but must you store brains next to my soup?" she said one time.

He was bringing brains home, slicing them on the patio or out in the hallway. She thought it was such a curious hobby. She took photos of him doing it and they laughed. "Perhaps you might get a separate refrigerator?" she asked. She had no idea what he was studying or why he would be studying it. She was busy with her own work. She had never heard of Mike Webster and had no idea what football was.

One night, Bennet was looking in the microscope and she heard him say, "What is this? What in the world—?" He was looking at a slide from a section of Mike Webster's frontal lobe, and he saw strange, dark splotches.

"What's going on?" Prema said, calling from the kitchen.

"I have no idea," he said, flipping quickly now through one slide, then another. "It doesn't make any sense."

"What the mind doesn't know," she said in a singsong voice. It was a shorthand version of the phrase Bennet had taken to repeating.

"—the eye cannot see," he finished. "Yes, yes, exactly, Prema!" A professor had once taught him the saying and he never forgot it. You can't know what you're looking at unless you understand it.

He flipped to another slide, saw the same dark splotches. He sat back in his chair. "What the—?" He consulted a medical textbook, then another one, then dug into a binder of journal articles he had collected. He went back to the slides, the books, the slides. He kept finding the splotches—in Mike Webster's brain and in the books. He became increasingly engrossed in the story unfolding on the slides, and in the books, the history of concussion and brain trauma, what people knew and when they knew it, the rhythm of the evolution of science, fits and starts and wrong turns and denial and more fits and starts.

Scientific proof of Martland's 1928 theory about punch-drunk boxers wouldn't come for another four decades. In 1973 the British neuropathologist J.A.N. Corsellis studied fifteen former boxers who had died of natural causes. He cracked open their skulls, took their brains out, and studied them. He called his brain bank the Corsellis Collection and he documented his findings, including the clinical information he was able to gather, postmortem, from family members.

Case 1 (R.H. 54/71.) This boxer's ex-wife, a sister, and a brother were interviewed. He was a bright, healthy boy who did well at elementary school and excelled at sport. His boxing career began at a charity show when he was 11 years old and he went on to fight as a professional for the next 14 years. The number of his fights [is] estimated at 400; he lost a handful and one contest was stopped. He fought in the United States and became a British and a World Champion. As a young man he was quiet, generous, and abstemious. He married in his early 20s when he had already become a social as well as a boxing success. Soon his life became more hectic and "he changed completely." He wenched and drank and gambled heavily. His memory began to fail him. He had three car accidents. . . . His marriage broke up and he drifted away from his family, only returning for the occasional embarrassing visit. He had violent outbursts, he was "knocked out" by only a small amount of alcohol, his behavior was "disgusting." His brother remarked that "his brain was not functioning—he made mistakes in reckoning." He could not settle in a job and he became a vagrant. . . . At the age of 62 he was found lying neglected and louse-ridden in the boiler house of a hotel.

Case 7 (R.H. 124/71.) In this case the wife was interviewed. Her husband came from a family of boxers. He was not good at school—"he could read and write but never did." He started boxing as a professional at the age of 16 years and during the next 20 years or so he fought an estimated 400 contests. He was a popular, successful man and he traveled on many boxing tours around the world. He retired from the ring after a particularly damaging fight, and started to teach physical training and boxing in boarding schools. He gave this up after a few years at a time when he was drinking heavily and beginning to become moody and violent. A few years later he lost a job in a printing works for hiding away to sleep and he seems not to have worked again. . . . He had spells of "going within himself" followed by aggressive attacks on his wife and his home. He complained of violent headaches; his sexual demands gave his wife little rest. He wandered, out, half-dressed, at night and would importune for money. He had "glassy-looking eyes"; he was doubly incontinent at times. . . . He could not be left alone. When 59 he was admitted to a psychiatric hospital and found to be grossly demented.

Case 13 (R.H. 125/71.) The patient's daughter was interviewed. . . . He joined the Royal Navy at 14 years and rose to Petty Officer rank. During this time he boxed as an amateur and won a Royal Naval Championship in his weight. He won "several cups and many canteens of cutlery"; he took part in exhibition bouts; he was knocked out several times. He had cauliflower ears and a deformed nose. His wife had described him as good-tempered and popular at that time with a keen sense of responsibility and strict personal standards. . . . He became "more vague" and "spoke more slowly." He began to neglect his appearance and he complained that he could not grip things or get on a bus. His sight and his memory seemed a little faulty. . . . He became violent after two pints of beer, sometimes "fighting with his wife." . . . He wandered away bemused and had to be taken to a mental hospital. He was then 53. On admission he was mildly confused and complained of blackouts. His wife, from whom he was separated, but who was still concerned for him, said that his personality had been changing for the worse. . . . He could not recall his address or the date . . . completely disoriented and needed help with dressing. . . . The deterioration continued. He became incontinent, paranoid, and aggressive. He ate off the table with his fingers; a cigarette packet he called a flower; he undid buttons when asked to put his tongue out. He continued to have blackouts and a few days after a convulsion he died from bronchopneumonia, aged 57 years.

"The Aftermath of Boxing," Corsellis titled his paper. He told the case histories and followed each with a description of what he found when he looked inside the skulls of the dead boxers: unusual and specific damage to the tissue. Bruised and bashed, swollen and atrophied, irregular folds in irregular patterns. There was no question, even before examining the tissue under a microscope, that the boxers had sustained cerebral damage. Corsellis called the disease "dementia pugilistica."

"A single punch," Corsellis wrote, "or even many punches, to the head need not visibly alter the structure of the brain but there is still the danger that, at an unpredictable moment and for an unknown reason, one or more blows will leave their mark. The destruction of the cerebral tissue will have then begun and, although this will usually be slight enough in the early stages to be undetectable, it may build up, if the boxing continues, until it becomes clinically evident. At this point, however, it could be already too late, for destroyed cerebral tissue can never be replaced, while the further danger exists that the process of degeneration could smoulder on even after the boxing had stopped."

In his dining room, Bennet looked at the photos of the Corsellis Collection; he had this article in his collection of journal articles in his binder. He looked at the photos he had taken of Mike Webster's brain before he sliced into it. He put these images side by side. The Corsellis brains were bruised and bashed, swollen and atrophied. Webster's was not.

Bennet had imagined finding evidence of dementia pugilistica when he looked at Mike Webster's brain. He imagined irregular folds in irregular patterns as in the Corsellis Collection.

But now he was looking at Mike Webster's brain under the microscope.

And now he was reading what Corsellis saw in the boxer brains under a microscope.

The hippocampal neuronal population was considerably depleted. . . . Many neurofibrillary tangles in the nerve cells of the frontal and temporal cortex . . . particularly marked in the anteromedial temporal gray matter including the amygdaloid nucleus, the hippocampus and the parahippocampal gyrus.

Corsellis could have been dictating Bennet's findings. These were precisely the changes he was finding in Mike Webster's brain under the microscope.

"Everywhere," Bennet said to Prema that night while he looked. "It's all over the place! *What are these clumps doing here?*" he said, in his highest-pitched voice, the squeak that came out when he was angry or excited or both.

The clumps he found in Mike Webster's brain were build-ups of a protein called *tau*. Tau belongs in a healthy human brain. It acts as a kind of lubricant. But in concentrated masses, it forms clumps called neurofibrillary tangles. With the proper staining, these tangles announce themselves under a microscope and show up as dark splotches, random stars spitting rays.

"Everywhere," Bennet said, flipping through a series of slides of Webster's brain. Tau tangles were kind of like sludge, clogging up the works, killing healthy brain cells—in this case cells in regions of the brain responsible for mood, emotions, and executive functioning. This was why boxers went crazy. This was why Mike Webster went crazy, too.

"Just everywhere," Bennet said again and again into the night. He was finding tau tangles in the same regions as the Corsellis brains—and in other regions, too. Maybe this wasn't dementia pugilistica, but it was similar.

What do you do with something you notice that no one else has ever noticed before? Do you believe your eyes? Why had no one reported seeing something like this before?

Because no one had ever gone looking for a disease like that in a football player's brain before.

Was a professional football career similar to a boxer's when it came to head injury? To the untrained eye—which Bennet definitely was when it came to both American football and boxing—it seemed similar.

What the mind doesn't know, the eye can't see. But what the mind knows too well, the eye can miss altogether.

. . .

It was a warm day in May 2003 when Bennet drove up to the University of Pittsburgh to see his former professor, the neuropathologist Ronald Hamilton, who had been his teacher through his two-year fellowship training.

"Bennet?" Hamilton said. He took off his glasses and extended his hand.

"You like the suit?" Bennet said, standing in the doorway with his arms outstretched, like, *ta da!* He had taken to wearing his best suits even to run errands.

"I see ol' Cyril is treating you well," Hamilton said.

"He taught me that a black man must dress impeccably to get respect," Bennet said.

Hamilton smiled. He had forgotten about this; Bennet had a way of blatantly referring to matters others considered indelicate.

"The gay life is good?" Bennet asked.

Hamilton shook his head. How do you even answer something like that? Bennet had never met a gay man before Hamilton, and he found the concept fascinating and culturally enriching.

"It's really great seeing you again, Bennet," Hamilton said.

"Your shirt is thin and lifeless," Bennet said. "Have you considered starch?"

"Please, Bennet, please come in."

"I have something for you to look at," Bennet said, and he handed him the tray of slides. "Take your time with it."

"Now?"

"Can you?"

Hamilton rolled over an office chair for Bennet and told him to sit and he turned to his microscope and began looking at the slides.

"You're not going to tell me what I'm looking at?" Hamilton said.

"No. Like the old days. See what you come up with."

This was sport for neuropathologists. A guessing game. Can you look at the pathology and guess what the patient was suffering from?

Hamilton flipped through the first two slides, then dropped his shoulders in boredom. "You're bringing me an Alzheimer's case?" he said. "You do realize I spend my day with these—"

"No, keep looking," Bennet said. And so Hamilton took his time. One slide after the other, while Bennet twirled in the chair like a kid on a playground. He needed Hamilton's read on this. Hamilton was the expert. He'd made a significant discovery about abnormal masses of proteins in the brains of Alzheimer's patients during his decades-long career looking in microscopes.

"Huh," Hamilton said, having finally figured the puzzle out. "So how did you end up with a boxer down at that morgue?"

"It's not a boxer," Bennet said.

"It's not a boxer?" Hamilton said.

Nope.

Hamilton returned to the slides. "Where else do you find tau tangles like this?"

"It's a football player," Bennet said. "Mike Webster."

Hamilton looked at him, his eyebrows popping up in disbelief.

"A professional football player," Bennet said. "Mike Webster was a professional football player who played football for the Pittsburgh Steelers."

"Bennet, I know who Mike Webster was," Hamilton said. "But this is crazy."

"Mike Webster was crazy," Bennet said.

"I know—"

"And this is why."

Hamilton went back to the microscope.

"I've been looking at it for a long time, and this is why," Bennet said. Now he spoke like a confident man. He knew this stuff.

Hamilton sat back in his chair. The simplest, most elegant discovery. Football players getting dementia pugilistica.

Bennet explained the major difference between dementia pugilistica and his finding. In this case, the brain doesn't look battered at all on gross examination. It looks perfectly normal. It wouldn't be something a pathologist would have cause to go looking for. There would be no signs of it in a normal autopsy. You would have to know the clinical history. You would have to know the guy went crazy. You would have to then go cut the brain, stain it with these particular stains, and then look at it under the microscope. You would have to go through all the steps Bennet went through, following no protocol, following the call of only his own blind curiosity.

"Good lord."

"Same pathology, different presentation."

"This is crazy."

"Mike Webster was crazy," Bennet said.

"Dementia footballistica," Hamilton joked. He kept going back to the slides. "This is crazy. This has never been identified before."

"I've been sitting with it," Bennet said. "I have no other way of understanding it."

"We need to take this upstairs," Hamilton said.

And so that day Bennet and his former professor paid a visit to the chair of the University of Pittsburgh Department of Neurology, Steve DeKosky, director of the Alzheimer's Disease Research Center, who was preeminent in the field of neurodegenerative diseases. Bennet had met him maybe twice before, and only in passing. He was the grand pooh-bah. He was fancy and political. He was just the type of guy Bennet never wanted to become.

But DeKosky knew brains. And he'd had his own questions about the NFL and brain trauma. Alzheimer's researchers in his circle of colleagues had been talking about retired NFL players reportedly having memory problems. He had decided to follow up. He reached out to the NFL Hall of Fame and suggested a design for a large longitudinal study that would track Hall of Famers over time. The suggestion was never acknowledged—no one from the association had even written back to him—and the slight had made DeKosky ever more curious.

And now Hamilton was appearing in his office with a former fellow—that odd man who chose to work at the morgue instead of pursuing an academic career—with something to say about the brain of an NFL player.

DeKosky respected Hamilton. That was about the only reason he agreed to entertain Bennet's seemingly random presentation. The three sat and repeated the guessing game, only this time DeKosky was the one looking in the microscope.

Mike Webster's brain.

This is Mike Webster's brain.

"You have my attention," DeKosky said, and he got up to close the door.

And so Bennet explained what he had done and what he

had seen, and under the buzz of a fluorescent light in an office in a hospital on a sunny hillside in Pittsburgh, the three scientists agreed that they were looking at something no one had ever found before, let alone gone looking for. They decided to write a scientific paper about it and present it the way they would present the results of any important scientific study.

Later, Bennet told Wecht about what he had found in Mike Webster's brain, and Wecht said, "What? What the hell are you talking about, Bennet?"

He had Wecht's attention, and soon he would have America's.

| | | | |

CHAPTER 8

BELONGING

Uche came to visit and then Mie-Mie did and then Uche again; in those first years in Pittsburgh while Bennet studied brains, the two sisters circled in and out of Pittsburgh on business travels and vacations. For Mie-Mie it was a chance to visit the big brother she had always called her best friend. She was now a newly minted PhD, working for Shell Oil in the United Kingdom; she had a fancy life, fancy friends, a boyfriend of considerable wealth who drove a Rolls-Royce. Hanging out in Pittsburgh with Bennet in his little condo grounded her, was a respite from all that, her quirky brother with the brains in his fridge, doing experiments, writing papers—she thought it was awesome, and kind of adorable, and she was proud of him. She loved spending time with Prema, this quiet, iron-willed nurse from Nairobi whom Bennet was seeing—or maybe not seeing. That still was not clear. But Mie-Mie and Prema felt they were becoming sisters and Bennet got to feel like the man of the family; it was his apartment, his car, his world they had entered. On Saturdays they all went to the Grove City outlet mall together, on Sundays to St. Benedict's together. Bennet was proud to introduce Mie-Mie to the congregation; the people had gotten to know Uche, and now here was Mie-Mie. It was like he had a growing family here, he had sisters, Prema, Wecht like a father, and Father Carmen like a brother. He had work he cared about, and all of it together was like a cradle rocking him in 2003 and 2004, slowly rocking him, as the depression that had strangled his youth was gradually losing its grip.

Out of the cradle and into the real world. That's what it felt like. Or maybe: out of the loony bin and back into the real world. Maybe that was more like it. He would drive his Mercedes through the streets of Pittsburgh with Bob Marley blasting through the speakers and he would think how good and mysterious it felt to be emerging, finally, from the hell that had been holding him. He thought back to secondary school. The track team. You're watching everyone running, for so long just watching, thinking, marveling at the kids whizzing by you. But then something happens—what happens?—and you decide to stand up and push your foot off the soft ground and you find out you can do it, you can participate, and *oh my gosh you have a lot to offer!* He thought about his sister Winny, her telling him about that strange howling noise that came out of his mouth that day he went back to grab the baton from that fallen boy, that great howl of determination that came out of him! Winny couldn't stop marveling at that sound he had made, and he had no idea what she was talking about. *I made a sound?*

You belong. That was probably the biggest thing he felt in 2003 and 2004. In those days of discovery, when the depression lifted, he felt he was finally able to belong to something, to somewhere, to someone.

That was the spirit and that was the strength he brought to the scientific paper he was writing about Mike Webster's brain. He was doing what a respectable scientist does, and he felt comfortable in those shoes. He did not think his research on Mike Webster's brain was any more brilliant than any of his other studies; all of them were the results of logic, so all of them were beautiful. He had at least a half-dozen works in progress. He never stopped being interested in suicide. Why do some depressed people kill themselves and others do not? He would talk to Prema about it. "Could there be something in the brain itself?" he'd say. "We should do a study." She said she would help. Together they worked on a ten-year retrospective survey of suicides in Allegheny County, tracking patterns of brain pathology.

Also, he was working on "Fatal Constriction of an 8-Year-Old Child by Her Parents' Pet Python: A Call for Amendment to Existing Laws on the Ownership of Exotic Wildlife to Protect Children from Avoidable Injury and Death," with Wecht. That was a doozy. A Wecht-branded doozy. He was working on "Fatal Fulminant Pan-Meningo-Polioencephalitis Due to West Nile Virus" with some other pathologists at the morgue, and he was working on "Postbariatric Surgery Deaths, Which Fall Under the Jurisdiction of the Coroner" with Todd Luckasevic, his new sidekick at the morgue. Todd was a medical student doing a rotation there, and Bennet was his supervisor. Todd was a delight, and so was his little brother Jason, a law student. Two brilliant guys who welcomed Bennet into their family, too, for Thanksgiving, for a beer after work, to hockey games; the community Bennet was creating in Pittsburgh was growing wide and deep, like roots under a sapling suddenly standing strong.

If he thought his paper about Webster's brain was special at all, it had little to do with the league Webster played for or the politics of big-money football. It was a personal thing for Mike. It was, Bennet thought, Mike Webster needing to tell us something.

Mike Webster spoke to us through the patterns of disease

in his tissues. I listened and translated what he said. He said it was not his fault. He said to us that he suffered from the effects of more than twenty thousand blows to his head while he played football. He told us to do something so that younger players who will come after him will not end up like him. He told us to be more compassionate, more understanding, and more patient with his peers who may already be suffering from what he endured.

Writing a scientific paper was like stepping into a loud and crowded room. There's a whole bunch of blabbermouths in there already, going on and on, and you have to figure out what everyone is talking about before you can figure out how to join in.

The national conversation about football and concussions had started in earnest in 1992. That was the year Al Toon, a three-time Pro Bowler—once the highest-paid wide receiver in pro football—retired from the New York Jets at age twenty-nine because of brain injury. "It felt like a cannonball hit me in the back of the head," he said of his final NFL play, in which he caught the ball, and got dinged. He had experienced many such hits. "I don't recall all of the concussions. There were more than five and probably fewer than twenty. There was a serious blow my last year in the league, another in the middle of the season, and then little bangs that everybody gets in every game. It was the cumulative effect of previous concussions. I remember clearly to this day the doctor saying, 'You have reached the point where we don't know what's going to happen next. You may never recover.'"

Two years later, the twenty-nine-year-old running back Merril Hoge—Mike Webster's roommate when he played for the Steelers—retired abruptly from the Chicago Bears after getting kneed in the head while throwing a block against the Buffalo Bills. He had received a previous concussion a few weeks earlier during a road game against the Kansas City Chiefs and had been cleared to resume playing during a telephone call with his team doctor. Hoge made the decision to quit football as he lay in intensive care unable to recognize his wife or his brother, or even to remember that he had a fourteen-month-old daughter. "I don't function, period," he said. "There is no control. I'm at the mercy of time."

At that point, people in the media started to question what was going on. Players had gotten so much bigger, so much faster, the hits so much harder. Guys were ending up in intensive care with head injuries, all these tragic stories playing out on TV. What was going on? And what was the NFL going to do about it? "The Season of the Concussion," headlines read, when, in 1994, three quarterbacks—Troy Aikman, Chris Miller, and Vinny Testaverde—were knocked unconscious on one Sunday alone. "To this day, I don't recall playing in the championship game at all," Aikman would later say. "I don't think I ever will." He took the Cowboys to Super Bowl XX-VIII, and they won it. "The Super Bowl isn't real clear—what happened during the game isn't clear to me."

The PR was terrible for America's game. Good clean fun. Family fun that began with peewee leagues in towns and farms and suburbs of America. High school dreams and letter jackets and cheerleaders bouncing. And then the NFL! Not just a league, but a whole entertainment industry. Bigger than any other sport. Way bigger. Bigger than TV. Bigger than music. Bigger than Hollywood. An $8 billion per year American success story. The hits were part of the fun. Fans loved them. The NFL sold "Greatest Hits" videotapes at Kmart for people who wanted to watch them again and again.

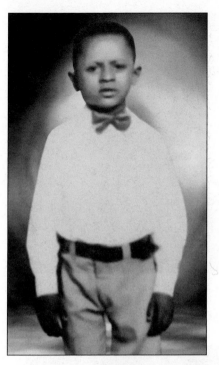

Bennet Omalu, age seven, on his way to mass in Enugu, Nigeria.

After a long day of autopsies, Omalu poses in scrubs.

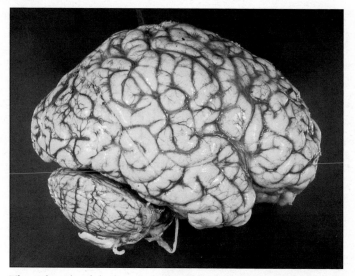

The right side of the brain of a football player diagnosed with CTE by Omalu. As the CTE damage is microscopic, the brain appears normal to the naked eye.

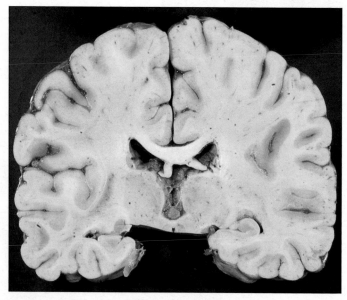

A cut coronal section of the same brain, which shows none of the damage typically associated wth traumatic injury or degenerative brain disease.

Omalu examines
a tissue sample on the
balcony of the condo
he shares with his
wife, Prema.

Tissue samples taken
from the brains of
athletes whose families
asked Omalu to check
them for CTE.

Omalu, left, and Dr. Julian Bailes examine tissue samples in the West Virginia University lab. © *West Virginia University Hospitals*

Omalu on vacation in Laguna Beach in 2014 with his daughter, Ashly, his wife, Prema, and his son, Mark.

URGENT!

Mr. Robert Fitzsimmons,

NO Matter what Happens, I will always Be Gratiful To Have Had Enough ability od Function To Be able Recognize & aware of Great art work, skill, professional Excellence ad Humanitarian Consideration ad The Cahuna's To Make a Stand when other People abuse Their unearned Position & Privileges of Power + Wealth By interfering ch Ives other Hardworking Concerned For all People people for the Great Efforts ad unselfish work that You Have Been Doing Flot Normally

The beginning of a letter from Mike Webster to his lawyer, Bob Fitzsimmons, in which he praises Fitzsimmons's "skill, professional excellence, and humanitarian consideration and the cahuna's [sic] to make a stand when other people abuse their unearned position and privileges of power and wealth." *Courtesy Fitzsimmons Law Firm PLLC, Wheeling, WV, and the Estate of Mike Webster*

Excerpt of another letter from Webster, featuring a depiction of how he envisions his mental deterioration. The circle on the left shows Webster's brain as it used to be—neatly organized—and the circle on the right reflects the breakdown of that structure over time. *Courtesy Fitzsimmons Law Firm PLLC, Wheeling, WV, and the Estate of Mike Webster*

A billboard commemorating the death of Bennet Omalu's father, John Donatus Amaechi Omalu, that was hung on the family compound in the village. Bennet's father was known as Oba, a title of honor.

Omalu and his siblings in prayer during a ceremony in the village that was held before his father's mass. The family is dressed in white at Oba's request. He wanted the funeral to be a celebration of life rather than an occasion of mourning.

Omalu's eldest sister, Winny, with their eighty-two-year-old mother, known by the honorary name Iyom.

Omalu wears custom fabric featuring portraits of Oba and a cap bearing his father's initials during the funeral week.

The funeral procession to the ancestral home of Omalu's father in Enugwu-Ukwu village.

But . . . *debilitating* hits? Surely that was an exaggeration. Or that was when you cut to commercial.

"There is an enormous amount of pressure on the player, the owner, and the doctor to get that player back out there," Hoge would later say, adding that the NFL had no guidelines at all for when a player should or should not return to play after a concussion. It was just: *Get back in there.*

And now America was saying: *Well, now, wait a second. Are you sure these guys are okay?*

NFL Commissioner Paul Tagliabue owed America a response. In truth, he thought this whole year-of-concussion business was a lot of hype—"a pack journalism issue," as he told one reporter. But he had a public to answer to, customers to satisfy, and so he would be a man of action. In 1994, he announced that the NFL was going to address the problem of head injuries in its players by putting together a committee. A team of doctors and scientists would do research and determine if football was truly harmful to players and their brains, and if it was, the committee would figure out what could be done about it. They would mount a series of rigorous studies, Tagliabue said. The team he assembled was called the NFL's Committee on Mild Traumatic Brain Injury. (The league had replaced the term "post-concussion syndrome" with "mild traumatic brain injury," a term it deemed "more academically appropriate.")

Tagliabue named Elliot Pellman, a New York Jets team doctor, who had been Al Toon's doctor, as the director of the fourteen-member MTBI committee.

The MTBI committee had been studying the problem of head injuries in football players for nearly a decade by the time Mike Webster died in 2002. They had been publishing their research in the scientific journal *Neurosurgery*. In 2003, Pellman compiled an overview of the committee's work to date.

"Although published information existed," he wrote in *Neurosurgery*, "most of what I—like other team physicians—knew about concussions was from on-field anecdotes passed on from other team physicians and athletic trainers who had been treating professional football players for many years. During my years of medical school, internal medicine training (including an extra year as chief medical resident), and fellowship, from 1975 to 1986, I had never received a single lecture on concussions. As I learned later, this was typical of physician training for what was then an often under diagnosed and little understood clinical condition."

Gee, Bennet thought, reading Pellman's account. He thought about his own dining room now littered with piles of books and papers about concussions dating back to Hippocrates. *It is not difficult to locate information if you are interested in the science of concussion. Have these doctors not read the books? Should I tell them about the books?*

"During my treatment of Mr. Toon," Pellman went on, "I quickly realized how few experts and how little prospective, scientific medical information were available regarding concussions. I decided that a novel approach would be necessary to gather information, particular for a professional sports league."

Gee whiz, Bennet thought. He had a library of scientific papers; researchers had been on this problem for a century or more. Perhaps he should call this Pellman and offer to share the materials he had accumulated on his dining room table? He felt increasingly excited about showing his own findings to this group that seemed to have a weak grasp on the basic science.

He wondered, too, what Pellman meant when he said his group needed to take "a novel approach" to studying brain injury. There were already plenty of research teams studying concussions. This was hardly some esoteric science. As early as 1982 brain injury in sports appeared as front page news in *The Wall Street Journal*. "A silent epidemic," the story said. Teams of researchers in Pittsburgh, Boston, North Carolina, and other places around the country had been looking into the problem and publishing their findings. Jeff Barth, Robert Cantu, Julian Bailes, Kevin Guskiewicz, Micky Collins, Bill Barr—these were some of the established names in the field of concussion research, and none of them was on the MTBI committee.

Were doctors on the MTBI committee talking to these experts? And if not, why not? It seemed the committee was on a parallel track, blazing a new path, oblivious to—or ignoring—the work of experts working on the same question: Was there a measurable link between football and long-term brain damage?

Yes, concluded the American Academy of Neurology in 1997. In fact, the AAN had established guidelines for concussed athletes returning to play. "Repeated concussions can cause cumulative brain injury in an individual injured over months or years," the AAN report stated bluntly. "The problem faced by the medical community has been developing a consensus on managing athletes with these injuries. . . . Frequently, the loss of objectivity on the part of the athlete, coaches, sports media, and spectators is an unfortunate and potentially harmful bias."

In the laboratory, scientists affiliated with the AAN were concussing rats to try to figure out how to manage the injury. The rat experiments confirmed the pattern they observed in people: Recovery varied from patient to patient. It depended on the severity of the blow, but also on how many previous concussions the person had had. Once you got one concussion, you were more likely to get another. After several concussions, it took less of a blow to cause the concussion and a longer period of time to recover. As a result of those findings, the AAN was able to define concussions in terms of three grades of severity: from transient confusion, Grade 1, to complete loss of consciousness, Grade 3. They recommended return-to-play rules based on the severity of the injury. Players who suffered a Grade 3 concussion should be withheld from play until asymptomatic for one week, they said, and if they got another Grade 3, they should be benched for at least a month.

The NFL had rejected these guidelines. They weren't supported by research, Pellman said in 2000.

Rejected the recommendations of the American Academy of Neurology? Bennet thought. Who was this Pellman guy? Rejecting existing science and choosing to start over with "a novel approach"? That is not in the spirit of scientific inquiry, Bennet thought.

In essence, Pellman had said team doctors knew better than independent scientists. They were, after all, *team doctors.* They would use "the art of medicine" to determine what was best for their players. As for research, that's what the MTBI committee was for. They were looking into this problem, accumulating data, and publishing their findings frequently, paper after paper in *Neurosurgery.*

Bennet worked on his own paper and thought, wow, talk about a stranger walking into a roomful of blabbermouths. It was as though the established scientists were in there saying one thing and the NFL was talking over them, ignoring them, saying another thing. And here comes some guy from Nigeria who had never even heard of football, here comes this man from nowhere saying, "Hey, guys! Look what I found!"

And: "*Guys!* My surname is Onyemalukwube. It means, 'If you know, come forth and speak.'"

Bennet studied the data the MTBI committee had accumulated. Most of it had to do with biomechanics studies and advances in helmet technology. They were using crash test dummies and measuring the impact of blows to the head. They were talking about inventing a super-helmet to protect the head, and they provided many charts and graphs and formulas:

> Concussion risk functions were computed by using the logist function in the Statistical Analysis System program developed by the SAS Institute of Cary, North Carolina. This function relates the probability of injury, *p(x)*, to a response parameter x on the basis of a statistical fit to the sigmoidal function $p(x) = [1 + exp(\alpha - \beta x)]^{-1}$, where α and β are parameters fit to the responses from the laboratory reconstructions of game impacts. The goodness-of-fit was quantified with the -2 log-likelihood ratio parameter, p value, and correlation coefficient (r).

Gee whiz, Bennet thought. *Helmet technology? Why are you people even going there?* He thought about Italian physician Jacopo Berengario da Carpi in the early sixteenth century. He thought about da Carpi and those hundreds of human cadavers, all those skulls, and the notion that "brain commotion" was caused by the thrust of the soft structure of the brain against the solid part of the skull. He thought: *the sixteenth century.* What good does a helmet do? It protects the skull from cracking, sure. But basic laws of physics told you that the brain sloshing around inside that skull was going to bash into the skull walls no matter how much padding you nestled the head in. Plenty of scientists had proved that one several times over.

Didn't these NFL doctors read?

Moreover, Bennet found one particularly glaring hole in the research the MTBI committee had done thus far. It was an area of research missing from the work of the independent scientists, too:

Autopsy. None of these scientists had ever examined an NFL player's brain in autopsy. They were missing the whole area of research Bennet was about to offer them.

Pathological findings were irrefutable. Concrete evidence, right there on the slides. Images. Splotches. Sludge. You could see for yourself exactly what had happened to Mike Webster's brain. It would help these established scientists finally get through to the NFL. It could act as a bridge!

He thought everyone would welcome a discovery as important as this: pathological evidence that showed that the kind of repeated blows to the head sustained in football could cause certain and specific debilitating brain damage in certain and specific regions of the brain. He figured the MTBI committee would be able to make use of his finding. It could help them course-correct the direction of their own research.

But I did not simply want to report it as a case report. I had to give my finding a name, a sexy name that was scientifically sophisticated but with a good acronym that could easily be recalled by a third-grade student. I had to come up with a comprehensive name that would mean something but at the same time would not mean anything, in case I was eventually proven wrong. There was a possibility, although minimal, that I could be wrong. I researched and researched on descriptive names and terminologies that had been used in varying combinations in the past and I decided I liked Chronic Traumatic Encephalopathy. Chronic stood for something that took long to develop; Traumatic stood for something related to or associated with trauma; and Encephalopathy stood for a sick brain. I thought CTE was a very sexy acronym, and it was easy to remember.

So in August 2004, nearly two years after he first met Mike Webster on the slab, Bennet put the finishing touches on his paper, "Chronic Traumatic Encephalopathy in a National Football League Player." He listed as coauthors Ron Hamilton and three geneticists from Pitt who had helped him with some of the science, and he put DeKosky's name last. The last name on a scientific paper was the big one. It was like saying: here's my mentor, here's the fancy one, here's who made this research possible.

"What the fuck?" Wecht said, when he saw DeKosky's name there. If anyone was the father of this endeavor, surely Wecht was. He had set the ball in motion. "Bennet, what the fuck?"

So Bennet tucked DeKosky's name into the list of others and put Wecht's name in the honored spot, even though Wecht had not been involved in the research beyond his crucial decision to allow Bennet to keep Webster's brain from disappearing forever into a grave.

Bennet stuffed the paper in an envelope and he licked the flap and then he addressed it to the editors of *Neurosurgery* and dropped it into the mailbox.

It would be three months before he would hear anything back.

. . .

Prema understood long before Bennet did what was happening in their relationship. She never said it out loud but she knew full well. Mie-Mie didn't say anything, either, even though she, too, understood—as did Uche and Father Carmen and most of the people at church. It seemed Bennet was the last to know what was going on in his own love life. He had shut that part of his life down; he had tried it in the past, tried valiantly, and it hadn't worked, so never mind. Just like deciding whether or not to be smart when he was a kid; it was something you put your mind to. You could turn different parts of yourself on and off like that, simple as flicking a switch. Well, his depression had put a hole in that theory. But still. He was done with romance. He was writing papers and studying and working his butt off on Wecht's private cases. He didn't need a relationship.

He worked on Wecht's cases on Sundays, after brunch. He and Prema would go to church together, then eat, and then he would have to drive out to some godforsaken county morgue in some town in Pennsylvania or Ohio or West Virginia and do an autopsy for Wecht and Prema would go with him. She worried about his being alone; she had taken to staying with him at the morgue in Pittsburgh when he would work until two and three o'clock in the morning. "You can't go there alone." A few times on the Sunday outings she watched him do autopsies, but she couldn't take the smell, so she would just find an office or someplace to sit. She brought books.

On New Year's Day 2005, they were in Bennet's condominium and the phone rang. It was Bennet's father calling to say happy New Year. Then he said: "This is the year you will marry, son."

"Sure, sure, Daddy," Bennet said. "Also, did I tell you I have applied to get my master's degree in public health?"

His father responded to this news with extended silence. "Why do you need that?" he said finally. His booming tuba voice brought Bennet back to Enugwu-Ukwu and kola nuts. He felt instantly small.

"If I want to open a clinic some day," Bennet said, "it will be useful to learn."

"Do you *want* to open a clinic some day?"

"No, but—"

"Then get married," his father said. "You are thirty-six years old, Bennet. It is time to have a wife."

"I know, Daddy."

"Remember I told you, marriage is not about love. Marriage is a business arrangement. You are picking a life partner. The love comes later."

"Okay, Daddy." He was so sick of the nagging. Everyone was nagging him about getting married. At church, people seeing him with Prema on Sundays, they would talk about wedding bells, Bennet ignoring their silly chatter. At the lab at Pitt one of the nurses had pulled him aside and asked him if he was gay. She said people were wondering. "Why aren't you married?" Wecht, too, was on him about it. "It's part of your professional profile," he told him. "It gives you clout politically. You need a wife, Bennet."

"Also I have applied to get my MBA at Carnegie Mellon University," Bennet told his dad that New Year's day on the phone. He was going to do that after the master's in public health.

"These degrees. Are you doing this for selfish reasons?"

"No."

"For self-aggrandizement and to inherit the world?"

"No."

"Will you use your God-given talents, blessings, and opportunities to make a difference, to enhance the lives of others?"

"Yes."

"Good," his father said. "And I would like for you to get a wife."

"Okay, Daddy."

Shortly after he hung up, the phone rang again and it was his brother Theodore. He told Bennet he had called to say happy New Year and then he said, "Bennet, this will be the year for you to marry."

"Okay, Theodore."

Then again his phone rang and this time it was Chizoba saying happy New Year and then, "This will be the year for you to marry."

"You had some emergency family meeting about this, Chi Chi?" Bennet asked.

"Well—"

"Tell the rest not to bother calling," Bennet said. "I'll handle it."

And with that amount of forethought, Bennet turned to Prema, who had brought her laundry over. She was standing behind the couch, folding a blue blouse with embroidery on the sleeve.

"Let's get married," Bennet said.

"Oh. Are you sure?" she said.

"Yes."

"Okay," she said, flattening the blouse and smoothing out the wrinkles.

"We can learn to love each other," Bennet said.

"Okay, Bennet," she said.

Why was it so difficult for him to admit that he already loved her? She would never understand his reluctance to surrender his heart in this one simple way, the simplest act in the world to her, to him so complicated and fraught.

In the coming weeks Bennet told Father Carmen about the engagement and Father Carmen made the announcement at church and everyone more or less acted as if they had not seen this painfully obvious thing coming; they put their hands in front of their widened mouths, saying "Oh!" and "Ooh!"

"Happily ever after!" Bennet said, giving everyone what they seemed to need, and soon Bennet himself came to believe in it and need it, too. Wecht and Sigrid took Bennet and Prema out for an engagement dinner at a ritzy downtown restaurant. Wecht barked orders at Sigrid about what kind of wine she should try and she shot back with lessons about salad dressing and Prema looked on somewhat aghast at the way that couple interacted. Bennet loved all of it. He felt proud of Prema for looking so smart in the winter-white suit he had bought her. He felt proud of all the ways in which he believed he had made Prema beautiful and he wanted to keep doing it more. "My wife," he practiced saying. "My wife."

"We will now go to the movies," Wecht said that night after dinner, because he loved movies, and he ordered people around exactly that way. "The show is at nine thirty, so let's get going." They went to see *Hotel Rwanda*, hardly a celebratory movie, but it was playing at the Squirrel Hill theater, Wecht's favorite, the one place on earth where he found he could relax, and the two couples sat next to each other and Wecht passed the popcorn, which Bennet dutifully munched—a boy with his dad and his mom and his girl, except now all grown up. He felt as if Wecht was treating him like a son, and he loved that feeling. He felt more like a son with Wecht than he ever did with his dad, and he did not experience sadness or conflict but instead focused on the warmth of family and the comfort of knowing he had found a home, in this city, with these people, living this life where optimism filled you without effort, just regular oxygen you breathed and there was plenty of it for everyone.

In a blink he realized how strange it was to feel so peaceful while watching people flee from the ravages of the Rwandan genocide. That was horrible. But that was no longer reality. That was just a movie. This was his new reality, this moment here, America and popcorn and people suffering atrocities on a screen in front of you. That was something you now stood back and watched. It was no longer the reality you inhabited.

At home one morning, on television, the bishops and the cardinals were dressed in their finest robes, crimson, gold, and silver shimmering in the sun, and they were chanting and praying:

> "Follow me." The risen lord says these words to Peter. They are his last words to this disciple chosen to shepherd his flock. "Follow me." This saying of Christ can be taken as the key to understanding the message which comes to us in the life of our late beloved Pope John Paul II. Today, we bury his remains in the earth as a seed of immortality.

More than four million mourners gathered in Rome for Pope John Paul II's funeral on April 8, 2005, just a few months after Bennet and Prema's engagement and the announcement of happily-ever-after. The couple stayed home from work to watch the funeral, both of them holding rosaries, rolling the beads and praying in accordance with the pattern. Prema was stoic, while Bennet said the prayers under his breath and wept openly. *Oh, Bennet.* He loved that pope. He had a framed photo of John Paul II on a bookshelf and he had all his books. The pope stood up for Africa when no one else did. The pope was in Nigeria when Bennet was giving up on Nigeria. "Respect for every human person," he said, "for his dignity and rights, must ever be the inspiration behind your efforts." The pope before that cheering crowd in Abuja, the pope calling for the release of Abiola. All those people cheering in thanks, and then the police, and then whips made of electrical wire. *Get back, damn you, get back!*

Bennet felt that the pope was his friend, his soulmate, which is sort of the point of the pope, and Bennet was a true believer. Saying his rosary that day, he was thinking *Thank you for trying to help Nigeria, most Holy Father,* and *Good luck in heaven,* and *Pope, please tell God I'm sorry for my sins,* and *Thank you, Pope,* and *A special thank-you to Jesus,* he was praying and his phone was ringing and he didn't want to answer it because he was praying along with more than four million mourners, and Prema next to him, and the bishop at the altar on the TV saying "When you were younger, you used to dress yourself and go where you wanted." But the phone kept ringing and so finally Bennet reached over and picked it up.

It was work. He heard strange cries from familiar voices at the morgue. A tech talking, and then another tech talking over her, and they were saying, "Bennet! Something is happening! Bennet!" Bennet held the phone, still momentarily locked in his prayer trance.

And he said to him, "Lord, you know everything. You know that I love you." Jesus said to him, "Feed my sheep." Amen, amen, I say to you.

Bennet could not understand what the techs were screaming about but it had to do with the FBI and the FBI was at the morgue ripping through boxes—and, hold on, *what?* That day of the pope's funeral, having nothing to do with the pope's funeral, a world away, in downtown Pittsburgh, a dozen FBI agents were storming into the Allegheny County coroner's office, and simultaneously into Wecht's private office, and they were grabbing boxes, logbooks, hard drives. Guys wearing FBI jackets, loading boxes and books and computers, and the TV news was there, cameras, Wecht arriving late from a talk he did at Fox Chapel Area High School, leaping out of a car, microphones in his face. "I just came in! I have to find out what's happening!"

"*What is happening?*" Bennet said, after he hung up with the tech and finally reached Wecht, who was standing in his office, mid-raid, watching these men in their jackets carrying boxes of autopsy records out to their vans.

"It's bullshit," Wecht said. "It doesn't concern you, Bennet. It's fucking bullshit like these cocksucking motherfuckers did to me before. It's *nothing*."

"But, sir, if you'll pardon me, it sounds like something," Bennet said, and he thought, *Wow, fathers are falling. In one day, fathers are dropping like flies.*

"Forget about it, Bennet. It will amount to nothing. They tried this before."

"But when you grow old, you will stretch out your hands, and someone else will dress you and lead you where you do not want to go." He said this signifying by what kind of death he would glorify God. And when he had said this, he said to him, "Follow me."

| | | | |

CHAPTER 9

ATTACK

Bennet's paper about Mike Webster's brain was published in the July 2005 issue of *Neurosurgery*. When it arrived in the mail, he held it gently in his hands, like it was parchment, like it was the original of the Declaration of Independence or something. Page 128. It was so handsome. "Chronic Traumatic Encephalopathy in a National Football League Player." It had his name and all the others in bold stacked on the left above their dignified bona fides in fine print. The words SPECIAL REPORT appeared in a red banner across the top, the letters bleeding to a fade as if they were moving, as if they had just zoomed in on a top-secret mission. It was hard not to feel proud of something like that.

> We herein report the first documented case of long-term neurodegenerative changes in a retired professional NFL player consistent with chronic traumatic encephalopathy (CTE). This case draws attention to a disease that remains inadequately studied in the cohort of professional football players, with unknown true prevalence rates. . . . Our case represents an extremely rare scenario whereby a complete autopsy was performed on a retired NFL player with a comprehensive neuropathological examination,

which revealed changes consistent with CTE. . . . Our report therefore constitutes a forensic epidemiological sentinel case that draws attention to a possibly more prevalent yet unrecognized disease.

It was beautiful. All of it. And Bennet marveled at it, the whole time in his mind talking to Mike Webster. *Here you go, Mike, look what we did.* It was a fabulous feeling of accomplishment. And then the phone rang.

Now he was sitting at his kitchen table with his head cocked to one side, balancing the phone against his shoulder; he was listening to some guy tell him that there was a problem. A big problem.

"*Retracted?*" Bennet said. "What do you mean they want it retracted?"

"I'm sorry this is happening," the guy said. He was from the journal's editorial board, and he was saying three doctors had written a letter to the board demanding that the journal retract Bennet's work.

"But you don't just retract papers," Bennet said. "It's published! It's right here in my hands!" His voice was in its highest pitch, a bicycle squeak. "Your board had it reviewed by a dozen or more professionals before it was accepted. We provided revisions. We provided data. The microscopic proof which are the photographs in the paper itself!"

"I know—"

"*It's already published!*"

"The demand is pretty forthright. From some notable doctors."

"Who?"

"I'll fax you the letter."

Retracted. You don't just retract papers. Retraction was

something you did if the author was found to be a fraud. Retraction would be a public humiliation.

"It is a highly professional paper," Bennet said, growing angry, his voice rising. "Written and reviewed by highly respected scientists!"

"We'll need a response," the guy said. "I'll fax you the letter. I'm sorry this is happening."

Bennet hung up, fired off an email to Hamilton and DeKosky. *Help!* He did not immediately tell Wecht. Wecht had enough trouble. Maybe Wecht was going to get indicted, maybe he wasn't. Maybe this. Maybe that. For nearly a year everyone at the morgue would live with that crushing anxiety, waiting for the FBI to *say something* about that preposterous raid, anything, and you didn't dare talk to Wecht about it because he'd blow. So you put your head down. Avoided Wecht.

Hamilton was upset by the news. A retraction was, yeah, like getting a dunce hat stuck on your head and people throwing pies in your face. It would mean professional ruin. Bennet would never be able to publish again, and Hamilton and DeKosky would probably go down with him. This was ridiculous. They were established names in the field. *Nobody gets retracted.*

Hamilton said the research was solid, completely solid, and Bennet said of course it was. And then they both took a deep breath and thought: *Wait a second. Who are these idiots demanding a retraction?*

Bennet stood by the fax machine in his condominium while the pages of the letter came spitting out, single-spaced, six sheets in all. It was longer than the original article. He gathered it and flipped quickly to the end page to see who had signed the letter.

Elliot Pellman, the chairman of the MTBI committee.

The NFL guy?

Ira Casson, also on the MTBI committee.

Oh my gosh, the NFL guys?

David Viano, also on the MTBI committee.

I thought, this football league is coming after me? I just did not understand this football league! I became very nervous and shaky. Why would they write so many words against my work? I believed my work could help them! I did not understand why they would react this way. I was sweating profusely. I reached out for my good old Johnnie Walker scotch whisky. The Scots are the best whisky distillers, oh my gosh! I poured two shots for myself and gulped it down. I sat in the kitchen and I began to read their letter, but by the second or third paragraph, I began to smile. I began to relax. At that moment I realized I knew the subject better than these so-called top physicians. Their understanding of the subject was embarrassingly naive and virginal.

"We disagree," the letter said.

"Serious flaws."

"Complete misunderstanding."

"A serious misinterpretation."

"A failure."

In tone, the letter struggled to remain calm, but the subtext was clear: *We own this field. We are not about to bow to some no-name Nigerian with some bullshit theory.*

The attack against Bennet was that he had misinterpreted his own neuropathological findings. In his calmer moments, Bennet considered the fact that neither Casson, Pellman, nor Viano was a neuropathologist. *How can doctors who are not neuropathologists interpret neuropathological findings better than a neuropathologist?*

But mostly Bennet did not remain calm.

In the coming days, as he prepared his response, he began to look into and question the integrity of the MTBI committee. It was one thing not to put a neuropathologist on your fourteen-member brain committee, quite another to have the committee headed by . . . a rheumatologist, as was the case with Pellman (who was also revealed to be Tagliabue's personal physician, since at least 1997).

Wait, he's a rheumatologist? They picked a joint guy to lead their brain study?

As a New York Jets team doctor, Pellman was of course on the NFL payroll, as were other scientists on the committee. *Were they being bought? Were they even really studying concussions?*

Looking back through the literature, Bennet saw that Pellman had put forth unwavering conclusions about concussions and football back in 1994 when the committee was first formed. "Concussions are part of the profession," he told reporters. "An occupational hazard." He said it was like steelworkers who get injured; it was something that came with the job. The players knew what they were getting into. And, besides, concussions were temporary.

Bennet wondered if this MTBI committee had been formed to control that same narrative. *No big deal.* He noted that the committee was churning out papers for *Neurosurgery* at an alarming rate. One a month for five months in 2005 alone. The research in those papers refuted much of the work that the mainstream scientists who were not on the NFL payroll were doing.

Was this some sort of orchestrated campaign? Even the guy running the journal *Neurosurgery*—Michael Apuzzo, the editor-in-chief—turned out to be on the NFL payroll.

"Professional football players do not sustain frequent re-petitive blows to the brain on a regular basis," concluded a 2005 article from the MTBI committee. And if they did sus-tain frequent repetitive blows to the brain, well, look at the statistics, the article argued: the statistics showed that con-cussed players were able to play again. These statistics, the MTBI committee doctors maintained, proved that the head injuries were simply not that severe. "More than one-half of the players returned to play within one day, and symptoms resolved in a short time in the vast majority of cases," another article said.

Bennet wondered what sort of rat's nest he had stepped into. A bee's nest. A hornet's nest. In those awakening mo-ments, he hoped that was not the case. He hoped this was not like Nigeria. No, this was America. This was a land where people played fair. This was a land where you did honest work and worked hard and harder still and because of your hard work you earned respect. Linear. Rational. *Christian!* God had blessed America. That's what Bennet grew up think-ing, and knowing, and that's why he came, and you don't just let go of something like that. Letting go meant you were wrong, you had it wrong, you were stupid.

He felt the warmth of whisky down his throat, soothing. He thought about Mike Webster, his body getting wheeled in on the gurney, those hands, that scar on his head, those burns on his thighs from the Taser he used on himself. Was this football league paying scientists to trick people into believing that players like Mike Webster did not suffer brain damage from football? If that was the case, then they knew.

They knew? He refused to believe that they knew. *That was un-American!*

And yet: They wanted his paper retracted. They wanted to

nullify the work of an independent scientist who had stumbled onto undeniable proof. They wanted to silence him.

One paper a month for five months, eventually a total of sixteen papers in *Neurosurgery* from the MTBI committee. That was a ridiculous number of papers from one group of scientists, Bennet thought. Anyone would think.

He wondered how to phrase his response to the NFL doctors trying to silence and humiliate him. He would have no trouble defending his neuropathological findings.

But he had something else to tell them, too. Something else for the MTBI committee to consider.

In his refrigerator, in a white bucket. Oh, Prema hated the way Bennet would always stash his brains right next to the milk like that. In the bucket he had pieces of the brain of another dead NFL player who had gone crazy.

Terry Long played right guard for the Steelers alongside Mike Webster. He grew up a shy boy in Columbia, South Carolina, helped his widowed mom raise the younger kids by getting a job laying bricks. He went into the army at nineteen, served two years with the Special Forces. He discovered football at Fort Bragg, got good at it, and was recruited by East Carolina University to play offensive tackle. He was short, not even six feet, but at 284 pounds was packed solid as dirt. The Steelers drafted him in the fourth round in 1984, and within a year he was starting on the offensive line with Webster. For five years, six inches away from Webster. They called him T-Bone. He was an affable guy who donated a football scholarship to his alma mater, became close to the legendary Steelers coach Chuck Noll. But six years into his career, something wasn't right with his head. He got moody. He had started taking steroids—maybe that was it. He failed a drug test in 1991, and Coach Noll suspended him. He took it hard. Way hard. He locked himself in his garage, in his car, the engine running, the carbon monoxide rising, breathing deep. He couldn't get enough poison in him to do the job. A girlfriend dragged him out of there. He got rid of her, and the next day he ate rat poison. That didn't work, either. They sent him to a psych ward. By 1992 he was off the team. He got married again, clung to his wife, needed her, clung to her, then turned on her. In paranoid rages, he became violent. She left, came back, left again. A cycle. He became a hermit. But then he would emerge and he would be normal again, charming even. He was a fantastic salesman. He started a lot of businesses. He couldn't keep any of them going, couldn't keep his head together, gave money away to anyone who asked. He swung between highs and lows, became impulsive and reckless. He bought a chicken processing plant in Pittsburgh's North Side. He wasn't good at processing chickens. Neighbors complained that the Value Added Food Groups building was giving off rank odors from rotting poultry carcasses. Then USDA inspectors came and said the place was in violation of federal regulations. Allegheny County plumbing inspectors came and found terrible sewage problems. Caving in, everything caving in on him. Two months later, the chicken plant blew up. Arson, the feds said, and indicted Long. He said the hell with it. He went home and drank a bottle of Drano. That didn't work. He got sent back to the psych ward. Then on June 7, 2005, he got a large bottle of antifreeze and drank it all and that's how he finally killed himself. He was forty-five.

Since his death was ruled a suicide, it fell under the jurisdiction of the county coroner. Bennet wasn't working the day Long's body was rolled into the morgue. His colleague Dr. Abdulrezak Shakir did the autopsy. Shakir could have put the brain back in Long's body, as he did with almost every other autopsy in his seventeen-year career, could have packed it up and sent the corpse off to be cremated or buried. But he didn't. He knew Terry Long was a football player. He thought about Bennet, his research, his excitement about brains. "Fix the brain," he said to the technician.

"But—"

"Fix the brain," he said.

Bennet was thankful for the vote of confidence. He said, "Well, let me see here." And when the formaldehyde had made the brain firm enough to slice, Bennet pulled Terry Long's brain out of the bucket and put it on the cutting board and took a knife to the frontal lobe and cut a section about the width of a stick of gum. He did this work at his apartment, outside on the balcony, because Prema hated the smell of formaldehyde. He took slices from the parietal, occipital, and temporal lobes. "Look at you," Prema said. "You are cutting brains on the balcony. Look at you." She thought: *This right here is my future husband in a nutshell,* and she took a picture of him.

He packed the four slices into plastic cassettes, put them in his briefcase, and took them up to Jonette at the lab.

"Another one?" Jonette said.

"If you please," he said.

Same stains, same tests, same routine.

And when Bennet looked in the microscope he found the same splotches, the same tangles, the same tau proteins. "This stuff should not be in the brain of a forty-five-year-old man," he said. "This is another case of CTE."

He told Wecht.

"Are you sure?" Wecht said. "A second case? Bennet, are you sure?"

"I am sure," Bennet said. "It's right here on the slides, Dr. Wecht."

And so Bennet immediately began working on a second paper to submit to *Neurosurgery*, while he was still composing a response to the NFL's demand that his first paper be retracted. He figured a second case of CTE would strengthen his argument, that the added evidence would encourage the doubters on the MTBI committee to listen to him.

But Wecht, because he was Wecht, said to hell with the scientific community and the whoever-idiots trying to prove Bennet wrong. "I have no patience for that bullshit." So before Bennet had a chance to finish a draft of his paper about Terry Long for *Neurosurgery*, Wecht went to his friends in the local press.

"Wait," Bennet said. A respectable scientist doesn't go to the mainstream press. A respectable scientist publishes papers in peer-reviewed scientific journals.

"No, I will not wait," Wecht said.

The headline on the September 14, 2005, story in the *Pittsburgh Post-Gazette* was just the kind Wecht liked—exciting, explosive, with Wecht's name in it.

WECHT: LONG DIED FROM BRAIN INJURY: HAD HEAD TRAUMA FROM NFL DAYS

Oh, no, Dr. Wecht. Please, no, Dr. Wecht.

Wecht did not have a full command of the science when he spoke to reporters, but it was close enough.

"A football helmet gives you an awful lot of protection," Wecht said, "but you don't have to be a doctor or an engineer or even a football player to realize that the helmet does not block out all the measured force produced when some 300-pound player with a hand the size of a Christmas ham whacks you in the head dozens of times a game, season after season."

Locally, a Steelers team doctor was enraged by the headline. Joe Maroon, the neurosurgeon on the Steelers roster, came out with a public statement. Maroon was a major player in the concussion business—and yes, he treated it like a business. He was a go-getter of the highest order. In addition to his post with the Steelers, he was a vice chairman at University of Pittsburgh Medical Center, cofounder of the hospital's Sports Medicine Concussion Program, and medical director of World Wrestling Entertainment (WWE). He had been front and center on the NFL concussion crisis since the beginning; he had implored Merril Hoge to retire back in 1994 after repeated concussions, telling him he risked permanent brain damage if he continued playing. It was hard to get a handle on Maroon. On the one hand, he probably saved Hoge's life. On the other hand, he was an adviser to the NFL's MTBI committee, one of the concussion experts who were saying concussions were not a problem in the NFL. Maroon was endowed with an entrepreneurial spirit. He and a colleague had come up with a computer-based test, ImPACT (Immediate Post-Concussion Assessment and Cognitive Testing), which people could use to help determine the severity of a head injury. He trademarked the test, sold it to the NFL, the NHL, and colleges and high schools across the country, and was making millions of dollars on it.

STEELERS DOCTOR SAYS CONCLUDING FOOTBALL LED TO LONG'S DEMISE IS BAD SCIENCE read the headline that came in response to the Terry Long news. Maroon attacked Bennet's finding. "I think it's just bad science to conclude that football caused his death," he said. He went on to say in another article, "The conclusions drawn here are preposterous and a misinterpretation of the facts. . . . To say he was killed by football, it's just not right, it's not appropriate."

Bad science. Preposterous. A misinterpretation of the facts. Apparently that was going to be a charge Bennet would have to get used to. *I own this science. I am not about to bow to some no-name coroner with some bullshit theory.* Now there was another hornet in the nest Bennet wished he had never stepped into.

Maroon kept at it. He told reporters that he himself had in his possession Terry Long's medical records and these records proved Bennet's findings were wrong. Terry Long had never had a single concussion, he said. "I was the team neurosurgeon during his entire tenure with the Steelers," he said. "I rechecked my records; there was not one cerebral concussion documented in him during those entire seven years. Not one."

"What the fuck?" Wecht said to Bennet. Wecht knew Maroon personally. Another Rust Belt guy from an immigrant family, rising up. He had his own outsized ego. Wecht knew all about Maroon's heroic and exciting triathlons; Maroon made sure everyone knew about his triathlons. He was big on self-promotion, a trait that Wecht had no room to criticize him for. But was Maroon right about Terry Long?

"He's wrong," Bennet said.

"Are you sure?" Wecht asked. "Bennet, are you sure?"

"Dr. Wecht, I am sure."

Bennet had Long's medical records, too. He opened the file, showed it to Wecht. There was a letter in the file, a letter written by Maroon himself, describing one of Terry Long's concussions.

"Holy goddamned Christ," Wecht said. "Well, you have to tell the newspaper."

"If you please, I will not talk to the newspaper," Bennet said.

"Do it."

"But—"

"*Do it.*"

So Bennet showed reporters Maroon's letter detailing one of Terry Long's concussions. Headlines ricocheted back and forth, Maroon publicly apologizing, then attacking Bennet again. "Fallacious reasoning," he said of Bennet's work.

Then Pellman, the chairman of the MTBI committee, jumped in and backed Maroon, launched his own attacks. "Speculative and unscientific," he said of Bennet's work.

Bennet did not like feeling that people were angry with him, and yet he himself was becoming angry. He felt the Igbo fire igniting inside him. He felt he was learning something very ugly about America, about how an $8 billion industry could attempt to silence even the most well-intentioned scientist and in the most preposterous ways. *A demand for a retraction? An outright denial of the facts? A personal attack on his validity as a scientist?*

Father Carmen read the press coverage. "Oh, Bennet, what have you gotten yourself into?" he said to him. "The NFL is one of the most powerful organizations in America. Please be careful."

A reporter showed up at Bennet's condo, said he worked for the sports pages, had a few questions. He saw Webster's and Long's brains sitting in tubs in Bennet's living room. "Dude!" he said. "Get these out of your house! Someone could come in and kill you and steal these brains! Do you know what you're *dealing* with?"

No, he did not know what he was dealing with. What he *thought* he was dealing with was a promise to Mike Webster, and to Terry Long. Guys who went crazy and no longer had a voice. He found something in their brains, and he had a duty to tell people.

Onyemalukwube.

He went back to his dining room table and his books and his laptop. He finished working on his scientific paper detailing his findings in Terry Long's brain. He called it "Chronic Traumatic Encephalopathy in a National Football League Player: Part II" and put it in an envelope and sent it to *Neurosurgery,* the prestigious peer-reviewed journal that did not, in the end, accept the NFL's request to retract Bennet's first paper. They agreed to publish this one, too.

Then, in the middle of this dark, confusing mess, there came a bright spot. At the time, it felt like the first sunshine of spring. Bennet got a phone call from Julian Bailes, a neurosurgeon of considerable renown who had worked for a decade as a Steelers team doctor. He had studied under Maroon. He was a southern guy, from Louisiana, had played football in high school and college, loved football as much as anyone. He was now chairman of neurosurgery at West Virginia University Hospitals. He had known Mike Webster well, was friends with the family. He knew Terry Long, too. He knew brains. He knew concussions. In his lab in West Virginia he was concussing rats, examining the resulting damage to brain tissue. Bailes had experience that touched and intersected and paralleled Omalu's research in the way of all fascinating coincidences.

On the phone, Bailes introduced himself. He said, "Dr. Omalu, I'm calling to tell you I believe you."

It was the first time anyone who had anything to do with the NFL had validated Omalu's work, had called him anything other than a quack.

"Thank you, Dr. Bailes," Bennet said. "Thank you very much."

"Julian," Bailes said. "Call me Julian."

Bailes gave Bennet his own understanding of the NFL's involvement in the concussion conversation—a topic that he himself had been trying for years to keep alive. And the NFL had been ignoring it. Ignoring the recommendations from the American Academy of Neurology, ignoring the research from independent scientists who had been finding evidence of a link between football and long-term brain damage. "A slew of independent researchers," Bailes said. "We've been pounding this issue now for two decades." They had been warning the NFL that there was a problem, a big problem. They were in effect screaming "Fix this problem!" And the screaming went nowhere, the screaming led to the MTBI committee and all that wasted energy.

"Then you come out with your CTE research," Bailes said. "And it's sort of like the whole story suddenly makes sense. You've given their boogeyman a name."

"I was just trying to figure out what happened to Mike Webster," Bennet said.

"Webby," Bailes said. "I loved that guy. We were all trying to figure out what happened to him. And T-Bone. Yeah, that's two. There are more."

"More?"

Bailes was cochairing a study at the University of North Carolina's Center for the Study of Retired Athletes. His group had surveyed thousands of retired players, and in 2003 had found that players who had suffered multiple concussions were three times more likely to suffer clinical depression. They reported their finding to the NFL.

"You told them about it?" Bennet said. "What did they say?"

"Flawed."

Bailes and his team did a follow-up study. This one showed that repeatedly concussed NFL players had five times the rate of "mild cognitive impairment," or pre-Alzheimer's disease. Moreover, it showed that retired NFL players were suffering Alzheimer's symptoms at an alarming rate—37 percent higher than the average guy walking down the street. They reported their finding to the NFL.

"What did they say?" Bennet asked.

"Flawed."

"Geez," Bennet said.

"Exactly," Bailes said.

The only experiments that were not "flawed," according to the NFL, were the ones conducted by their paid scientists, all of which happened to disagree with a growing number of independent researchers.

"And I don't have to tell you," Bailes said, "but that's just unprecedented in science. That would be like the American Heart Association saying, 'Hey, if it's not our sponsored research, we don't acknowledge it or comment on it. Only *we* can figure out heart disease!'"

Or it would be like the tobacco industry in the 1980s—denying that cigarettes caused cancer despite mounting evidence that they did.

It would have been laughable, if it weren't so irresponsible.

At stake, after all, were people's lives. Athletes suffering head injuries, pressured by a league and, in fact, a culture that said, *Get back in the game! Man up! Don't ever show it hurts.* This was not just an issue for pro football players. It was an issue for college football players, high school football players, all those peewee leaguers who dreamed of going pro.

On the matter of the NFL's responsibility to the larger

sports community, Julian Bailes was a man who could go ballistic:

"Here we have a multi-*billion*-dollar industry," he said in an interview. "Where does their responsibility begin? Say you're a kid and you sign up to play football. You realize you can blow out your knee, you can even break your neck and become paralyzed. Those are all known risks. But you don't sign up to become a brain-damaged young adult. The NFL should be leading the world in figuring this out, acknowledging the risk. They should be *thanking* us for bringing them this research. Where does their responsibility begin?

"There was a seminal study published by the University of Oklahoma. They put accelerometers in the helmets of University of Oklahoma players. And they documented the g-force. So we know the g-force for a football player being knocked out is about sixty to ninety g's. To compare, a fighter pilot will pass out at five or six g's, but that's over a long period of time. These football g-forces are just a few milliseconds, very brief—boom! And they found that in the open field, the dramatic cases of a receiver getting blindsided is about one hundred g's. It knocks them out. Very dramatic, everybody sees it. But the linemen? They were actually getting twenty to thirty g's on *every play*. Because they bang heads. Every play.

"Helmets are not the answer. The brain has a certain amount of play inside the skull. It's buoyed up in the cerebral spinal fluid. It sits in this fluid, floats. When the head suddenly stops, the brain continues, reverberates back. So when I hit, boom, my skull stops, but my brain continues forward for about a centimeter. Boom, boom, it reverberates back. So you could have padding that's a foot thick, but it's not going to change the acceleration/deceleration phenomenon. And a lot of these injuries are rotational. The fibers get torn with rotation. You've got a face mask that's like a fulcrum sitting out here: You get hit, your head swings around. That's when a lot of these fibers are sheared—by rotation. A helmet can't ever prevent that.

"And have you seen helmets lately? In the old days, you had this leather cap to protect your ears. That was it. You'd never put your head in the game. You'd be knocked out after the first play! Even in the sixties, the helmet was a light shell. The modern helmet is a weapon.

"So I told the NFL, I said, 'Why don't you take the head out of the game? Just take it out of the game! Let the linemen start from a squatting position instead of getting down for head-to-head. Have them stand up like they do on pass protection. So there's not this obligatory head contact.'

"Nothing. They had nothing to say. Who am I? I'm only a guy who has concussed hundreds of rats in the lab, a player for ten years, a sideline doctor for twenty years. What do I know? Some stupid neurosurgeon.

"Instead of answering anything we bring to them, the NFL is ducking and shooting arrows at us. Criticizing us. Saying our work is a bunch of bunk. They have only attacked us."

Bailes was worked up. Bennet was worked up. They compared notes, shared their outrage. Eventually, they reached out to another guy who was worked up: Bob Fitzsimmons, the lawyer from West Virginia who had given Bennet permission to study Mike Webster's brain.

Fitzsimmons's case against the Bert Bell / Pete Rozelle NFL Player Retirement Plan was still winding its way through the courts. *Still.* Three years later. Because Fitzsimmons would not give up. He would fight for Webster even long after his death.

So Bennet, Bailes, and Fitzsimmons formed a team, a kind of brotherhood with a mission: to learn more about the disease, to understand the NFL's obstinate, perilous denial, and to break them of it.

In December 2005 Bennet was on a plane, trying to put all this stuff out of his mind. He had his eyes closed and he was once again glad enough that he was not himself flying the plane; he thought about his childhood dream to become a pilot and smiled. He had noise-canceling headphones on, blasting "If You Don't Know Me By Now."

"What?" he said, feeling a jab.

"The dinner cart," Father Carmen said.

"Oh!"

"You were singing," Prema said.

"I was singing?"

They were seated together in coach. They were headed to Nigeria to get married, and Father Carmen was in tow to officiate at the wedding. For Bennet it was already overwhelming. So many layers of intersecting thoughts and emotions: his history, Nigeria, his father, his bride-to-be, his priest. On the plane, mostly what he was trying to do was clear his mind of America, to make sure he was not carrying any anger or disillusionment with him over the sea and into the clouds. All the worldliness of the NFL. The stuff he'd stepped into. The other ugliness he found in America. He didn't want people back home to know about it, the wickedness of corruption, he didn't want to tarnish the image so many people back home had of the land of milk and honey.

"Africa," Father Carmen said. *"I am going to Africa!"*

He had been making this point continuously ever since Bennet and Prema asked him to come along. For him it was the trip of a lifetime, a chance to touch the soil that so many of his parishioners had once touched, or their grandparents had, or their great-grandparents had. The Africans and the African Americans, his whole congregation had ultimately come from that land so far away from his tiny world, his tiny neighborhood in Pittsburgh.

"Africa!" he said, when they landed in Lagos. "*I am in Africa!*"

Theodore was in baggage claim, pointing and shouting, holding a thick roll of naira.

"You three stand over here!" he barked, and he handed out money to strangers, got passports and visas stamped, got the luggage, and when they got to the car he introduced Bennet and Prema and Father Carmen to the police officer he had rented, a skinny guy with a huge, long gun, and everyone smiled politely and climbed into the backseat. Theodore drove, six hours into the countryside, while Bennet sat motionless watching Nigeria whiz by, and Prema slept, and Father Carmen sat there with Prema's wedding dress on his lap, saying, "This is amazing, this is beautiful, this is fantastic," while Theodore pointed and told stories.

The wedding was at a church in Enugu, the city where Bennet went to medical school and where hotels are large enough to accommodate the hundreds of people who came to celebrate. It was a busy church, in a busy city, and weddings were scheduled back-to-back, some on top of each other. Three at once, right before Bennet and Prema's wedding, and Father Carmen was nervous as he put on his vestments.

"Let's get started," the priest in charge of the church said. "Um—"

Bennet and Prema had not yet arrived. None of the wedding party had yet arrived.

"Oh, don't worry about it," the priest said. "I do it all the time. It's a long line. Just start the service and they'll show up."

"I—can't," Father Carmen said. *For heaven's sake!* He stalled. He made pleasant conversation. *Get here, Bennet! Where are you, Prema?*

At last they arrived. Bennet's short, solid mom, and Mie-Mie and Winny and Uche in light blue gowns, orange beads, and explosions of blue silk on their heads, wrapped and folded into the headdresses of happiness. Then Oba and Theodore and Ikem and Chizoba in their fine black suits. Then Bennet in his designer tux with a bright red vest and a bright red silk tie done in a presidential full Windsor knot.

Prema appeared like a swan all in white, her hair high off her head, a delicate veil, a string of pearls, a bouquet of red roses.

The church was hot and people fanned their faces with the programs they handed out, and Winny had tears of joy rolling down her cheeks. Mie-Mie and Uche wrapped their arms around their mom, then around Prema's mom, who had traveled from Nairobi. Afterward, after a formal reception at the hotel and a good long sleep, they all went back to the compound in Enugwu-Ukwu. They gave Father Carmen a gray caftan to wear. "My first caftan!"

Oba sat in his obu saying the prayers over the kola nuts and he wore his high red hat with the feathers. Theodore and Chizoba wore their short red hats, because now they were Obas in training. Bennet did not have a hat. The elders honored Oba for being a man who now had all seven of his children married. That was an accomplishment, and it cemented his status in the village ever more firmly. The men drank cognac and dipped the kola nuts in peanut butter and chewed, while the two-day wedding feast was prepared in the yard behind the house by teams of sweating cooks wearing green smocks. Prema and her mother and Mie-Mie and Uche and Winny and their mom sat in the room beside the kitchen, hoisted their skirts and put their swollen feet up, and laughed and waited for the food to come up from the yard. The cooks in the yard slaughtered a cow and several goats and chopped and chopped vegetables and stirred huge pots of rice over red-hot embers. Hundreds of villagers came to the feast. They brought dancers and drummers, and people threw money in the air, and you could hear the drumming like thunder rumbling over top and through Enugwu-Ukwu for two days.

CHAPTER 10

SCRAMBLE

The Wecht news was an earthquake. WECHT INDICTED BY GRAND JURY, read the headline in the January 21, 2006, *Pittsburgh Post-Gazette*.

> After a yearlong investigation, a federal grand jury yesterday indicted nationally renowned Allegheny County Medical Examiner Dr. Cyril H. Wecht on charges that he misused his public office for private gain.
>
> The 84-count indictment . . . outlines charges of mail and wire fraud. The government also alleged that . . . Dr. Wecht asked employees of the coroner's office to perform personal errands for him on county time, including dog-walking, picking up personal mail, purchasing sporting goods and hauling away trash.

Dog-walking? Bennet thought. *Trash?* He was just returning from the wedding in Nigeria, and the headlines were making him sick. Eighty-four felony counts of piddly shit. *Who cares about this piddly shit?* Sending personal faxes, misusing mileage vouchers and office stationery. *So, he was sloppy. So?* It seemed crazy to presume that a guy whose private practice took in more than a million dollars a year would resort to stealing office supplies. But it didn't matter how crazy it seemed. It was all there, in a forty-five-page indictment.

Wecht resigned from the Allegheny County coroner's office the same day the indictment came, the end of an era. A guilty verdict on any of the counts could ruin him completely. He'd lose his license and his private practice and his TV appearances and his heroic headlines. A guilty verdict on the more serious counts could mean a twenty-year prison term.

Most people in a situation like that roll over, make a deal. Ninety-five percent of people who are accused of federal white-collar crimes in the United States plead guilty, reach a settlement. But this was Wecht. He would fight. He would spend $8 million defending his name. The FBI would take two years preparing for the trial; they wanted to talk to Bennet about testifying, along with about two hundred fifty other witnesses. Bennet already knew what he was going to say to the FBI. This was his American father. This was the first person in the world to give him a voice. *Get the fuck out of here you goddamned motherfucking cocksucking pieces of motherfucking shit.* That's what he would say to them.

Dr. Shakir, Bennet's senior colleague, was named acting director of the morgue while the county bigwigs sought Wecht's permanent replacement. Father Carmen, who knew nothing about county politics, said, "Hey, Bennet, maybe they'll promote you; you can be the new Dr. Wecht!" Bennet said, "I can't think about that right now," but the more he thought about it, the more he thought, *Sure, why not?* and started to want it. He had no idea that people would laugh at him for even wanting it; the county bigwigs had a plan and it certainly did not include the guy from Nigeria.

The ground was shaking even as Bennet and Prema were

committing to a future in Pittsburgh. They imagined a secure position for Bennet one way or another at the coroner's office, and Prema, with her nursing degrees, in a hospital; and if and when Wecht survived the trial, Bennet could continue working on private cases with him, maybe even become his legitimate partner in the business, make enough money to continue to fund his brain research, continue with Bailes and Fitzsimmons to study CTE, to maybe find a cure for it, *oh my gosh, how about a vaccine!* He felt his career was on solid footing in Pittsburgh, so he and Prema decided to buy a house. They found a beautiful redbrick colonial in Sewickley, an ivy-covered old-money neighborhood on the banks of the Ohio River, and they put a down payment on it. The next day, the real estate agent called. "I'm sorry," she said. "No deal."

No deal?

"They don't want black people living in that neighborhood," Bennet said to Prema. "That is why they refused our money." Prema would never accept that explanation. But the agent provided none of her own. Bennet turned into a bulldozer after they refused his money. *Well, then I will build my own fucking house. I will build the biggest, most beautiful house in the world. This is America!* He bought a one-acre plot in Moon Township, in a neighborhood where brand-new McMansions were going up. A place for him and Prema and the baby that Prema was making in her belly to live out their happily ever after. So much was happening. So much was happening so *fast.*

Increasingly, Bennet came to view his CTE research as the urgent work of angels, partly because he is a person inclined to see angels, and partly because these angels were so *active.* The spirit of Mike Webster calling him, and then the spirit of Terry Long endorsing him: "Yes, you are correct; please proceed." And then Bailes, out of nowhere, believing him. He, too, was an angel. *And now there were more.*

In November 2006, the same month Bennet's second CTE paper appeared in *Neurosurgery,* there was another dead football player.

This one was in Tampa. This one had shot himself in the mouth. His name was Andre Waters but they called him Dirty Waters because he hit so hard, so hard he had put one guy out of the league permanently. He played ten seasons for the Philadelphia Eagles. He once hit a guy so hard the NFL came up with a rule—nicknamed the Andre Waters rule—that prohibited defensive players from hitting quarterbacks below the waist while they were still in the pocket. The focus was always the other guy, how bad the other guy got hurt. Never Andre Waters, his aching head. He had a seizure on the plane once; they said it was cramps and he was back on the field the next week. He got fifteen diagnosed concussions, then stopped counting. Bone-jarring hits. Such awesome hits! He felt them in his head. All in his head. Everything packed in tight, tighter, no release. After he retired he bought a .32-caliber Smith & Wesson and he sat on his back deck in his Tampa home and he put it into his mouth and pulled the trigger. He was forty-four.

Bennet had never heard of Tampa and he did not know what a Philadelphia Eagle was. The Andre Waters news came to him via yet another angel, a man who identified himself as Chris Nowinski.

Prema was like, whoa, whoa, whoa, Bennet. Stop! Please, stop with the angels! "You must pause. You must pause and be rational." As if angels understood rational.

"How do you know this Nowinski guy is legit?" Prema said. "It could be a trick!"

Prema was becoming increasingly fearful. She didn't like any of this NFL business. She didn't like her husband poking into this hornet's nest with a stick like this. She reminded Bennet of the reporter who had showed up that one day and said, "Get these out of your house! Someone could come in and kill you and steal these brains! Do you know what you're *dealing* with?"

"This guy Nowinski," she said. "Be careful." She had a book in her lap and a pen behind her ear and she was sipping a Coke. "I don't trust any of these people, Bennet. We should no longer answer the phone."

Bennet took his shoes off and parked them neatly at his feet. "It's not a trick," he said. "This new guy has his heart in the right place. I feel sorry for him."

A heart being in the right place doesn't tell the whole story of a person's motives, Prema thought. But she agreed; it was easy to feel sorry for Chris Nowinski.

He was neither a doctor nor a scientist. He was a guy from Boston with his own very bad headache who had become a self-appointed brain advocate. He was a former WWE wrestler who had wrestled under the stage name Chris Harvard—the only Harvard-educated wrestler in the WWE, he would point out. He had played football in college, but it was the head bashing as a wrestler that did him in, especially that last bash, at the Pepsi Arena in Albany, when a Dudley Death Drop ("3D") engineered by the Dudley Boyz sent poor Chris Harvard's head smashing through a table to the cheers of thousands. Vision loss, ferocious migraines, loss of balance, memory problems; he was twenty-four years old and feeling like a feeble old man. He went to eight doctors before anyone really listened to him and took the time to tell him what was going on. Those were *concussions*. All those times. Not just the times he had become unconscious, but all those times, perhaps one hundred of them, that he saw stars, suffered a "ding"—any loss of brain function induced by trauma was a concussion, and all of them were serious, all of them were brain injuries, all of them required attention, not the least of which was the time to heal before suffering another one. No one had ever told him that. No one had ever told him that the job he returned to each day was potentially brain damaging. No one, that is, until Nowinski met Dr. Robert Cantu, a Boston-based concussion expert, and then Nowinski quit the WWE, started sniffing around the shady world of concussion in sports, and decided to write a book about it. He had read Bennet's paper about Webster, and now he wanted to talk to him about what he had just heard on the news.

He told Bennet about Andre Waters's suicide; he said he wondered if perhaps Andre Waters, too, had CTE.

"I wonder," Bennet said.

Nowinski said, *Let's look*. He said, *I'll talk to the family and get permission, and you look at the brain, okay?*

Deal. That was the deal Nowinski hoped he and Bennet could build a partnership around. Nowinski would help Bennet get more dead NFL player brains, and Bennet would study them.

The brain was sent on December 19, 2006, by overnight delivery. Several cut pieces of Andre Waters's archival brain fixed in formalin. Very tiny pieces. Upon receipt, I examined the brain first on my balcony, in fact, my wife again took pictures of me examining the brain. When I could not stand the cold any longer, and when I needed a rigid platform/table to cut, carve, and shave the brain tissues, I took it to my kitchen counter. I had to do these examinations in silence, in the quiet oblivion of my condominium, since at this time I was becoming very weary, if not paranoid, of everyone, especially the NFL. I perceived that I was being treated as an outsider who should not be trusted, like a persona non grata, a nonentity, a person of no consequence, possibly because of my heritage. I did not want anyone to know what I was doing. I was afraid of becoming crushed, and my efforts to unravel CTE quashed. I sent the tissues to the same brain laboratory where I had sent Mike Webster's and Terry Long's brain tissues. Jonette, the technician, was especially enthused since she was becoming part of history. At this juncture, I knew my CTE stuff. I had read thousands of papers. Honestly, at that time, I may have been the most knowledgeable person on CTE.

In January I went to the lab to pick up the slides to examine them. Unlike Mike Webster's case, I was eager to find out the results. Epidemiologically, a third case of CTE would make it a case series and would move it up in the hierarchy of medical evidence from statistical aberration to mounting evidentiary epidemiological trend. I had asked Jonette to expedite the tissue analysis and she did. The day I picked up the slides, I immediately came home and looked at them and called Mr. Nowinski and told him about the results. He was ecstatic. He was yelling on the phone and asking me if I knew what this meant. He said this was big, very big! In my naïveté, I did not foresee what he was referring to; little did I suspect his motives or plans. That was the beginning of my regrettable quagmire.

Chris Nowinski knew a guy, a journalist who freelanced for *The New York Times*. Alan Schwarz was admittedly an accidental journalist—he was a mathematician who liked to write about baseball stats. But he was interested in Nowinski's story. Here was an unlikely folk hero on a personal mission to uncover the truth about concussions in the NFL. Nowinski was pushy. He had told Schwarz he was going to have some big news soon. He had told him about Andre Waters's brain before the results were in. In a few days, he said, we will know. So of course when Bennet called Nowinski with the results, of course Nowinski was ecstatic, and he ran to tell his friend, who said "Wow," and who said that Waters's diagnosis was exactly the kind of peg that would make for a great feature story.

A feature story about Chris Nowinski.

Bennet had no idea this was going on. All he knew was that shortly after he found CTE in Andre Waters's brain, someone from *The New York Times* was calling him. Such a strange call, seeing as he had not yet had a chance to tell anyone but Nowinski about Andre Waters's brain. The *Times* wanted a photo, and some quotes. When the story came out the next morning there were two pictures, Nowinski on top and Bennet underneath. Bennet was not sure he was ready for all of this, no, he was not at all sure, and he did not like the feeling of losing control of information about his own research.

EXPERT TIES EX-PLAYER'S SUICIDE TO BRAIN DAMAGE was the headline that ran on the front page of *The New York Times* on January 18, 2007. Bennet had not figured on anything like that when he examined Andre Waters's brain. Bennet had figured on a far more sober "Chronic Traumatic Encephalopathy in a National Football League Player: Part III" in *Neurosurgery*.

At that point, Bennet did not understand that the angels were unruly. He did not realize that the hornet's nest he had stepped into when he first started looking at NFL player brains would attract more hornets. It would take him years to understand and untangle all that. At that point, he still trusted Nowinski. He thought Nowinski was simply a loud and brash angel. He admired loud and brash angels. He figured he and Nowinski were alike in that way, outcasts fighting for legitimacy and finally finding some.

The *Times* story shot the issue of the NFL's concussion troubles into public awareness. Specifically, "the NFL's tobacco-industry-like refusal to acknowledge the depths of the problem."

The NFL was like Big Tobacco! A corporate cover-up! People were starting to say things like that. They were saying outright that people were dying because of what the NFL had done for so long, hiding the truth, not telling their own players what was happening to their brains. That was a narrative the news media could get its head around. That was the story, and that was juicy.

But the *Times* story also began a quieter narrative, a subtext: this was Chris Nowinski's heroic journey. "He chose Dr. Omalu," the *Times* article said. "He chose Dr. Omalu both for his expertise in the field of neuropathology and for his rare experience in the football industry. Because he was coincidentally situated in Pittsburgh, he had examined the brains of two former Pittsburgh Steelers players who were discovered to have had postconcussive brain dysfunction."

He *chose* Dr. Omalu. *Chris Nowinski chose Dr. Omalu?* Because Dr. Omalu was *"coincidentally situated."* In two sentences Bennet's contribution to CTE was reduced to that of a minion, his five years of research little more than a fluke.

What happens in stories is what happens in stories: the telling and retelling simplify and reduce. History gets written in the wind that keeps blowing; if it's not too strong you don't even notice it. The lights are bright and there's so much shouting and scrambling. A war is starting, and it doesn't matter if you never wanted to fight, you wake up one day and you're somebody's soldier.

As for the NFL, its MTBI committee scientists responded to the *New York Times* story with more denials.

"Preposterous," they said, about the Andre Waters finding.

"Not appropriate science."

"Purely speculative."

The NFL was on defense, the media had picked up the offense, and Bennet was scrambling to do what was beginning to feel like Nowinski's bidding.

Schwarz got a full-time job at *The New York Times* after his story about Andre Waters's brain was published, and he started digging, pumping out more stories challenging the NFL—groundbreaking stories that unpacked and challenged the work of the MTBI committee. He rarely mentioned Bennet Omalu again. If there was a hero of the narrative, it was Chris Nowinski.

NFL Commissioner Paul Tagliabue retired at sixty-five in September 2006. His successor, Roger Goodell, had risen in the ranks, had started his career in the NFL as an intern right out of college. Perhaps things would change under his tenure as commissioner. He was not even fifty, part of a generation more attuned to the issue. Perhaps he would bring a fresh perspective. Perhaps he would straighten out the mess?

No.

The situation only got messier the more the news media dug. Pellman, the chairman of the MTBI committee, the rheumatologist, was found to have significantly embellished his own bio. No, in fact he didn't have a medical degree from SUNY; in fact he had attended med school at Universidad Autónama de Guadalajara, and no, he wasn't *exactly* a professor teaching at Albert Einstein College of Medicine as he had said, but he had, like, an honorary position there, but, well, no, he didn't technically teach there, no. But anyway, his secretary screwed up. It was all her fault.

Goodell got rid of Pellman as chair of the MTBI committee and appointed two cochairs from within the committee: Dr. Ira Casson, the committee's lone neurologist, and Dr. David Viano, a self-described "biomechanics consultant." Casson would now lead the charge in speaking to the press. He was, by all accounts, an accomplished neurologist. He knew brains. He had found brain damage in Muhammad Ali's CT scans back in the 1980s; he had published a landmark study about boxer brains and chronic brain damage in 1984. The link to football was hardly far from his mind: Casson was the one who had urged Al Toon to retire back in 1992, the dawn of the NFL's "Season of Concussion."

But there was something bewildering about Casson. He was a knot of contradictions. Now that he was leading the MTBI committee, he denied that the NFL had any concussion problem at all.

"No," he said on a 2007 HBO *Real Sports* special, when the interviewer asked him if repeated football-related concussions could result in brain damage, dementia, or depression.

"No," he said a second time when the interviewer rephrased the question.

The blatant denial was problematic on a number of levels. Even the courts had ruled, by this point, that concussions among NFL athletes could lead to brain damage. That happened in Mike Webster's disability case. Fitzsimmons finally had his verdict. On December 13, 2006, eight years after the initial filing and four years after Webster's death, the U.S. Court of Appeals for the Fourth Circuit upheld the ruling that Webster had been totally and permanently disabled as a result of brain injuries from playing professional football. The ruling, a 3–0 decision, resulted in an award of more than $1.5 million to Webster's four children and former wife. It was the first time the NFL had been successfully sued by an individual.

"No," Casson said on the HBO special after a third, a fourth, and a fifth attempt to rephrase the question about the possibility of football causing debilitating brain damage.

"Is there any evidence, as of today, that links multiple head injuries with any long-term problem like that?" the interviewer asked, finally.

"No."

People started calling him "Dr. No."

The NFL was on defense, the media was on offense, and Bennet was a reluctant soldier.

The public attacks on Bennet enraged some of his friends, most notably Jason Luckasevic. He was the younger brother of Todd, the med student at the morgue whose family would host Bennet for Thanksgiving dinners. Todd and Jason would take Bennet to hockey games and out for beers. Now Jason was fresh out of law school, working with a small firm in Pittsburgh, and he was brimming with the same kind of do-gooder optimism that drove Bennet. He had hired Bennet to testify in a few of his asbestos cases, and Bennet had hit them out of the park, so he kept bringing him back for more. The two were becoming close, meeting in Jason's office a few blocks from the morgue.

"What are you going to do about this?" Jason said one day. He said Bennet needed to protect his reputation. He said the NFL was making a mockery of his work and he couldn't stand listening to it.

Bennet made the point that his reputation was hardly the issue. "The question is, how many more guys with CTE?" he said. "Think about how many more there must be, Jason. Even Dr. Bailes said it's probably every guy playing the game.

"Someone needs to sue the bastards," Bennet said. He put his chin down, gave Luckasevic a sideways glance, signifying "Somebody?"

Luckasevic laughed. First of all, Bob Fitzsimmons had already done that, on behalf of Mike Webster. He had taken his disability claim all the way to the appellate court and won $1.5 million.

"Small potatoes," Bennet said.

"Bennet—"

"This could go way beyond disability claims," Bennet said.

Luckasevic let out a good long sigh, tossed his pen on his desk, leaned back in his chair. He set his gaze on his bookshelf, rows and rows of law books, red, blue, brown, and green. "Well, there *is* fraud," he said, finally. "You know, what they've done to these guys is fraudulent. Lying to them about what football could do to their brains."

"Now you're talking," Bennet said. "Thousands of players. *Billions of dollars!* That's what the NFL owes these guys."

Luckasevic looked at Bennet, blinked, caught himself. This was getting silly. He was thirty years old, a lowly associate making $40,000 at a small firm catering to blue-collar guys in Pittsburgh with asbestos problems.

"Yeah, I'll sue the NFL, Bennet," he said. "I'll get right on that."

"I'm *serious*," Bennet said. "What's your hang-up?"

For God's sake. "Well, to file a lawsuit you need a client with a complaint first," he pointed out.

"You can find thousands of clients," Bennet said. "Football is a very popular game and there are many professional players!"

"Right."

"Well, you're the lawyer," Bennet said. "You'll figure something out."

Luckasevic had to admit it was fun imagining something like that. Like a young Bill Gates and his pals tinkering in his garage. Like a young Steve Jobs doodling on a napkin. Ideas have to be born somewhere.

To compile a case history on Andre Waters for his next scientific paper—"Chronic Traumatic Encephalopathy in a National Football League Player: Part III"—Bennet decided to travel to Tampa to visit Andre Waters's family. Nowinski said he would come, too; they would meet at the airport and drive together.

It was the first time they ever met face-to-face, which was weird, considering their recently shared history making front page news in *The New York Times*.

"You're much younger looking than I expected," Nowinski said, smiling. Bennet's photo in the *Times* had him looking so . . . professional in his white lab coat with his name embroidered in blue cursive on the pocket. This live version of

Bennet, all the quirks and the cackle-laugh, was not what Nowinski was expecting.

"And you are very tall!" Bennet said. He thought Nowinski was the picture of TV-commercial America. Towering, blond, boyish, clean-cut, charming.

They drove out into the flat, marshy landscape of south Florida. They joked together, traded skepticism about the guys on the MTBI committee. Nowinski told Bennet about his headaches, and Bennet told Nowinski about Wecht, about Prema and the baby coming, and about how frustrated he was that the NFL was discounting his research. Nowinski made the point that Bennet did have a "believability problem." Maybe if he was an old gray-haired guy in his seventies, with a name like O'Malu, with a resume replete with Ivy League stamps and badges, maybe people would have believed him about CTE.

I began to feel that I had been deemed an outsider. I did not think people took me seriously, and since they did not take me seriously, my message was not taken seriously. The problem was not the message, but the messenger, and if the messenger is not liked, trusted, or respected, the message is null and void, no matter how true the message is.

It was a good point. And as they drove together, Bennet talked about the partnership he was forming with Bailes and Fitzsimmons. Fitzsimmons had been talking about doing the legal work, was going to put up the $10,000 seed money. Nowinski said he also had been thinking about a partnership with Cantu, the doctor who had first shown him the light about what was happening in his own bashed head.

In the car, Bennet and Nowinski discussed the idea of their joining forces. They even came up with a name, the Sports

Legacy Institute. Bennet liked it because it had a good acronym: SLI.

They would collect brains and study CTE. They would challenge the NFL's repeated denials. They would help the families of former players. It would be an unbeatable power team. Bailes and Cantu had the medical clout, years of concussion research behind them, and Bailes had the inside track on the NFL. Bennet had the discovery and the encyclopedic knowledge of the science. Nowinski had the face, the smile, the unbeatable schmooze. Nowinski had in spades what none of the others had or understood or cared to acquire. He had the missing ingredient. Nobody understands showmanship better than a former WWE wrestler.

When he got home, Bennet told Bailes and Fitzsimmons about the idea of an expanded partnership with Nowinski, and they agreed.

"I think I have another case," Bailes said. "There's another brain we should get."

CHAPTER 11

| | | | |

ODDBALL

Keana Strzelczyk spoke about her former husband this way: "If I had still been married to him I could have 302'd him, put him in a mental hospital involuntarily. But I wasn't married to him anymore so I couldn't.

"I was like, 'What do you want?' And he's like, 'Nothing. Never mind.' And I was like, 'Justin, what's wrong? What's wrong?'

"I met him in 1993. We got married shortly after. He was so much fun to be around. He didn't judge people. He could fit in anywhere. Black tie or seedy biker bar. I mean, he was just very chill.

"As far as his career goes, he never had concussions that I knew about. He was never diagnosed with concussions on the field. Or off the field, for that matter. I never felt anything one way or the other when he played. I mean, it was great. We were in Pittsburgh the whole time and the Steelers organization was, you know—the women I was with, they were just like family, which was, it was great. I felt as wives we did a lot of good. I loved doing the charity work. But, you know, now, looking back . . . Now how I feel about it is that I don't even—I can't. There's just too many lies.

"Murderers, liars, thieves. I just—I just don't.

"He wouldn't come home. He wouldn't call. He went to take the trash out one night and he didn't come back until five o'clock in the morning. I had no idea where he was. One time he said 'I'm going to Vegas for the weekend, I'll be back Monday.' I was like, okay. He didn't come back for six weeks.

"That was one of the reasons that we split was because of him doing stuff like that. I just couldn't deal with it anymore.

"I thought maybe he had bipolar, because he started to get angry. He was scaring me. My daughter wouldn't go anywhere with him. She was afraid of him. I bought my son who was in fourth grade one of those disposable mobile phones and hid it in his bag because I was afraid. Then I just stopped sending the kids.

"I really thought he had bipolar.

"Had I known this was from football, I think I would have behaved differently. You feel some sense of guilt for kicking them out, for kicking them to the curb, because, you know, you're blaming other things. That's what always gets to me. That this game, this thing that he loved so much, that gave us so much comfort, you know? Financially, it let us have a great life, and yet it was the downfall of him and that's kinda like . . . I still don't even know what to think about that, like that still kind of just blows my mind. Something that was such a big part of our lives, and that gave us so much—it took him away.

"I'm like, 'Justin, what's going on? What's wrong?' And he started crying and he's like, 'God came to me just now here at the garage and he spoke to me.' And I was like, *what?* And he was like—and then he paused, and then he got real angry and he was like, 'Never mind, never mind.' And I go, 'Justin, do you want me to get the kids on the bus and come over there to the garage?' And he's like no, no. And I said, 'I can come over.' And he was like no. And then he said 'I love you' and hung up.

"How these owners sleep at night, I have no idea. I just feel like the NFL is run by murderers, liars, and thieves. They can sugarcoat it, and do all the charity they want. And that kills me because I think: Why aren't you doing something for these men? Forget breast cancer awareness. Forget colon cancer awareness. Forget, I don't know, whatever you're doing. Concentrate on these people that you've wronged. You could build a whole entire hospital and facility dedicated to these men. You have enough money! You could have a whole staff! You could have a retirement home for these men. You could build five retirement communities. And have them each with their own personal doctor.

"I don't think Justin committed suicide like they said. I just—I don't know. In my mind, he knew. He knew he wasn't going to be here anymore. He knew he wasn't coming home, wherever he went. I don't know what he had in his mind, but he wasn't coming back."

Justin Strzelczyk was thirty-six when he drove away on that cool autumn morning in 2004, the sky streaked with clouds. He didn't tell Keana where he was going; he just hopped in his truck and drove. He stopped at a gas station on a highway outside Buffalo, New York. He tried to give some guy three thousand bucks and told him, *Head for the hills! The evil ones are coming!* Then he got back in his truck and sped away, ninety miles an hour, eventually with the cops chasing him on Interstate 90. The cops chased him for forty miles, threw metal spikes, blew out his tires, but he kept going and kept going, a hundred miles an hour, until finally he steered over the median strip, into opposing traffic, and smashed into a tanker carrying corrosive acid and everything exploded.

Strzelczyk had been dead nearly three years when Julian Bailes started thinking about him in light of CTE, Webster, Long, and Waters. Bailes had been on the Steelers sidelines during Strzelczyk's playing days, and he had been deeply troubled by his tragic death; he told Bennet and the others the story of that death, and they agreed it was worth asking whether perhaps the local coroner had saved a piece of Strzelczyk's brain tissue, which in fact he had. Bennet looked in the microscope and again found CTE.

"It's making me sick," Bailes said. "All of this, it's making me sick."

"I'm sorry, Julian," Bennet said. They were in the conference room adjacent to Bailes's office at West Virginia University Hospital in Morgantown, about an hour south of Pittsburgh, where the mountains were blue and round on top.

"They called him Jughead," Bailes said. "Did I tell you that? That was Justin's nickname."

"I don't understand Jughead," Bennet said. He was wearing his wide-pinstripe suit and his cologne filled the room like sassafras.

"After the guy in *Archie*. Because he was just so goofy and so lovable. That was Justin to a tee."

"Archie?"

"Wow," Bailes said. "It's a comic book, Bennet." He rolled his chair back, put his feet up on the long, wide table. He was in his scrubs, just out of the OR, and he was drinking a Diet Coke.

"Comic book," Bennet said, trying to be present for his new friend.

Bennet had come down to Morgantown to go over a PowerPoint presentation that Bailes was taking to a meeting in Chicago. Bennet wanted to make sure Bailes got everything right, was there to help prep him. But the news of Strzelczyk's diagnosis was hitting Bailes hard, and Bennet was trying to give him the room a grieving man needs to reminisce.

"Jugs," Bailes said. "Everybody loved Jugs. I would go to his apartment. I rode his motorcycle. Did I tell you about his Harley?"

Bennet nodded. "The hat with the spike coming up," he said, motioning with his hands. "He had the hat?"

"The helmet!" Bailes said. "Like a Prussian helmet. He had this box on the back of the Harley. He filled it with candy. Seriously, this was a guy who would drive around and give kids candy. Friggin' Santa Claus."

"You knew these guys," Bennet said. "It is very different for me looking at a slide."

"He had a banjo and that big beard, like a mountain man, a big lumberjack on a Harley strumming a banjo. Seriously."

"A character," Bennet said. He had so little to offer. He had no reference point. Also, he was better talking about dead people as either just dead people or as spirits moving on. The land of the living was not his forte.

"And it's like, why?" Bailes said. "With all these guys. And where does it stop? I'm really wondering if every single football player doesn't have this. Some more, some less. And if they have it, who else does? What about the soldiers coming home, killing themselves? I don't know who all. It's staggering, and it's just . . . it's football. A game. All this for a game?

I played football. I love football. But mankind does not need football."

He stood up, fumbled with the cord on the laptop. Fidgety. More and more, Bailes's southern veneer was falling away. Cool preppy kid, his dad a Louisiana Supreme Court judge. Privileged kid. Brilliant kid. Brain surgeon. Steelers team doctor. It was as though the more the light came on about CTE, the more someone else was crashing through and inhabiting Bailes, compassion was crashing through, or maybe he always had it, yeah, he has to always have had it, Bennet thought. Compassion bottled up.

"And you know, with Webster," Bailes said, his mind churning. He sat back in his chair. "I was always like, *Why, Mike? Why is this happening to you?* I mean, if you knew Mike Webster in his prime. I used to sit with him at my mother-in-law's house . . . he would come over. He was fine. Then one time he was holed up in the Hilton and I had to come get him out, he was slipping, he was slipping and I was like, *What happened?* He was a warrior. I was like, *Why is Mike doing this? Why?* I would think, that's not Alzheimer's disease. I'm trained. I know Alzheimer's disease. I was heartbroken watching him. And then Justin just goes off. Bam. *Why?* I can't believe it. I think about all this and I can't believe it."

"They couldn't help themselves," Bennet offered.

"I'm the *doctor,* Bennet," Bailes said. "The doctor is supposed to help."

"You couldn't have known."

Bennet leaned forward, picked a speck of lint off his sleeve. He took the opportunity to switch the subject to Jesus and forgiveness. He talked about God working in mysterious ways and he talked about angels. He said just being friends with these guys, knowing them the way Bailes did, loving them the way he did, that was God's work right there.

"Do you want something to eat or something?" Bailes said.

Bailes was converting to Catholicism but it wasn't something he talked about easily. His wife was Catholic. They had five kids. That was how he found Catholicism. Because of that he was converting, not because of this, not because of Bennet and the truth on the slides.

But maybe, yeah, maybe part of the reason was because of this.

"We could order sandwiches," Bailes said. The Jesus talk had forced him to collect himself. He wasn't one to get all emotional with remorse or touchy-feely talking about himself or talking about God. If he admired Bennet for one thing it was for his ability to show unabashed vulnerability. All that emotion he wore—Bennet was a man transparent, a man without filters, a man who exploded with love, God, rage, joy, envy. And then he had all that intellect on top.

What an oddball, Bailes thought. That was their friendship. Bennet thought Bailes was an angel with compassion bottled up, and Bailes thought Bennet was an oddball. Someone who needed protection. Because oddball was not, after all, the kind of personality that won fans in academia, or in the medical community. And oddball was exactly the kind of personality that a multi-billion-dollar entertainment behemoth like the NFL could ridicule, discredit, and dismiss.

"Julian, why did they not invite me to Chicago?" Bennet said to Bailes that day.

"I already told you everything I know," Bailes said.

Everyone who was anyone in concussion research was invited to Chicago. Goodell had convened the meeting in June

2007, the first leaguewide concussion summit. All thirty-two NFL teams were ordered to send doctors and trainers to the meeting. It would be a chance, finally, for the NFL to talk openly about this unfolding crisis and to hear from independent scientists, many of whom they also invited to the meeting—three hundred participants in all.

They asked Bailes to come. They asked Cantu to come. They did not ask Bennet Omalu.

"They hate me?" Bennet said.

"They don't hate you," Bailes said. It was more like they had successfully orchestrated a way to marginalize him. Should he tell him that?

"Okay, should we go over the PowerPoint one more time?" Bennet asked.

"I think I'm good," Bailes said. "I'm ready for this. In fact, I can't wait."

If Bennet wasn't invited to the meeting, then Bailes would bring Bennet's science. He would present Bennet's work to the NFL and the nation's top neurosurgeons, slide by slide. He would say "Dr. Bennet Omalu." He would say "Here's who you need to listen to."

"You know, it's now even more ironic that I am not going to Chicago," Bennet pointed out. "Because for the first time in many years, I have time on my hands."

Bailes put back the last of his Diet Coke. "Did you tell Prema yet, Bennet? Did you tell her that you no longer have a job?"

"No."

"You have to tell her."

"I'm not going to tell her, Julian."

. . .

It wasn't just that Bennet didn't get chosen to be Wecht's replacement as Allegheny County's new chief medical examiner, it was who the county bigwigs chose when their plan was enacted: Dr. Karl E. Williams, a longtime Pittsburgher, a seemingly innocuous fellow with a bow tie and round wire-rimmed glasses. To Bennet he was hardly an innocuous fellow. The bow tie. The wire-rimmed glasses. Bennet knew him.

Williams's career trajectory had intersected with Bennet's in one especially unpleasant way. Williams had served as a forensic pathologist at a small hospital up north, Ellwood City Hospital, which most people even in Pittsburgh had never heard of, but Bennet had heard of it. Back when Bennet got the guy off death row. The Thomas Kimbell case. *Show me whose hands those are, and I will show you who the killer is!*

What are the chances? Williams was the prosecutor's expert forensic pathologist on the Kimbell case, duking it out with Bennet. Williams was on the team that, in the pretrial hearing, had said this guy trying to get Thomas Kimbell off death row was not credible, they said there was no scientific way that some *forensic pathologist* could determine, all these years later, who killed that woman and her kids.

"Yeah, there is," Bennet had said, in so many words. *"I'm the way."*

The judge sided with Bennet.

Bennet was hardly the picture of humility back then. Bennet was all showmanship, newly schooled by his mentor, Dr. Whizbang himself, Cyril Wecht. And there Bennet was with his applause line, *Show me whose hands those are, and I will show you who the killer is!* There were all the media glorifying him, Bennet beaming like a triumphant prizefighter.

Williams sat there, on the losing team.

This was the guy who became Bennet's new boss at the Allegheny County coroner's office. Here was the dawn of a new day at the morgue, a place that had been raided by the FBI, scrutinized by investigators, and put in the spotlight by media beginning to suspect literal skeletons in the closets. Williams was the man appointed to clean up the mess. If he had followed any of Bennet's career after that trial, what he heard had done nothing to improve his opinion of the guy from Nigeria.

For three months in the office I don't think Dr. Williams ever said one word to me.

Then he sent the slides of Webster and Long to somebody I did not know.

Then he began to send my work to be reviewed by other pathologists. I think he was looking for some type of mistake so that he would have a reason to fire me. He did not find any mistakes.

I moved swiftly and obtained signed consents from Webster's family and Long's wife for the brains which were fixing in formalin in my office. Still Dr. Williams refused to release the brains to me.

It was only after Long's wife got involved that Dr. Williams released the brains to me, without the slides. He said the slides were not available so I told him to keep them, as long as I had the brains, I did not want to be bothered with him.

To this day, I do not know what he did with those slides.

I moved the brains to the coat closet in my condominium, so at some point I had Webster's brain, Long's brain, Waters's brain, and then a wrestler, Chris Benoit's, brain in my coat closet at home. The work environment at the medical examiner's office was becoming threatening, antagonistic, and hostile. I was treated with ignominy and I was beginning to be painted and branded as a troublemaker. I was referred to with all types of adjectives and nouns, and suspected that many called me the N word behind closed doors.

One Sunday morning in March of 2007 I received a call from my former professor and teacher at Pitt, Dr. Wiley, asking that I should come see him first thing on Monday morning. I asked why. He wanted to help me. He said he did not want me, his former student, to be professionally incapacitated at such a young phase of my career. First thing on Monday morning I went to his office. I met with him and Dr. Hamilton. Dr. Wiley suggested I should leave the medical examiner's office, and possibly leave Pittsburgh.

I wept in his office and asked him what I had done to deserve this. He looked at me and said he did not know. I got home that day, still with tears in my eyes, knelt down and wept to my God. I resigned my job at the office that week. I was now also in trouble with my immigration status, since at that time my immigration status was based on my employment. I went back into a state of acute depression, and I started seeing a psychiatrist, an older guy who was in his seventies and semiretired. I saw him every Wednesday morning at eleven o'clock. I saw him for about six months and built such a wonderful friendship with him. While all these things were happening, my wife did not know anything. She was pregnant with our first child, Ashly, and I did not want her to worry. I was out of a job for six months, and she did not even know. I had savings, so our standard of living was not affected. I began a nationwide search for a new job. Every *morning I would pretend that I was going to work, and I would go to the library or to church and work on my private consultation cases and CTE.*

To feel that you're running away. To feel marginalized. To feel you don't belong. Once again, here he was. And the builder was calling about the house in Moon Township. The drywall was up and where did he want the flatscreen in the bedroom? Could he come out and look at the size of the pantry in the kitchen? Because it could be bigger if they took off a foot or two from the powder room; there was still time. He answered the builder's queries and drove with Prema out to the house. She held up paint chips for the baby's room and swatches for living room drapes. She began to regard that house as her own loving creation, her work of art, and Bennet could not allow that to be taken away from her. He prayed for a miracle, stood in the backyard and imagined a swing set and prayed for a miracle.

So Bailes going to Chicago with his research, with his PowerPoint presentation, to stand up for him, *to be his voice,* that was a significant moment in Bennet's life. That was a kind of rescue.

But, honestly, at that point Bennet needed so much more rescue. Wecht wouldn't talk to him. The FBI was after him to testify. His precious slides had vanished. He'd lost his job. His American dream was collapsing. It felt like monsters were growing out of the earth, pushing up from under his feet, pushing up and toppling him over and getting ready to swallow him.

The meeting was in an amphitheater in Chicago's Westin O'Hare. Maybe two hundred guys in suits holding awesome folders with the NFL's awesome logo on them. Inside the folder, like a prize in a box of Cracker Jack, was a CD holding all the journal articles about concussions that the MTBI committee had produced. Goodell got up and thanked the MTBI committee for such important work.

Pellman was there.

Casson was there.

Maroon was there.

Apuzzo, the editor of the journal *Neurosurgery*, was there, too. He had not accepted Bennet's paper about Andre Waters's brain, "Chronic Traumatic Encephalopathy in a National Football League Player: Part III" for publication in the journal. He had accepted the first two, but this one he had turned down without explanation. He was on the NFL payroll. He had served as a consultant for the Giants since at least 1997.

It was awesome to be affiliated with the NFL.

It was standing room only in the amphitheater, mostly white guys in suits, and the morning session started off politely enough. Members of the MTBI committee were praised for their hard work as guys showed slides and other guys clapped, and there was much doodling on notepads. Then a former New York Jets neuropsychologist, Bill Barr, cut through the crap and all but accused the MTBI committee of fraud. He told everyone in the room that the committee had excluded available data—his own data—from its studies, thereby skewing results and promoting a false narrative. He went after the committee, and committee members fired back, and by the time they broke for lunch the tone of the summit had turned dark.

Bailes spoke after lunch. "Does Concussion Lead to Pugilistic Dementia and Alzheimer's?" was what he titled the talk, going straight for the heart of Bennet's work. He figured the science would elevate the discussion, move it forward, enable the group to think about building on Bennet's work. Not that Bennet's work was news to them. By now they all knew about it, as reported in *The New York Times*. Bailes figured just saying it out loud, showing the slides, would wake everyone up. At a minimum, it would make the statement that, hey, guys, there's work to be done here, there's a whole lot more research we need to do. Because *look* at this: it's scientific proof that the kind of concussions sustained in football can lead to debilitating brain damage.

Bailes clicked through the slides, told the stories. This was personal. Webster, Long, Waters. And Bennet, too. He thought about how Bennet was as pure a scientist as anyone could bring into this equation—no government and no institution funding him, doing no one's bidding but his own.

Bailes stood up there and he showed pictures of the tau tangles, the sludge that did Webster in. He showed it in Long's brain and in Waters's brain, too. He was solemn, his heart heavy. The game he loved so much, had played in high school and college, had felt privileged to be part of as a sideline doctor with the Steelers, he was telling all those like-minded men that their beloved game was causing brain damage.

He saw a guy near the front, smiling. Except, no: it was more of a smirk. He saw Casson, the infamous Dr. No. The guy with the smirk was looking at Casson. The guy was looking at Casson because Casson was rolling his eyes. Like, *Here we go again.* Like, *Can you believe this bullshit?* Like, *What a fucking idiot.*

They were mocking him.

Bailes had never before been mocked. Certainly not in his professional life.

"And I'm thinking, 'This is a new disease in America's most popular sport, and how are its leaders responding? By laughing at the guy presenting it. Alienating the scientist who found it. Refusing to accept the science coming from him.'"

Bailes felt a burning inside him, a volcano.

At a press briefing afterward, Bennet's name kept coming up—this was Bennet Omalu's research—and so Casson made a statement about that stupid Nigerian's work: "The only scientifically valid evidence of chronic encephalopathy in athletes is in boxers and in some steeplechase jockeys. It's never been scientifically, validly documented in any other athletes."

A total dismissal of Bennet's work.

"I'm a man of *science*," Casson said, implying that Bennet Omalu was not.

As for the commissioner, Roger Goodell, he said: "I'm not a doctor."

One final thing happened in 2007 that turned Bennet's world sour. Maybe he suspected it would happen, the way you can feel a storm coming even before the wind blows. There's a stillness in the air. There's that feeling on your skin. Something was not right.

Nowinski was on the phone. It was a conference call. Nowinski, Bennet, Bailes, and Fitzsimmons. The four would gather for regular weekly calls about SLI, planning research, discussing how to move forward to promote concussion awareness and how to pierce the wall of NFL denials.

Nowinski was talking and he was saying he needed money. He said he deserved to be paid for his efforts to bring CTE to the public's awareness.

"What do you mean, money?" Fitzsimmons said.

A salary, Nowinski said. He said he wanted to make at

least $110,000, and he wanted it paid retroactively, starting from the day SLI was formed.

Fitzsimmons made the point that the group had no money, that it was a *nonprofit,* that he himself had already put $10,000 of his own into it, to say nothing of all Bennet's personal assets that had gone into the research, the foundation upon which SLI was built. They would of course need to seek funding to continue the research, but that was a long way off.

"There's no money," Bailes chimed in.

"Nobody's getting any money," Bennet said.

Nowinski did not back down. Maybe he didn't even need them; that's the way he was talking. He could go solo. He didn't need the scientist who discovered the disease. He didn't need the brain surgeon who had been studying the subject for decades and knew his way around the NFL. He didn't need the one attorney in the world who had ever successfully sued the NFL for disability claims.

In fact, maybe he had all he needed: *The New York Times.* And he'd been talking to other people. Better people. He didn't say anything about that then. He just said he needed to be paid, and the others said they couldn't pay him, and the conversation got heated and Fitzsimmons couldn't believe what he was hearing. *The wrestler wants money? For what?*

Fitzsimmons had never felt good about Nowinski joining the group. He found him bossy and impertinent and he believed he was trying to turn Bennet's science into the Chris Nowinski Show. Using Bennet to make himself famous. "Why should we put up with this?" Fitzsimmons would say to Bennet and Bailes. What did Nowinski even bring to the table? And now he was asking for money. And now on the conference call, Bailes and Nowinski were fighting. A power struggle. A battle for turf. Nowinski wanted SLI headquartered in

Boston, where he and Cantu were based. Bailes thought it belonged in West Virginia, where he and Fitzsimmons were based. The argument got heated, and then the money issue came up again, and Fitzsimmons just couldn't take it anymore.

"I'm resigning," he said. "Good luck to you guys." He hung up.

Bailes couldn't take it anymore, either. He hung up.

It was just Nowinski and Bennet left. *"Who do you think you are?"* Bennet said, his voice high and angry. *Who?*

They both hung up without resolution. Bennet would remember Nowinski calling him a few days later, calling to tell him that his brain analysis services were no longer needed for SLI.

Nowinski wouldn't remember it that way; he would say he wanted out all along. He would say his request for money was just a ruse, an exit strategy, and it worked. Whatever it was, and whoever was right and whoever was wrong, the fact was that the alliance was over. Nowinski took off. He had an idea for a different neuropathologist to be the face of CTE. A better face. And a better whole team of people who would maybe *behave*. And he had *The New York Times*.

Bailes and Fitzsimmons and Bennet still gathered each week for their conference calls. They gathered in collective wonderment.

What just happened?

CHAPTER 12

| | | | |

COMFORT ZONE

The witness box is an almost perfect square, heavy oak coated again and again in shiny shellac, so thick you can dig your fingernails into it. On his second day of testimony at the Wecht trial in Pittsburgh in 2008, Bennet is resisting the urge.

I'm sorry, Dr. Wecht. You have to know I am not here by my own choosing.

Wecht won't even look up, his arms crossed, biting his thumbnail, staring at nothing.

The jurors are settling in, shifting, trying to get comfortable in their seats, and a few of the alert ones exchange glances: *Is this Nigerian dude going to talk slower today?*

Bennet just wants to go home. California—that's where he lives now. That's where he does his CTE work now. In his garage. After being unemployed in Pittsburgh for six months, never telling Prema a thing about it, faking it, thinking fast on his feet so she wouldn't find out, he landed the medical examiner job in San Joaquin, and he and Prema bought a house in the sleepy town of Lodi, and it's wonderful, really. Living in obscurity is wonderful. *On the outskirts!* That's where he belongs. Just like when he was a kid. Watching the other kids. Not getting into the fray, sitting on the edges of the action, dreaming about becoming an airline pilot and soaring forever away. And then in med school, not fitting in. Seattle, New York, never fitting in. No, of course, sitting on the edges of life was not wonderful back then. It was depressing as hell. But he's a man now, and he understands that God placed him on the outskirts like that for a reason, to gain strength, to get used to it, because that's where he belongs. The outskirts. With dead people.

If he had to point to a single reason why he chose to spend his life with dead people, he would point to this trial in Pittsburgh in 2008. Living people are messy. Dead people are clean. There is no politics with dead people. His retreat from the real world—his necessary retreat—enabled him to be right where a guy like Mike Webster needed him to be. It was his retreat that enabled him to find CTE in Mike Webster's brain. That worked out just fine.

But this mess here, this is not working out fine. Stuck in a witness box in a pair of too-tight cap-toe oxfords, dreading what's to come.

"Good morning, Doctor," the defense attorney says. He's a dapper enough guy, properly attired in a sharp blue suit; he has a bushy mustache and a flap of gray hair sitting on his head like a doily on an old lady's coffee table, but otherwise he's completely put together.

"Good morning, sir."

"We have not spoken before, have we, sir?" he says to Bennet.

"Sir?"

"We have never spoken?"

"No, no, this is the first time I'm meeting you."

Today it's the defense attorney's turn to question Bennet about the eighty-four counts of piddly shit, now reduced to forty-one counts of piddly shit, that threaten Wecht's livelihood and future.

The defense attorney wants to know, truthfully: Was Bennet hoping to become a famous pathologist just like his former boss, the defendant sitting before us today, Dr. Cyril Wecht?

"No," Bennet says, answering way too fast, as if to squelch the part of him that thinks: *Yes! Of course, yes.* There is so much of Wecht he wanted to be like. Of course. *Oh my gosh, yes! Are you kidding me?* All those things he learned from Wecht. Slamming down the phone, *motherfucking cocksucking ass-kissing bastard.* How to dress, where to buy the best car, how to think about race, prejudice, being a black guy, being a Jewish guy, one of those gays. How to stay centered and confident even when the world around you treats you like shit. But that is not the stuff the defense attorney is referring to.

"Now, you were kind of a bargain for Dr. Wecht, weren't you?" the attorney asks.

"If you say so."

"Doctor, do you recall, sir, how much you were paid as an employee of the coroner's office when you were a full-time pathologist?"

Oh, geez. *Relevance, Your Honor?* This could get embarrassing. "I was started at a low level of ninety thousand dollars," Bennet says. "Why I say low, is comparatively, compared to what people of my education and level were paid, ninety thousand dollars for a board-certified forensic pathologist, neuropathologist was . . . low."

"Did you ever go, Dr. Omalu, to Dr. Wecht to express your concern about your salary and to discuss it with him?"

"Yes. Many times I went up to Dr. Wecht, and I brought it up. In my mind, it wasn't good."

"Do you remember what you said to him, how you engaged him on the topic of your salary?"

"Many times he would tell me, 'Bennet, there is nothing we can do,'" he says. "'It is not up to me. It's up to the county.' I recall there was once we were talking and he said to me, 'Sit down, Bennet, and let me explain something to you. If you're paid a competitive salary at this county, administrators will be monitoring you, looking across your shoulders to see what you do. But if your salary is low, you have greater liberty to do what you want to do. So choose being paid a lower salary, and we are free to do whatever we want to do.'"

"Did you get a raise?"

"No."

Look, the guy used me, okay? Bennet looks at the jury, tries to say with his eyes all that he needs to say. *But I agreed to be used! He gave me so much more than money.*

"Sir, let's switch gears for a moment here," the attorney says, approaching with a slow saunter, like he's pondering, like he's just thinking this up right now. This is for dramatic effect; Bennet knows that. The closer he gets, the more Bennet can tell the doily thing is not fake hair, it's just the way he combs it. Such an easy fix.

"Had you ever indicated that you were scared as a result of the FBI investigation?" he asks.

"I wouldn't say that I was scared," Bennet says.

"Were you afraid?"

"Afraid?" Bennet says. On this point he needs to ponder. He leans forward, sits on his hands, can't wiggle his damn toes. "If you would pardon me," he says, leaning into the microphone. "The most frequent thing Jesus said, do not be afraid. I'm never afraid. What is it to fear?"

The people on the jury exchange nervous glances. *How did Jesus get in on this?*

Wecht allows a smile, and so does one of the guys from the morgue, in the galley. It's easy to forget what it's like to be around Bennet, until you're around Bennet again. The Jesus crack, that is so . . . Bennet.

The attorney goes back to his table, looks at his notes.

"In terms of your immigration status, sir, am I correct that when you entered the country, a part of the permit to enter the country was after you completed your medical education you were to return to Nigeria for at least two years to practice medicine?"

"Yes, sir."

"Immigration and your permit status in the United States was an issue from the day you joined there, correct?"

"If you say it was an issue, that makes it look like a bad thing."

"Nobody is making anything sound bad, sir. From the moment you came to the coroner's office did that man, Dr. Wecht, do everything he could to help you with your immigration status?"

Bennet looks at Wecht. "Oh, definitely! When everyone looked away, he helped me. And that is why I hold him in the highest regard. I've said it before, what I am today, Dr. Wecht made me. He supported me. He gave me the opportunity. He gave me a place to stand to express myself. He made me what I am today."

Bennet pauses. Waits for Wecht to look at him, acknowledge him. Or Sigrid? *Hey, guys?*

Nothing.

Bennet leans closer still into the microphone. "And I love him, if I could say that," he says.

Love?

Love. Jesus. The words hang in the courtroom like wayward party balloons. Bennet knows that. Americans are not always comfortable with these words in public. But Bennet is just going to be Bennet, and to hell with everyone and everything else. He is almost forty years old. *Bennet can only be Bennet!* He puts his feet flat, firmly on the ground, collects himself, straightens his back.

"Dr. Wecht was my adopted American father," he announces loudly to the court. It feels good to say. Just being honest and frank like that. It feels like a lot of pressure letting go.

"Are you under subpoena to be here, sir?" the defense attorney asks.

"Yes, sir. I had no choice."

"You didn't want to be deported—"

"Nigeria is corrupt. It's like the Mafia. I had to run."

So, yeah, the FBI had threatened to send him back, and he caved. Wecht would have to understand. It wasn't as if he had anything earth-shattering to offer the prosecution. He could use his testimony to slip in positive words for Wecht. And Wecht would understand.

"When all this is done with," Bennet says, looking straight at Wecht, "we will reestablish our friendship."

Wecht looks up. For the first time in two days he looks at Bennet. He shakes his head.

It feels like a shot. It feels like his hero just shot him through the heart. *Are you not listening? Bennet Omalu is telling the world that Cyril Wecht is a good man,* that he loves him like a father, that he is grateful to him, that he wishes everything could go back to the way it was when he was his loyal sidekick, Junior Wecht.

Again Wecht shakes his head. No. A dismissal. *I'm done with you, you piece of shit.* Wecht is not a forgiving man, and when it comes to betrayal, no, he is not going to forgive.

Bennet turns to the judge. "Can I ask Your Honor, please, I was hoping we could finish today so I can go back home to California."

Please, Your Honor.

"Well, it doesn't look like that is going to happen," the judge says.

"I have been here since Sunday," Bennet whispers, deflated.

"I couldn't hear you?"

"I have been here since Sunday. I left my house at three A.M. on Sunday morning."

"I didn't ask you to come here Sunday, sir," the defense attorney says. "May we have Government Exhibit 365, Page 797?"

The clerk hands over the pages.

Just let me go.

"Are you going to be featured on the Canadian Broadcasting Corporation this week?" the defense attorney asks.

"Oh, I'm surprised—" Bennet answers. "I don't know, really."

"You don't know?"

"I discovered a disease. Has there been media attention on the disease discovered? Yes."

"You have been involved in a lot of publicity for that discovery of yours, correct?"

Publicity? Canada? *Am I supposed to do something in*

Canada? What does this have to do with anything? Can someone please object? Relevance?

"I have not been involved in the publicity, but my discovery has attracted so much publicity," Bennet says. "When I discovered this disease, it was by accident. I never knew in my wildest imagination that it would attract the publicity it has attracted and the publicity it has generated."

"And just so the jury knows what we're talking about," the attorney says, "you claim that you discovered, while you were working at the Allegheny County coroner's office on Mike Webster's case, a phenomenon called CTE, correct?"

"Yes, sir."

"And you have been all over the national airwaves in America on that phenomenon this past year?"

"It went internationally, not just this past year—"

"And publicity is good for your name and reputation, isn't it?"

"No, I truly, if you ask me, really, I don't like it. I wish—I really wish I never touched Mike Webster's brain. Why? Because it has generated so much—with publicity comes the effects of human behavior, jealousy, envy, rancor, meanness, which actually I do not need, truly."

He does not need the bullshit, this real-world bullshit. People claiming credit. People running to the press. People stealing credit. Right now he just wants to go home to his garage in Lodi. The garage has floodlights, and big doors to open for fresh air. And a wall of brown cupboards for storing stuff. He wakes up, reads his Bible, says his rosary, goes out and cranks some Pendergrass or Bob Marley, and he examines brains. Before he leaves for the office he makes Prema eggs. Mashes carrots for Ashly. It's wonderful. He's been trying to come to peace with it, trying to convince himself that getting kicked into obscurity is wonderful, and mostly it is, of course it is, there is plenty to like about obscurity. It's the kicked part that he's still struggling with.

He wanted to stay in Pittsburgh. He wanted to be the new Dr. Wecht. He wanted to move into the big, beautiful house in Moon Township he was building, live happily ever after there with Prema and the baby. His dream house—they never even got a chance to move into it. Never once slept in it. The builders finished it the week they moved to California. The same week. That beautiful house, two white columns, brown brick, giant windows. Flatscreen TVs. Imported tile. Marble. Granite. Every single decision his and hers. The real estate agent said wait until the market goes up to sell it. He said fine, I'll wait. He doesn't want to sell it, and Prema can't bear the thought of selling it. So they still own it. It sits there vacant, like: There's the life we were supposed to have. There it is. He drove by this morning before he came to the courthouse. He stopped there, got out of the car, felt the bitter air on his cheeks. He marched up to the front stoop like he owned the place. *I own this place.* He kicked snow off the stoop with his shiny new shoe. He sat there, blew steam. He considered calling Prema. Calling her to say, "Hey, honey, I stopped by the house." But there was no way he would do that to her.

"Now, sir," the attorney is saying. "Have you referred to yourself as a brain chaser?"

Huh?

"No."

"Never?"

"I'm sorry. No."

"Dr. Omalu, do you recognize Exhibit 369, what that might be from?"

He looks at it. Some announcement or something from SLI. Where did this come from? What does this have to do with anything?

"I resigned. This is outdated. I resigned. It has nothing to do with— I resigned."

"Did you draft a portion of the description?"

"No. Chris Nowinski did. N-O-W-I-N-S-K-I." *Motherfucking cocksucking ass-kissing bastard!* Now, if we are going to talk about Chris Nowinski, Bennet's head is going to explode. Is that what everyone wants to see here in this courtroom today? *Is that why we are here?* "I was not in support of so many things that he did—"

"So you are no longer affiliated?"

"*No.*"

Deliberations in the Wecht trial drag on for ten days and end in a hung jury in April 2008. "Call and cancel your luncheon appointments," Wecht says to the press hovering outside the courthouse; he's beaming, full of life again after two years living like a raisin. "All that I built up, and all that my wife and I saved, is gone, and I am very much in debt," he says, and then he turns to Sigrid, huddled next to him in tweed. "I shall continue unfettered in the next, what, honey? Twenty years?"

He doesn't speak to Bennet, doesn't answer his plea for forgiveness even though Bennet's testimony was anything but damaging. Bennet confirmed dates of autopsies, receipts, payments, and other records that had hardly been questionable. On balance, he probably helped the defense more than the FBI, providing a portrait of his boss that was of a loving and generous man. It would take seven years for Wecht to finally speak to Bennet again.

. . .

A few months after the Wecht trial, in his garage in Lodi, Bennet finds CTE in another fallen football player. Tom McHale, a former offensive lineman for the Tampa Bay Buccaneers. A steep postretirement decline ended with his taking a lethal dose of oxycodone and cocaine. He was forty-five.

Still partnered with Bailes and Fitzsimmons, Bennet reports his findings to the group, now named the Brain Injury Research Institute, BIRI, headquartered at West Virginia University. "Tom McHale is positive," Bennet tells them. They tell McHale's family. This time, Bennet doesn't want to wait to release the news. He doesn't want to risk the rigmarole of NFL doctors demanding retractions or trying to humiliate him. He's prepared to go public with it.

"Please don't," the family says. They're still reeling, trying to understand.

Bennet is in his own way reeling, trying to understand. In a blink the whole CTE landscape has changed. Ego has erupted. Now there are competing scientists and arguments about turf and press releases and media training and money and ulterior motives.

If you make a discovery, you're supposed to tell people, because the discovery is important. But then what? Are you supposed to hold on to it, run around asking for glory? No, you are not. So what happens if someone else runs off with it, claims it as his own? Are you supposed to argue, try to get it back? Does anyone really care?

No. The important thing is the discovery, and what it can do for the world, and how it can help people. Not you. You were just the messenger. You were God's tool. Or, you were Mike Webster's voice. Hey, you did the right thing, now let it go.

But still.

Nowinski has started a new version of SLI. He's teamed up with the Boston University School of Medicine, and he's still working with Dr. Cantu, and they've added a newcomer to the scene: Dr. Ann McKee, a BU neuropathologist who has been studying Alzheimer's disease her whole career. CTE in football players comes as no surprise to her, although like others in the field she had never gone looking for it. She agrees to examine the brains that Nowinski says he will be able to bring to her. They create the Center for the Study of Traumatic Encephalopathy and start a brain bank. One of the brains Nowinski gets her is half of Tom McHale's.

Half to Bennet, half to Nowinski, that's what the McHale family decided. Bennet asked first, then Nowinski came. Two competing groups asking for a brain. How does a family even understand something like that?

The whole CTE landscape has changed.

Meanwhile, the NFL ups its damage control operation. In October 2008, the league makes what seems like one final attempt to discredit Bennet's work. The request comes via Maroon to Bailes. He says that the NFL would like to send an independent researcher to West Virginia to look at Bennet's slides and make his own judgment of the validity of Bennet's so-called "discovery." The league is still not willing to talk about Bennet's work as anything more than a weird fluke of some sort, an exaggeration, wishful thinking on the part of an uppity young scientist trying to make a name for himself. They want to put the issue to rest, once and for all.

"They want to send out a guy to look at your slides," Bailes tells Bennet, who has had new sets of slides made up from the brains in his coat closet.

"Forget it," Bennet says.

"No, don't forget it," Bailes says. "You don't want to be the guy who doesn't share his research."

"Julian, *I've shared*."

"Just come out and show the guy, Bennet."

Peter Davies of the Albert Einstein College of Medicine in New York, a thirty-year veteran of Alzheimer's disease research, is said to be the consummate pro. He will take no money from the NFL, not even parking reimbursement; he will just look at Bennet's slides and form his own opinion. Davies is more than a little doubtful; he will go on to speak of his skepticism countless times in the media. He has examined thousands of brains, and he's never seen anything close to the degree of tau accumulation that Bennet has described in his papers. Bennet, he thinks, is well-intentioned but naive. Bennet's claims are just too far-fetched; he must be mistaken about what he's looking at. Davies has to be reminded that Bennet is a real scientist, a neuropathologist, not just some guy at a morgue doing autopsies and playing with a microscope.

Davies, Bennet thinks, is an old white guy with silver hair who commands so much respect on the strength of being an old white guy with silver hair.

"Nice to meet you, sir," Bennet says, in the microscopy room down the hall from Bailes's office at the West Virginia University Hospital.

"Pleased to meet you," Davies says.

"Please, gentlemen," Bailes says, "please sit down."

"Sit down, Joe," Bailes says to Maroon. No one knows what to do with Maroon. He discounts Bennet's work, then accepts it, then discounts it again. It seems he's on his own private mission.

The microscope has multiple eyepieces so several people

can look at the same time. Davies takes one, Maroon another, and Bailes another.

Bennet sits on the sidelines, tapping his foot. He did not get new shoes for this event. He is wearing loafers, the shoes of a man who refuses to care.

"Whoa," Davies says, focusing on the slide.

"I told you," Maroon says.

"Wow," Davies says. "What the hell is this?"

"I told you," Bailes says.

It goes on like this for two days, slide after slide, the NFL's independent expert saying "Wow." Davies is transformed into a believer. It gets to the point where the only doubt Davies has is the staining of the slides themselves. (*Jonette! Oh my gosh, you do not second-guess Jonette!*) Perhaps the technicians were not using state-of-the-art equipment, Davies says. He asks Omalu if he could take some of the stuff home. Tissue samples, pieces of brain to take back to his lab in New York, where he could make new slides with his own equipment, his own technicians, his own stains.

"Sure, sure, sure," Bennet says. "You take some pieces home, talk to your guys, see what you think."

So in his lab in New York, Davies runs his tests, and when he looks in the microscope, he is stunned all over again. The tau pathology is even worse—even more pronounced—than what he'd seen in West Virginia.

He doesn't believe his own eyes. He has his techs make new slides.

When he looks in the microscope he sees the massive collection of tau tangles again.

"Come look at this!" he says, calling in his team of researchers. "What the hell am I looking at? This will blow your socks off! And it's not just in one case. I have three separate cases here. Bucketloads of tau pathology, and the one guy wasn't even forty years old."

It is far more severe than anything any of them had ever seen in the most advanced Alzheimer's cases—and in completely different regions of the brain.

So Davies fires off a letter to Bailes and Maroon, confirming what they all witnessed in West Virginia. He tells them that he believes Bennet, that Bennet was right all along. He tells them he had been skeptical but now he's a believer.

He writes a report for the NFL, detailing his findings, saying yes, Bennet was right. He speculates about the role of steroids, and of specific genetic markers, and other possible contributing factors worth pursuing, but the bottom line is that Bennet Omalu is right.

He writes to Bennet: "I remain convinced that you have discovered something, a new phenomenon. . . . This discovery could prove of great importance to the field of neurodegenerative disease research. . . . This is amazing stuff: you really have opened a major can of worms!"

The NFL never releases Davies's report, never makes it public.

Instead, the league commissions a new study, tries a whole different approach. They send a team of researchers at the University of Michigan's Institute for Social Research off to do a survey of retired players. More than a thousand retired players. The researchers are to ask the players about health issues, whether they have heart disease, cholesterol problems, cancer, and they are to ask them if they have ever been diagnosed with "dementia, Alzheimer's disease, or other memory-related disease."

They wait for the results.

Then, at the 2009 Super Bowl in Tampa, Nowinski and McKee hold a press conference.

"A press conference?" Bennet says to Bailes.

Tom McHale, offensive lineman for nine seasons, had CTE, Nowinski and McKee report. They say they have proof! Dr. Ann McKee of Boston University has found CTE in Tom McHale's brain.

"That's my brain!" Bennet says, watching the coverage on CNN. But of course it was Nowinski's brain, too. Half to each. And Nowinski will later claim that his group tried to call Bennet's group multiple times, and Bennet's group never returned the calls.

The infighting doesn't matter to the media. The wires pick up the headlines. CTE! Brain damage in football players! The story gets murky. Who discovered this new disease? Fact-checking slips. Ann McKee discovered CTE? Chris Nowinski and Ann McKee discovered CTE! That is how the narrative slowly gets rewritten, while Bennet struggles with his place on the sideline, convincing himself, yeah, sure, this is where he belongs. No, really, obscurity is fine.

In September 2009, a year after they began, the University of Michigan's Institute for Social Research reveals its findings from the survey the NFL commissioned them to do. They find that Alzheimer's disease, or something very similar, is being diagnosed in former NFL players nineteen times more often than in the national population among men ages thirty through forty-nine.

Nineteen times.

Their own study. It's like Big Tobacco ordering a study that ends up showing that smokers get cancer.

The Michigan study makes headlines. It's one more thing on top of one more thing about concussions in football players. It gets Congress activated. *What is going on with brain damage and the NFL?* The House Judiciary Committee announces that it will hold hearings. They want Roger Goodell to answer for this mess. They want Casson. They want the NFL's MTBI committee. The committee is still publishing papers in *Neurosurgery*—it has just come out with its *sixteenth* paper concluding that there is no worrisome link between football and dementia. *What is going on?*

Everybody who is anybody in CTE research gets the call from Congress to come to Washington to testify.

Bailes, Maroon, Cantu, Nowinski, McKee.

Everybody who is anybody in CTE research gets the call.

Bennet Omalu does not get the call.

"Why am I not invited, Julian?" Bennet asks Bailes. It will become a refrain—"Why am I left out?"—in the coming years, as Bennet struggles to earn entry to the circles, circles pushing against circles.

Professional sports. Science. Medicine. Politics. Law. Families suffering, guys going crazy, guys beating up wives, guys killing themselves. Bennet watches from the sidelines. He works on convincing himself he belongs on the sidelines, that he's happy there, not quite knowing what to do with the fact that if not for his contribution, his determination, his discovery, none of the circles would have collided, the sparks would not be flying, the CTE light might never have come on.

What are you supposed to do with knowledge like that? Sing your own praises? Stay involved in the national conversation just because hey, you're the one who figured it out? Demand respect because, hey, *you're the guy who figured it out?*

Exactly how does one do something like that?

. . .

*I try to understand, and I can't come up with an explanation
as to why the messenger is not listened to. And this is where I
have questions of: Could it be related to racism? Could this be
nothing more than racism? Where blacks are systematically—
and systemically—excluded from mainstream American life?*

*People have said that to me. They have said, "Bennet, you
know, if you were white, if you were a white guy, with the
work you have done, the whole world—they would have
lifted you so high." Even Nowinski said it that first day I met
him. He said I didn't have, what do you call it, "the believability factor." That I'm young. I'm black. I'm from Nigeria.
That if my name was O'Malu, an Irish guy with gray hair, a
white guy who is in one of the Ivy League schools, everybody
would have embraced me when I told them about CTE.*

*I do think there's a mind-set—no matter how much we
may want to deny it in this country—about the perception
of blackness. And sometimes it's a subconscious mind-set.
Where anything associated with blackness has a negative con-
notation. This mind-set has a very fundamental assumption.
A false assumption that black people cannot be intelligent.*

*I think this is my story, to an extent. It's a manifestation of
a way of thinking.*

*Like Albert Einstein has said. He said, "The world as we
have created it is a process of our thinking. It cannot be
changed without changing our thinking."*

*When I was in Nigeria, I was not aware of the concept of
racism. I was not. When I came to America, it was so alien to
me. That why would somebody who does not know me—the
mere fact that he sees that I'm a certain color, he would pi-
geonhole me? And then when it comes to creating opportunities for me to express my talent and become who I want to*

become, he would try to deny me those opportunities. To keep me down!

That disappointed me about America. That disappointed me so much.

What have I done? Can somebody tell me? If there's something I have done wrong, I want to find out what it is so I don't repeat it. I want to learn from it. But the more I search, the more convinced I am that I have not done anything wrong. I have done my part in the CTE world. I was able to make the impact I did while being unnoticed.

I think the NFL was totally confused on how to address the CTE issue. They globally mismanaged it, because they dismissed me.

On a cold and rainy Wednesday morning in Washington, D.C., in October 2009, politicians and scientists and business men and women gather in the Rayburn House Office Building, wearing polite expressions of anticipation.

"There appears to be growing evidence that playing football may be linked to long-term brain damage," the House Judiciary Committee chairman, Representative John Conyers, says, opening the session. He's in his eighties, broad, hunched over, smooth. He's the longest-serving current member of the entire Congress, one of the founding members of the Congressional Black Caucus. He's a walking monument; he was in Selma in 1963 on Freedom Day, he's the guy responsible for Martin Luther King Day. He's a no-bullshit guy, and he starts the three-hour morning session with blunt focus. "I say this not because of the impact of these injuries on the two thousand current players and more than ten thousand retirees associated with the football league and their families.

I say it because of the effect on the millions of players at the college, high school, and youth levels."

It's an issue that warrants federal scrutiny, he says, especially given the insidious fact that the NFL is tax-exempt. Technically, according to the books, the NFL is a trade organization, an unincorporated nonprofit 501(c)(6) association made up of and financed by its thirty-two member teams, and as such, it is required to pay no federal taxes. (Individual teams are for-profit entities, so they have to pay income taxes.) The NFL's tax-exempt status was bestowed in the 1960s when Congress allowed the then American Football League to merge with the National Football League, granting the newly formed group antitrust waivers. That gave it a monopoly on broadcasting rights—and that's largely how the league now makes about ten billion dollars every year, and how it can afford to pay Goodell's annual salary of about $44 million. (In 2015 the NFL will decide to end its tax-exempt status, explaining that the nonprofit designation had become a "distraction.") Meanwhile, state and local tax dollars go into funding stadiums—about 70 percent of the capital cost of NFL stadiums has been provided by taxpayers.

America funds America's game, and the NFL rakes in the profit.

So, yeah, Congress has every reason to stick their nose into this business.

"Is there a link between playing professional football and the likelihood of contracting brain-related injury such as dementia?" Conyers asks Goodell, who is sitting across from him like a schoolboy, rosy-cheeked, his blond hair parted on the left, slicked over, his blue eyes set deep as if tucked beneath a shelf. He's wearing a powder-blue tie.

"We know that concussions are a serious matter," Goodell answers. "Our goal will continue to be to make our game as safe as possible." He goes on like this, like a salesman, polished and vague. No one cares more about concussions than the NFL, he says. In fact, they put a team of doctors together to study this very issue. "We have published every piece of data," he says. "We have published it publicly, we have given it to medical journals, it is part of peer review."

"I asked you a simple question," Conyers says. Is there a link between playing professional football and the likelihood of contracting brain-related injury such as dementia? "What's the answer?"

"The answer is the medical experts would know better than I would with respect to that," Goodell says.

The dodge does not go unnoticed. Especially given the fact that the NFL's medical experts are not here to help answer the question.

Ira Casson, the current head of the MTBI committee?

Not here.

Why is he not here? the committee wants to know.

Nobody asked him to come, Goodell says, in so many words.

Oh, yes, they did.

An aide comes scurrying up to Goodell, hands him a slip of paper. Goodell reads it, leans into the microphone, says he'll need to get back to the committee on the Casson issue.

"From my experience, the NFL is a model in concussion management," Maroon adds, when given the floor. He's as close as the NFL comes to having a medical expert at the hearing. He talks about how honored he was to work with Super Bowl coaches Chuck Noll, Bill Cowher, and Mike

Tomlin. He talks about ImPACT, the concussion test he trade-marked that is now sold around the world.

Representative Maxine Waters can't stand listening to this crap. She knows the NFL. Her husband, Sid, played for the Browns. A charade, she says of the MTBI committee. "We've heard from the NFL time and time again," she says. "You're always 'studying,' you're always 'trying,' you're 'hopeful.'" And she points her finger at Goodell. "Let me say this to Mr. Goodell and everybody who is here today. I think you are an eight-billion-dollar organization that has not taken seriously your responsibility to the players. The fact of the matter is, yes, people want to play. The fact of the matter is they are going to be injured. And we know no matter what kind of helmet you build, or what kind of equipment you have, it is a dangerous sport and people are going to be injured. The only question is: What are you going to do? Are you going to pay for it? Are you going to pay the injured players and their fam-ilies for the injuries that they have received in helping you to be a multi-billion-dollar operation? That is the only ques-tion."

Goodell blinks.

Representative Linda Sanchez hops on the bandwagon. She knows dementia. Her dad had Alzheimer's disease. She knows labor. She used to be a labor lawyer. She wants to con-front Casson personally. She has a lot of questions for him, says she wishes he was here. She cues the video. She shows a clip of Casson on TV, the clip of him being interviewed in 2007 saying "No," and "No," and "No," all those times, denying the link between dementia and football.

"A blanket denial!" she says. "It reminds me of the to-bacco companies pre-nineties when they kept saying, 'No, there is no link between smoking and damage to your health.' And they were forced to admit that that was incorrect through a spate of litigation. Don't you think the league would be better off legally, and that our youth might be a little bit better off in terms of knowledge, if you guys just embraced that there is research that suggests this and admitted to it?"

"Well, Congresswoman, I do believe that we have embraced the research," Goodell says.

"You are talking about one study, *and that is the NFL's study*," Sanchez says. "You are not talking about the independent studies that have been conducted by other researchers."

The comparison is made explicit in the first session, and repeated in the second: Big Tobacco. The NFL is like Big Tobacco. The MTBI committee is a charade. Nowinski piles on. McKee piles on. Bailes piles on. He mentions Bennet's name several times, says he's the guy who figured this out. None of the other scientists mention Bennet.

It's a PR nightmare for the NFL.

Three weeks after the hearing, Casson is relieved of his duties with the MTBI committee, and the committee itself is scrapped. The league announces it will start over, with new researchers, actual independent scientists.

Then, two months later, the NFL does something that catches everyone off guard. On December 20, 2009, they announce a gift of one million dollars to Nowinski's group at Boston University. One million dollars for them to go ahead and study CTE. In addition, they will encourage their players to pledge their brains to BU's new brain bank.

The gift appears to flummox even Nowinski.

"A million dollars, Julian," Bennet says, calling Bailes after hearing the news. "The NFL is giving Chris Nowinski *a million* dollars?"

"Something like that," Bailes says.

"They're buying support."

"That's too simplistic."

"It's the NFL again funding concussion research," Bennet says. "It is what it is, Julian. The NFL paying for science."

Nowinski's group throws Goodell a party after he gives them the million dollars. At the Boston Harbor Hotel, they present him with the Impact Award. They have a big cake. It has a brain on top, made of frosting, in the shape of a football.

"A cake, Julian," Bennet says. "A *cake*."

CHAPTER 13

| | | | |

WORD

Just because politicians, scientists, and business execs are raging about it, and newspaper headlines are screaming it, doesn't mean the message sticks—or that people care. It takes more than that to change a culture.

In the wake of the congressional hearings, the NFL announces that coaches will start putting posters in locker rooms. "CONCUSSION: A Must Read for NFL Players. Report It. Get Checked Out. Take Care of Your Brain." The text explicitly warns of personality changes, depression, and dementia that could happen if you keep banging your head into guys. "Concussions and conditions resulting from repeated brain injury can change your life and your family's life forever."

The media heralds the poster as a seismic shift in the NFL's handling of head trauma, and yet, at the same time, it's . . . a poster.

In a single weekend in October, despite the poster, four players are knocked out cold with concussions. That's when the league announces it is changing the rules: it will start handing out fines and suspending any player judged to be guilty of "devastating hits" and/or "head shots."

This announcement finally activates football fans. The

concussion issue is starting to become a serious buzz-kill. Like a looming player strike or something—one of those things you hope won't happen. You hope the guys work that buzz-kill thing out so that your Sundays—your tailgate parties, your beer and Dorito and wing ding gatherings—are not ruined.

But fining guys for big, awesome hits? From a fan's perspective, it's now getting personal.

Discussion boards light up:

This is not good. Freaking women organs running this league.

The NFL is turning into a touch football "Nancy Boy" League. Steer your kids that have talent into baseball, basketball, or any other sport that will still have dignity left in two years.

The pussyification of the NFL continues. Every single goddam year the rules get more and more VAGINIZED.

Right about the time the NFL starts penalizing players for violent hits, it also quietly removes from its website the popular DVD *Moment of Impact,* which it sold for $14.99. The package copy for *Moment of Impact* put you on the scrimmage line. *First you hear the breathing. Then you feel the wind coming through your helmet's ear hole. Suddenly you're down, and you're looking through your helmet's ear hole. Pain? That's for tomorrow morning. . . . 'Moment of Impact' takes you . . . into the huddle, up to the line, and under the pile with some of the game's roughest customers.*

Because it's *you.* This violence is for *you,* a chance to imagine yourself taking it, absorbing punishment you never actually would. A vicarious thrill. The violence is virtual.

The last thing you want to be reminded of is the fact that it's not really virtual at all, that these are actual people doing the bashing and getting bashed, people with families and histories and dreams.

You don't have to be a brain surgeon to recognize the stark contradiction that begins to befall the NFL. The violent nature of the sport, the very thing it's built on, is now called into question. Even sportscasters struggle to reconcile what football *is* with what it's doing to its players.

Postgame commentary following *Monday Night Football* in 2010 gets at the heart of the dilemma:

STEVE YOUNG: If you do something that's devastating—a big hit—you're going to probably be exposed to being suspended.

STUART SCOTT: But isn't that *football*? I mean, seriously. A devastating hit—isn't that, hasn't that been *football*?

MATT MILLEN: Listen, this bothers me, what we're talking about right here. It's wrong. You can't take the competition and the toughness and all the stuff that goes into making the game great—you can't take it out of the game.

YOUNG: What they're worried about is that Darryl Stingley hit. They're going to legislate it out.

MILLEN: That is stupid.

TRENT DILFER: This game was built—and people love it— because of the gladiatorial nature of it. Those are guys out there, and they're sacrificing their bodies and laying it all on the line, and that's what people enjoy. And the league is going to rob us all of that. . . . It's an absolute joke. First of all, every week we're talking about thousands of hits. Eventually the head is going to get hit. This is part of football.

MILLEN: *It's the game.* It's the way the game is played.

DILFER: It's just gonna happen! These guys are gonna get blown up. It's a physical game and you can't take it out of it.

YOUNG: A defenseless player, you're gonna have to take it easy on him.

MILLEN: You can't!

YOUNG: You're going to have to! Or you're going to sit out for a couple weeks.

SCOTT: *That's not football!*

It's the game. It's the way the game is played. There is, of course, a whole feeder system of guys who want to play it. What of those players? What is happening to their brains?

On April 26, 2010, Owen Thomas, a twenty-one-year-old University of Pennsylvania defensive end, hangs himself in his apartment. He's the youngest person yet to be diagnosed with CTE. His mother tells reporters that her son had started playing football when he was about nine, and he had never been diagnosed with a concussion, had never shown any side effects normally associated with brain trauma.

Thomas's diagnosis sheds light on a crucial fact that keeps getting lost in all the hoopla. *He never had a recorded concussion.*

But CTE is not about the big hit, or not only. A player doesn't have to be knocked out cold and taken off the field on a stretcher to be in danger of getting CTE. The subconcussive collisions may, in fact, be the real culprit. The little hits. Thousands of them, the little hits that look like nothing, that look like . . . football. All those linemen starting out every play, banging heads. Bennet's findings, and the ones others make after him, suggest it's these *subconcussive* collisions, all those regular bashes that linemen absorb in practice, twenty to thirty g's on *every play*—it's the accumulation of those hits that ends up making guys go crazy.

It could, for all anyone knows, begin at the peewee level.

It's the game.

"I hope you're listening to everything that's going on out there," Jason Luckasevic says to Bennet, calling him from his law office in Pittsburgh. The two have remained close, have become confidants over the years. "Because everything they're finding, everything they're doing to help these guys, it's all because of you."

"Thank you, Jason," Bennet says. "Thank you."

Luckasevic never let go of the lawsuit dream he and Bennet hatched together back in his office that day in 2007. In fact, he let his imagination run wild with it, and one day he took the idea to the senior partners at the firm. They laughed. A case that huge would require every lawyer in the building, first of all. And what, exactly, would be the case? That football damaged football players? Every player knows it's a dangerous game, long before they decide to go pro. What was the case?

"The case is that they were lied to about the possibility of brain damage," Luckasevic said. *"The NFL lied to them."*

Maybe. The partners didn't know the subject as intimately as Luckasevic did, and what's more, they weren't too sure about that Omalu guy making all those claims. Hadn't he been run out of town or something?

"Forget it," Luckasevic told them, and when he told Bennet that he had been laughed out of the office, Bennet said, "Oh my gosh, that's how you know you're on the right path. Such experiences should only strengthen a man's resolve!"

Luckasevic felt the push and the pull. On the one hand, there was the rational, grown-up world his partners represented. And then there was the decidedly more emotional Bennet approach. Maybe he was a fool for going with his gut, but he couldn't quite help himself. The righteous indignation that drives a kid to go to law school was still a part of him, and Bennet had a way of fueling it. So Luckasevic asked the partners at the firm for permission to float the idea about suing the NFL to other lawyers around the country; maybe someone would be interested and would help him. The partners granted the request. *Let the kid go humiliate himself if he wants to.*

So that's what Luckasevic did, he started cold-calling guys. Dozens of lawyers across the country. Everyone turned him down. Nobody wanted to team up with a junior lawyer from Pittsburgh who wanted to sue the NFL. Just, no.

"Sorry, son."

"No."

"I don't think you know how naive that sounds."

But by 2010, Luckasevic had met a few former players. He couldn't tell even Bennet their names because they were in the shadows, struggling with memory, struggling with addiction, and they didn't want to be known. Luckasevic took his time with them, befriended them, explained CTE. He explained Webster and Long, Waters and Strzelczyk, explained how the madness wasn't their fault; it was a disease, and it was almost certainly because of football. Luckasevic told them the NFL had lied to them, he told them, hey, what the league did to them was not right.

"And, you know, they're starting to *listen* to me, Bennet," Luckasevic tells Bennet one day.

"I told you!"

"It's still a pretty far-fetched plan."

"If you say so," Bennet says. Then he tells Luckasevic about a woman he just talked to. She reached out to him. "Her husband is suffering. You should talk to her. She's coming to the meeting in Las Vegas next month. I'll introduce you to her."

"See you in Vegas," Luckasevic says.

Tia McNeill was Googling one night. She was trying to figure out what the hell was wrong with her husband, Fred.

What the hell is wrong with you, Fred?

What Fred would do was hold a knife to his wrist; he would sit in his Los Angeles apartment and he would hold a blade to his wrist and look at it. That's when he would start thinking. It wasn't "Oh, everyone will be upset if I do this" or "I hate my life." Nothing like that. Instead, he would feel the cool blade on his skin, and he would think how thin and baby soft that skin was, he would think, *This is going to hurt like hell.* It might have actually been quite simple if not for the pain part. *Now, how can I do this so it doesn't hurt?* He just needed to get past the pain part.

Tia had no idea about the knife, and she was surprised when her son Gavin, with whom Fred now lived, told her about it. "We have to get him help, Mom. I'm afraid of what he might do."

How many guys are out there like Fred? Tia wonders. Not famous. Not glorified. Talented guys good enough to make it to the pros, played the game for the love of the game, and the paycheck, then went on with their lives . . . and then?

Fred used to be brilliant. He played linebacker with the Minnesota Vikings for seven years in the 1970s and 1980s, but football was secondary to his dream of going to law school. Tia encouraged him. She wasn't so big on the football thing, wasn't part of that world. He started law school during his last year with the Vikings, studying on the plane to and from games while the other guys slept. The day Fred graduated from law school in 1987 was the happiest day of his life. He was an emerging star attorney, quickly made partner. They built a five-bedroom house in Minnetonka. Fred was popular. A former Viking right there in the neighborhood! He and Tia had two sons and Fred coached them in youth football.

Fred's memory started failing as early as the mid-nineties, when he was in his forties. He never told Tia; he didn't understand it himself. Even when he got voted out of the firm. And then at the next firm, when he got fired, and the one after that—fired again. Everything was just taking so long. Something that should take an hour was taking him four. Reading a brief. The simplest tasks. He blamed his deteriorating eyesight. He went to an eye doctor—the only medical help he ever sought. He got glasses, then stronger ones, and stronger ones still. He kept forgetting things. He was supposed to pick up Freddie at school. Forgot. So many thoughts just—*poof!* He learned to compensate. He learned to say "Nice to see you" instead of "Nice to meet you." The latter was simply too risky. Apparently some of those people he had been saying that to were *friends*. But he had no memory of them. Blank. So it was "Nice to see you," always, just in case.

The boys were so young they thought their dad was just acting dumb when he would forget things. They thought he was being funny, and when he did that, they would punch him in the gut.

That was important information, the gut punch. That

meant: *You just messed up, Fred. You messed up bad. Come on, get it together. Act like you know what the hell is going on.*

As for Tia, she would scream when he would forget things. She didn't have a lot of settings, just on or off.

"You think I'm stupid!" he would say to her.

"I don't think you're stupid!" she would say. She didn't. She thought maybe he was depressed. She thought she understood. All the excitement of being in the NFL, all that hoopla—the transition back to regular life was hard for those guys. She urged him to get help. She would make the shrink appointment herself, but the day would come and he would bail. "I have to work on my cases," he'd say.

They left Minnesota in 1999 at Tia's urging and headed home to her family in L.A. Fred got a job with a general-practice firm but was fired after a year and a half. He got a job with another firm and was fired again. He was hired to do legal work for an insurance company, but they fired him, too. Within a year of moving to California, the family filed for bankruptcy.

After that, Tia gave up. It was all those years of urging Fred to go to a doctor, years of him promising and then not going, before she said "I'm done" in 2007, and walked out of the marriage. She didn't know that Fred's refusal to get help wasn't really a refusal. It was more about forgetting, about living in a fog and all the energy of trying not to show it. It was clutching for dignity and losing it, constantly losing it, feeling it dissolve.

Tia had no idea how sick he was. Would it have made a difference if she had known? Of course it would have. But you can't think like that. And you can't give a shit about people whispering behind your back. *You hear about Fred McNeill? Linebacker for the Minnesota Vikings back in the seventies and eighties. Ended up going crazy, and his wife couldn't handle it, so she walked out.*

The guilt, the people whispering, the financial worries, the effect on the boys, life has been a living hell pretty much since Fred lost his mind. Pretty much.

How many guys like Fred? How many wives and sons and daughters? In all, there are about sixteen thousand retired NFL players living here and living there.

With all the politicians, scientists, and business execs raging about it, and the newspaper headlines screaming it, you'd think people like Fred and Tia, former football families, would have heard all about CTE.

But Tia hadn't. It would turn out that the vast majority hadn't. Everybody was alone, as if on islands, trying to figure out what the hell was going on.

It had never occurred to Tia that brain damage from football could have anything to do with what was wrong with Fred. He wasn't a guy who suffered concussions. And anyway, that was so long ago. Why would you think: *football*?

"Fred?" Tia was saying one day recently. She was calling him on her cellphone. "Are you coming down?"

"Am I what?" Fred said.

"Are you coming down? I'm waiting outside in the car."

"You're waiting?"

"Fred, I'm out here waiting!"

"Oh, okay, I'll come down."

"Don't forget the suitcase," she said.

"Suitcase?"

"Remember I need my suitcase back?"

He did not remember anything about a suitcase.

"Fred, I just told you ten minutes ago that I am outside waiting for you and to bring me the suitcase," she said.

"It's too early for karaoke," he said.

"Coffee," she said. "Remember? I am taking you out for coffee. Now, come on."

"Coffee. That sounds good."

"Please hurry, Fred."

"So what I'm going to do is, I'm going to put my shoes on," Fred said, "and I'm going to get my briefcase, and I am going to get you the suitcase, and I am going to come downstairs, and we are going to get coffee."

"Why are you bringing your briefcase?"

"I need to go to the office."

"No, you don't, Fred."

He thought he was still a lawyer. He still dressed like one. He carried a white notepad, stained and smudged, covered top to bottom with phone numbers.

"Can we stop by the office?" he asked.

"Just come downstairs."

Five minutes went by. She honked. No Fred. Her next call went to voicemail: *You've reached the law offices of Frederick Arnold McNeill. Please leave a brief message.* She hung up. She reached into a bag of trail mix, popped a handful, and chewed. She stared forward and shook her head slowly in that way that speaks of tragedy, of comedy, and the insidious fine line.

Day after day like that, that's what life was like with Fred. Then Gavin told her about the knife, and that's when she started Googling, looking for answers. *What the hell is the matter with Fred?*

She read about CTE. *Football? This is because of football?* She dug deeper, read about Dr. Bennet Omalu. She found his phone number, dialed.

"Hello? Hello!" she said. She didn't expect anyone to answer, much less the doctor himself. "Hello!"

"This is Dr. Omalu."

She told him about Fred. "Could this be CTE?"

"It sounds a lot like CTE," Bennet told her. Not that he was in the business of diagnosing. Living people were not his thing. But he had heard this story so many times by now, the same story.

He told Tia about the upcoming conference in Las Vegas. Former players and family members like Tia had just started to find one another online, had started discussion boards, had started comparing notes. It was the beginning of awareness. The families decided to get together to learn more. They invited anyone who knew anything about CTE to come and talk, help them understand.

The Independent Retired Players Summit & Conference in the South Point hotel just off the Vegas Strip is a full-on immersion into the world of football and dementia—a vast, confusing, seemingly infinite parallel universe. It's the spring of 2010, and word is just beginning to spread. There are maybe fifty guys like Fred at the conference, wives like Tia and daughters and sons like Freddie and Gavin thinking, "Football? This is because of *football*?"

Yeah, it was likely football.

Here in Vegas there are scientists, and doctors, and salesmen, and opportunists, and all kinds of people getting into the brain trauma act for all kinds of reasons. One guy is hawking fish oil and other home-brewed brain trauma remedies, and some people, like Bennet, are here with real science to explain. Bennet presents his slides, stands up there explaining tau tangles. Nowinski, too, is here, and he tells of his team of researchers from Boston. He passes out forms: *Sign up to donate your brain to our group when you die.*

Fred sits next to Tia. He has a long, gentle face, a blocky brow, sprouts of gray hair shooting this way and that. He's wearing a windbreaker, baggy jeans, and sneakers, and he's listening to the speakers. Well, Fred always looks as if he's listening, but the truth is, he's able to zoom in on only a few key points.

"My *brain,*" Fred says to Tia. "I don't want to give my brain away."

"That's for after you die, Fred," she says. "Like, I'm an organ donor on my driver's license."

Fred fixates on the brain donation part. Tia has to admit the brain donation guy is kind of creepy; he reminds her of a guy doing an infomercial. Fred will continue to fixate on the brain part—over and over again they will have the brain donation conversation.

"A person still exists when the body stops working," he'll say. "I don't want to be surprised. Like, 'Oh, God, I wasn't supposed to feel this! Ooh, oww!'"

"You watch too many movies," Tia will say.

"No one gets to tell what happens. You don't get to say to the guy that buries you, 'Do you know what really happens down here?' You've lost all communication at that point, Tia."

"Okay, Fred. Okay." She understands. She understands that for most people there's living and then there's dying, but for Fred the whole gig has become more like being slowly buried alive.

"You can try, but there's no one who can hear you down there. 'Hello, it's me down here, ow, ow, ouch—'"

"Okay, Fred. Okay."

When the speakers break for lunch, Tia goes up to Bennet, thanks him for his work. He's in his blue pin-striped suit, unsure how to respond. It doesn't feel like a "You're welcome" moment. He shakes Fred's hand. It's the first time he's met a living guy who probably has CTE. He is not in the living-people business, so he does not know what to say.

"Nice to meet you," Bennet says, looking into Fred's vacant eyes. "Um, hello there, Fred."

"Do you need legal assistance, sir?" Fred asks him. Why exactly is Tia introducing him to this man?

Tia calls over Gavin and Freddie, introduces them to Bennet, and Bennet calls over Garrett Webster, the son of the great Mike Webster, whose brain was Bennet's first. "Talk to Garrett," Bennet tells Gavin and Freddie. "You guys have a lot in common."

The three sons sit for a long time, straddling folding chairs. Garrett tells them what it was like trying to care for his dad when things got bad. His dad pissing in the oven, his dad Super Gluing his teeth, his dad shooting himself with a Taser, his dad living out of his truck, and Gavin and Freddie nod and nod some more.

Person by person the awareness spreads like that, person to person, lightbulbs going on.

"Football. It's because of *football*?"

After lunch, a woman goes up to the podium to speak. She's Eleanor Perfetto, the wife of retired Steelers and Chargers lineman Ralph Wenzel, and because of her husband she's been on this subject of brain trauma for a while. Wenzel's dementia is the reason he's been institutionalized since 2007, she explains. He's no longer able to coordinate his body, to feed himself. But Perfetto brings some good news. She explains the NFL's "88 Plan," a bright spot of humanity. The 88 Plan is the result of a letter written to the league by Sylvia Mackey, wife of Hall of Famer John Mackey, who wore number 88 for the Colts. His existence, she wrote, had become a "deteriorating, ugly, caregiver-killing, degenerative, brain-destroying, tragic horror," and his monthly $2,450 pension didn't come close to covering the cost of the care he needed. The 88 Plan was created to help foot the bill for caregiving. It's not nearly enough, but it's a symbolic something. Since the plan's inception in 2007, 149 retired players suffering from dementia had been approved to receive benefits.

It's something. A trickle is better than nothing.

A trickle.

Jason Luckasevic, on the other hand, has a tsunami in mind. Tia meets him at the conference. His lawsuit idea is growing more credible by the day. Luckasevic has by now found a lawyer, a heavy hitter from Miami, who wants in. And another lawyer—an even heavier hitter from L.A., the guy who filed and won the famous Erin Brockovich lawsuit. He's interested, too. And now Luckasevic has seventy-four players and their families interested in suing the NFL, and at the conference, Tia makes it seventy-five.

In 2011, Luckasevic finally files his lawsuit. The complaint, co-authored by his new all-star legal team, is eighty-six pages long, and it charges that the NFL was involved in a scheme of "fraud and deceit." It says the NFL lied to its players about the link between football and dementia, and that it created a fake research arm, the MTBI committee, to perpetuate the lie.

Within a month, a Philadelphia lawyer files on behalf of seven more players. In quick succession the number of players suing the NFL grows to three thousand, representing nearly a quarter of all living players. Then it nearly doubles again, the lawyers consolidating the suit into one mass tort involving nearly six thousand players suing the league.

In the next two years, almost twenty-five thousand kids drop out of Pop Warner, the nation's largest youth football program—a 10 percent drop in participation, the largest in its eighty-five-year history.

During the same period, college football players are found to be *three times* more likely than the general population to have symptoms related to CTE. In a survey conducted by the *Chronicle of Higher Education,* nearly half of all college trainers say they feel pressure from coaches to return concussed players to the field before they're medically ready. In 2012, the NCAA finally comes up with an official concussion protocol—its first since the organization was formed at the turn of the twentieth century.

President Barack Obama says if he had a son, he would not let him play football.

A growing number of former NFL players—including Joe Namath, Troy Aikman, Brett Favre, Mike Ditka, and Terry Bradshaw—say that had they known what football could do to their brains, they would not have played. In 2015, 49ers rookie star linebacker Chris Borland, age twenty-four, retires from the game after one season, saying the risk of traumatic brain injury isn't worth any amount of money. He volunteers to give back three quarters of his $617,000 signing bonus.

"I hope you're listening to everything that's going on out there," people like Lukasevic continue to say to Bennet. "Everything they're finding, everything they're doing to help these guys, it's all because of you."

People in Bennet's circle know it. Does it matter that the rest of the world does not know that a shift in twenty-first-century American culture started with a no-name guy from Nigeria, a lone voice in the wind?

He works on convincing himself it doesn't matter. *I belong on the outskirts; that's my comfort zone.*

As for Fred, he never gets the chance to slit his wrist; Tia gets him into a nursing home. It's not ideal, but he's safe. It's not ideal because he's barely sixty, and he's an athletic guy who wants to do karaoke, play some hoops or something, and he's surrounded by ninety-year-old ladies who won't play, to say nothing of the fact that he needs medical help no one knows how to give. How do you treat guys with CTE? Is there even a protocol? Tia, like Keana Strzelczyk before her, thinks the NFL should man up and create care facilities for guys like Fred, facilities for athletic men who have turned into suicidal toddlers. The league made billions of dollars off them. And now they're simply tossed aside?

The other thing Tia does is sign Fred up for a pilot study. Something Bailes and Bennet have started developing. A test to try to diagnose CTE in a living person. If you can identify CTE in a living person, then you can start thinking treatment and maybe even cure. That's the direction Bennet starts to move in, while Nowinski and the Boston group, the Center for the Study of Traumatic Encephalopathy, continue to build their brain bank—hundreds of NFL players pledging to donate their brains after they die. Both groups continue to diagnose CTE in deceased players' brains—the combined total count reaches twenty in 2011—when one case makes particularly jarring headlines.

Dave Duerson, a Chicago Bears Pro Bowler who played eleven seasons in the NFL, turns up dead at fifty in a pool of blood in his condo on the outskirts of Miami, a Taurus .38 special by his side. The wound is in his chest, not his head. He has left a suicide note. "My mind slips. . . . I think something is seriously damaged in my brain. . . . Please, see that my brain is given to the NFL's brain bank."

The chilling realization that Duerson chose to shoot himself in the chest, and not the head, leaving his brain intact so that researchers could figure out what football had done to him, brings a new level of intensity to the conversation so much of America does not want to have. Duerson's suicide lingers in the national consciousness for reasons that go well beyond the fact that, yes, his brain tests positive for CTE. Duerson had served for years on the NFL's disability board, the Bert Bell / Pete Rozelle NFL Player Retirement Plan. He was one of the guys who had denied claims players made for disability payments, claims like the one Mike Webster made and would spend his last breath on earth trying to win. The six-member pension board repeatedly and unanimously said no to Webster, and Duerson was one of the six. He was one of the guys who would go on to vote no, over and over again, no, whenever guys tried to make the claim that football caused them to suffer mental decline. Duerson said those claims were false: football wasn't the reason guys were going crazy. *It wasn't football.*

Not until his suicide note did Duerson ever tell anyone he was suffering. But looking back, of course, looking back you always see signs. Like that time in 2005 when he threw his wife, Alicia, out the door of a hotel room, out the door and into a wall. "A three-second snap," Duerson explained when he pleaded guilty to domestic battery. He wasn't like that. He was not a violent man. Fans soon looked past that stupid three-second snap. Hey, a lot of NFL guys beat up their wives.

Domestic violence was becoming a rising issue among players. Was CTE at the root of that, too?

. . .

I was unraveling something that would enhance the lives of other people. In a way, I was helping people who could not help themselves, and like my father said, I should use my talent, my equity, to make a difference in the lives of other people. It was not about natural intellectual acumen or creative capacity, but rather an acquired intellectual capacity invested upon by unending specialized education.

In my yearbook in the final year of medical school, when I was asked what I wanted to become, I simply said: "I want to become myself."

People laughed, asking, was I not yet myself?

Well, no, I was not.

As a young man I became overwhelmed by low self-esteem and depression that could have destroyed my life—could possibly have led me to commit suicide. If I overcame all that, who was the NFL, or the Boston group, or anyone who thought I was no good, to overwhelm me and make me lose my focus and my ground on CTE?

Overcoming my personal issues emboldened me and made me believe in who I was.

The more attacks I got from the NFL, the more resolved I became to be myself. And every time I smelled racism, I even became angrier and more determined to be myself and stand for what I believed in, which in my mind was the truth.

I did not need anyone to legitimize me. I recognized I was an outsider. Racism even made me better at that. No one can be better at being Bennet Omalu than Bennet Omalu. There can only be one me, just like there can only be one you.

I do not have to fit in to be myself.

CHAPTER 14

| | | | |

DADDY

In July 2014, new billboards hang all over Enugwu-Ukwu. THE EXIT OF AN ICON, they read. They feature giant images of Oba in his red hat looking down from a gleaming blue-and-purple night sky. These advertisements are intended to act as reminders to villagers to pray for Oba on his journey through the gates of heaven.

"*Obaaa!*" Theodore yells, as he drives past the first one at the edge of town, and Bennet cranes his neck out the window, waving at the giant image of his dad.

Oba's embalmed ninety-one-year-old body waits at the morgue, and Bennet will dress it.

Theodore honks wildly as he pulls into the compound, and Bennet gathers himself. He's in his traveling clothes, linen shorts and a pink Ralph Lauren polo with the collar flipped up. He sees all three sisters come rushing out of the house, their arms wide open, and Bennet's mom with her shy smile, and Ikem and Chizoba beaming, and nieces and nephews in spinning circles.

"Oh, my sweet little baby brother," Winny says, wrapping herself around Bennet tight, swaying, while the rest of the family fires out the chatter of welcome. "It was a good flight?

Do you want something to drink? Let me take your bags. Wait till you hear who's coming! Wait till you see the crowd!"

"Look at this place!" Bennet is saying, squished inside Winny's embrace. *"Oh my gosh, look what you've done!"* The old dirt driveway has been paved with handsome tan and pink tiles, and floodlights and speakers have been brought in. Trees were removed from the back hill and all the vegetables were ripped up. The ground there was terraced to accommodate dozens of rows of tables. Bright white canopies hang overhead like angel's wings.

Another Oba billboard has been mounted on the eastern compound wall and Mie-Mie is pointing to it. *Turn around, Bennet, turn around and see!*

"Daddy!" Bennet says, eyes popping wide, Uche clapping, the whole family together in a double-exclamation-point re-union inside these walls.

As soon as Oba died in May 2014, the family began planning, made a spreadsheet, decided on a budget of $100,000, and got to work. Three months later and here we are, not really a funeral so much as a festival celebrating a revered patriarch—the orphan boy who made good and survived the civil war, an esteemed engineer who educated and married off all seven of his children, and who, as an old man, worked to create new village roads and infrastructure while offering wisdom to all who entered his obu.

More than a thousand mourners are expected over the course of the five days, an enormous number even by village standards, but wholly fitting for a man of Oba's stature.

Villagers have written tributes:

The towering colossus, born of fine steel, a man of candor and panache, Oba J.D.A. Omalu, moulded by destiny to be great . . . an inspiration to us, exuding an unraveled conviviality to both young and old. Merchant of joy, I know that the day you were made, heaven was gladdened. You fearlessly unleashed yourself on the fury of all life like a hard-boiled Spartan. The storm of life could in no way surmount you, a great whale shark who surmounted with angelic precision.

Oba! Oba! Obaaa!! You were the quintessence of justice, truth and firmness, you were always ready to say, stand by and defend the truth no matter whose goose is gored. . . . We are grateful to God almighty for the gift of an icon like you to the family and mankind.

Oh! A great star has salted the firmament. The great trail blazer of his generation has bidden goodbye to mother earth. The man of the people, Oba Gwa m n'iru is a father to us by the way of his teaching and ideas.

The tributes have been published in an eighty-page, four-color glossy magazine; then more tributes came in so the family had to do an addendum as a separate thirty-page black-and-white chapbook. All the mourners will get copies. Certain mourners will get T-shirts with Oba's picture on them, or mugs, water bottles, ceremonial hats, a thermos to take your lunch to work in, a "Divine mercy" exercise book with a picture of Oba and Jesus on the cover. There will be plenty of souvenirs to go around. As is the tradition in the region, many people will come dressed in the funeral fabric the family has designed: dark purple with yellow swirls, images of Oba in his red hat inside a circle, and the words THANKSGIVING IN A CELEBRATION OF LIFE OBA GWA M N'IRU

OCHI IGEW NZE 1923–2014. You order the fabric in advance and make your own dress, scarf, shirt, jacket, or trousers.

"Well, brother, I hope you're ready for all this," Chizoba says to Bennet, helping him with his bags.

"You're in charge of the brandy?" Bennet asks him.

Bennet decided not to bring Prema or Ashly or their three-year-old boy, Mark, to Nigeria for his father's funeral. Nigeria would be too hard on them. The rigors of travel through a developing nation, for one thing. But also, all this village hoopla. Bennet is proud to be the son of a man whom everyone holds in such high esteem, of course he is. But do his kids really need all this?

He wants, anyway, for his kids to be American. At home he buys them every toy they could ever want, every outfit, every treat, spoiling them unapologetically despite Prema's urging for moderation. He can't seem to stop himself. He bought Prema a Mercedes SUV to drive them around in.

If Bennet has any emotional ties to Nigeria, to the nation or the culture, he can't find them. Maybe that's typical for an immigrant in America. People expect you to have some measure of longing for the land you left, and you don't want to disappoint anybody, but frankly all that stuff is dead. That's like weeds you pulled. Nobody misses a dandelion.

Prema just got her American citizenship; Bennet's will come through in six months. If he is proud of one thing in his life, it is that he is about to become a citizen of the United States of America.

The Nigeria that Bennet left twenty years ago isn't doing great. Ebola has just hit, and no one quite knows how to talk about it yet. On the radio they hold a contest: "Who do you

love enough that you would kiss him and risk getting Ebola?"
On the news, they're saying that in 2014, Nigeria had the
highest number of terrorist killings in the world, 3,477 people
killed in 146 attacks, mostly at the hands of Boko Haram.
The terrorists have taken the schoolgirls. Two hundred
seventy-six girls kidnapped from a school in the northern city
of Chibok. The Boko Haram leader Abubakar Shekau said he
plans to convert the girls to Islam and sell them as wives to
militants, twelve dollars each. The name Boko Haram trans-
lates to "Western education is forbidden." It started tiny, in
2002, a group of frustrated men who believed in purity. They
wanted to establish an Islamic state in Nigeria, decided on a
method that included car bombs, suicide bombers, and IEDs
aimed at politicians, religious leaders, security forces, and civilians. They are targeting Igbo Christians who now, in a new
century, are once again fleeing the region.

Theodore and the others say don't worry about Boko
Haram; those terrorists are all way up in the north. A whole
different Nigeria up there. Totally different. Nothing to do
with people here in Enugwu-Ukwu.

You have to deal with what's in front of you.

There's a custom in the village and people can't say for sure
where it comes from. The custom says that after a man's body
is lowered into the ground, his widow should be the first to
pour dirt on his casket. It could be a sign of honor. Or it could
be an act of contempt. It could be a woman saying *Here, I'm
done with you, and now I am free to sleep with other men.*
Mostly, these days, it doesn't mean anything at all; it's just a
leftover tradition from a primitive Igbo era.

But the idea of contempt seems to be the most popular

interpretation of the ritual's origin, and one time when Oba and Iyom, Bennet's mom, went to a funeral, they both remarked on how distasteful they found the practice to be.

"I'll never do that at your grave," Iyom said to Oba.

"Thank you," he said, "I would appreciate that."

It wasn't much of a conversation, so it's hard to think it matters so much now. But this dirt-throwing matter has become a bone of contention.

Months ago, when Theodore and the others were preparing the celebration of Oba's life, a letter came from the parish priest. The letter included the funeral schedule, and it listed the dirt-throwing part at the end. The family looked at the schedule and said everything looks great, except the dirt throwing. Bennet's mom had told her children she didn't want to do it, and so Theodore told the priest to nix that part.

"But it's a law," the priest said.

"A law?" Theodore said. "It's a village custom."

"I said it's the law," the priest said.

"Whose law?" Theodore said.

"It's the law."

Theodore made the point that there's a difference between old-world rituals and Catholic doctrine. A widow throwing dirt on a casket is not part of Catholic doctrine.

The more Theodore protested, the more that priest dug his heels in. He said if Iyom didn't agree to throw dirt on Oba's casket, Oba couldn't have a Catholic funeral. "And if he doesn't have a Catholic funeral, he won't go to heaven," he said.

Oh, for God's sake. So Theodore called a family meeting. Emails flew around the world, brother to sister to sister to brother, all of them united in the matter of their mother not having to throw dirt on Oba's grave if she didn't want to.

"If she doesn't want to do it," Mie-Mie said, "then she doesn't have to do it. End of story."

"Exactly," Winny said.

"*What is with this priest*?" Uche said.

"Power hungry," Theodore said.

"Throwing his weight around."

"Forgetting he is a man of God."

"We need to do something about this crazy priest!" Bennet said.

They all chimed in.

"We can't stand for this."

"No, we cannot!"

They understood the larger implications. In a tiny village like Enugwu-Ukwu, so cut off from the rest of the world, those village priests could get arrogant and start thinking of themselves as gods. The Vatican is supposed to have safeguards in place so Roman Catholic priests around the world remember that their loyalties are to God, and to Jesus, and not to their own egos. But supervision in a remote place like Enugwu-Ukwu is lax. Priests in the village had been going rogue. In fact, more broadly, self-appointed gods had been turning up in the name of all sorts of religions, all over Nigeria, a country where corruption had become the norm in business, politics, and even worship.

Throw dirt, give me money, do what I say. It's God's law! You want to go to heaven, don't you? Kill somebody, kill yourself, kidnap some schoolgirls, marry them, it's the law. There are villagers who don't know any better. There are villagers who don't read or write. Everybody wants to go to heaven.

"The pope is going to lose Africa if he doesn't do something about this," Mie-Mie said to the others.

"We need to do something about this!"

"We should write to the pope."

"Let's write to the pope!"

"We owe it to the pope to report this and help him."

Emails flew. It was the principle. An Omalu stands for principle. An Omalu thinks he can help the pope save Africa. An Omalu is obligated to do his and her share to help the world rid itself of religious militant terrorist organizations. Onyemalukwube is the name in its full version. "If you know, come forth and speak."

Theodore made the point that there was the more pressing matter of arranging Oba's funeral celebration, and Oba needed a proper Catholic burial.

So the family agreed to sign whatever the parish priest wanted them to sign. They approved the priest's schedule for the funeral day, including the dirt-throwing part. They would deal with that priest later.

Alone at night, lying in bed in the dark listening to the familiar screech of crickets, Bennet thinks about how trivial these village matters might seem to people back home in America. Then again, a lot of American affairs would seem preposterous to villagers. *Football?* Everyone getting all upset over . . . a game?

It's good to see things from a distance, he thinks. It's good to have two points of view like that, to see your tiny village from the viewpoint of America and to look at America from the viewpoint of a tiny village. That kind of perspective stretches you.

Recently, back home in America, Bennet got a job offer to become chief medical examiner of Washington, D.C. It's a huge honor. Probably the fanciest title a forensic pathologist

could get. The office has a $9 million budget, provides foren-
sic services for everyone from local crime victims to senators
to foreign dignitaries.

Prema had a hard time breathing when she heard about
that one.

"*Outskirts*, Bennet," she said. "You belong on the outskirts, remember?" A high-profile position like that would be
a political nightmare, she said.

"Okay, Prema."

Bailes got excited when he heard about the offer. "Are you
kidding me?" he said. "Bennet, that's an amazing opportunity. You'll end up dining with Obama!"

"Okay, Julian," Bennet said.

After thinking about it for two weeks, after flying back
and forth to Washington to get wined and dined, Bennet decided Prema was right. A political nightmare. Four of the last
six guys who had held the post had left in scandal.

He turned the offer down.

"I belong on the outskirts," he told Bailes.

"I don't understand you at all," Bailes said.

Oh, Julian, Bennet thinks, lying in the darkness of his
room in the compound. *A guy like that will never understand
a guy like me.* He kicks the sheet off, wishes there was a fan
or something to put in here. The only air-conditioned room in
the compound is Oba's old room. Theodore's in there now.
Theodore is head of the family now.

Bennet folds his hands under his head, thinks how different his life in America would be if he made the move to D.C.
He searches his heart and finds no regret. He likes working
out of his garage in Lodi. *I really like it!* He's still trying to
figure out suicide, why some depressed people kill themselves
and some, like him, do not. He no longer suffers debilitating

depression, but he recognizes the fragility, feels the lurking; there has to be something in the brain. Most of his CTE research continues to be geared toward finding a way to diagnose the disease in living people; he and Bailes and Fitzsimmons have teamed up with a guy at UCLA and they now have a patent for the test. People still contact Bennet and ask him to autopsy brains and look for CTE, and he'll still do it, although he is less inclined to drop everything and jump at the chance than he once was.

The last time he jumped at the chance was May 2012, and the experience did not go well.

It was a Saturday and Bailes was calling him with the news that one of the hardest-hitting linebackers ever to play the game, the NFL superstar Junior Seau, had just committed suicide.

"Who?" Bennet said.

Bailes explained the significance. Seau was a league institution—he had played for twenty years—a ferocious tackler with charisma for the ages, beloved off the field as much as on. A first-round pick in 1990, Seau spent most of his career with the San Diego Chargers. He racked up fifty-six career sacks and was named to twelve Pro Bowls, but his end-zone dance and signature smile were what captivated fans. He had a way of making you love the game as much as he did. San Diego embraced him. He started a foundation for disadvantaged kids, he had a TV show, a restaurant, a clothing line, and a three-million-dollar home. His decline after his retirement in 2010 was gradual at first; only those closest to him could see what was happening. His memory slipping, crippling insomnia. Then his temper started flaring, and he became reckless. He gambled away his money. In 2010 he beat up his girlfriend and got arrested for it, and that same day drove his Cadillac off a hundred-foot cliff. Somehow he survived. He said he fell asleep; he wasn't trying to kill himself. But then on May 2, 2012, alone in his Oceanside, California, home, he pulled the trigger on a .357 Magnum revolver. He shot himself in the chest, as Duerson had done. He was forty-three. They found a paper in the kitchen on which he had scribbled lyrics to the country song "Who I Ain't."

Seau's celebrity status made his brain the most coveted specimen yet, and as soon as Bailes heard the news, he suggested that Bennet go get it and look for CTE. So Bennet called Seau's son and got permission. He booked a flight to San Diego and he brought a cooler. He assisted in the autopsy, took the brain out, cut it, and put it in a jar of formalin, as usual. But there in that dank, windowless morgue, before he even took off his rubber gloves, the chaos started.

Other people were calling the Seau family, telling them not to give Omalu the brain. Nowinski was calling, saying he wanted the brain. The Boston group had, after all, been designated the NFL's official brain bank.

The Seau family was confused. Two different groups wanted Junior's brain? Who were these people? How does a grieving family, still in shock, even begin to understand that?

At the same time that Nowinski was calling, the NFL was calling the Seau family. Despite the fact that Boston was the league's designated brain bank, the NFL didn't want Seau's brain to go to Boston. They were fed up with Boston. By this time, Boston was diagnosing CTE in brains with regularity, and with each new diagnosis came more bad PR for the NFL. In a study Boston commissioned, seventy-six of seventy-nine player brains showed signs of CTE.

The NFL wanted to take the narrative back. They would start with the Seau brain.

The Seau family was confused. *Three* different groups wanted Junior's brain?

Bennet stood in the San Diego morgue with his gloves on and his open cooler. "If you please, the family said I could take the brain," he said.

"I'm sorry," the chaplain for the medical examiner's office said. He said the Seau family had just called to rescind its consent. "The brain is going to the NIH."

"The NIH?" Bennet said.

The NIH? people like Nowinski wondered.

It was the first time during this whole saga that people had heard of the NIH expressing an interest in CTE research. Where was this coming from?

It was coming from the league's new concussion committee—the group it formed after it disbanded the deeply flawed MTBI committee. For its newly created Head, Neck, and Spine Committee, the NFL had chosen a brain expert to lead the research: Dr. Russell Lonser, chief of surgical neurology at the NIH.

So the NFL and the NIH were now partnered.

"I'm sorry, Dr. Omalu," the chaplain said, while Bennet pulled off his gloves.

"But," Bennet said, "I don't think you want to give this brain to the NFL."

"The family has decided," the chaplain said, and he showed Bennet the door.

Alone in the taxi, Bennet sat next to his empty cooler and he broke down and wept. He would learn later that the San Diego Chargers' team doctor had told the Seau family that Bennet was a fraud, that "his research is bad and his ethics are bad."

. . .

Shortly after the NIH got the Seau brain, the NFL gave the NIH $30 million, the largest philanthropic gift in league history. Goodell made the announcement the same day the league kicked off the 2012 season. "Our goal is to aggressively partner with the best scientists to understand more about the brain and brain injuries," he said, sounding very much like his predecessor, Paul Tagliabue, who had set up the MTBI committee back in 1994 with the same stated mission. And yet NFL-funded research had only derailed the national conversation—its paid scientists seeking to silence independent researchers who disagreed with its findings. Was it going to be different this time around?

The $30 million gift to the NIH put the NFL back in control of the science of concussions. It would be like the tobacco industry leading cancer research.

In January 2013, Junior Seau's brain tested positive for CTE. Like so many, the Seau family started understanding that the problem wasn't the fault of the man who seemed to have gone crazy. A disease. Junior had had a disease. The Seau family learned about other players, so many other families, with similar tragic stories. Football caused the disease. Football made them crazy. And the league had known about it.

The Seau family joined the consolidated lawsuits against the NFL that had started with Luckasevic's initial filing. The massive tort—a combined effort of more than forty law firms representing thousands of former players—was winding its way through the courts and was now headed by David Frederick, a high-profile Washington lawyer who had argued cases in front of the U.S. Supreme Court. The NFL's chief outside counsel was, notably, Covington & Burling, a major player defending Big Tobacco in the tobacco wars in the 1980s. Tagliabue now worked for the firm.

The NFL stood to lose $2.5 billion if it lost its fight against the players. On the other hand, the players, some of whom urgently needed help, might not live long enough to collect anything if the suit was allowed to continue to crawl through years of legal proceedings—to say nothing of the time on appeals if the players won.

The federal judge, Anita Brody of United States District Court for the Eastern District of Pennsylvania, ordered mediation. The two sides would have to compromise to resolve the fight. In 2013 they reached a settlement: the league would pay $765 million plus legal fees.

The players and their lawyers did the math. Would there be enough money to go around? Even the judge was skeptical. She ordered the NFL to produce actuarial data. How many players were we talking about, in the end? How many NFL players were likely to go crazy as a result of football?

One third, the report showed. One third of all NFL players were likely to develop football-related dementia, and at "notably younger ages" than the general population. And that was by the NFL's calculations.

Brody sent the league back to the table to come up with a better deal for the players.

On April 22, 2015, she approved a new "uncapped settlement" that would cost the NFL about $1 billion over the next sixty-five years. The players did the math again. Under the terms of the agreement, the average award a player will receive is about $190,000.

Plenty of people will say the deal stinks. Luckasevic will say the deal stinks, and his heart will sink because of it. He will tell anyone who cares to listen that the attorneys handling the negotiations failed to do right by the players. (When lawsuits are consolidated into one massive class action suit, the individual attorneys who originally filed yield to the appointed leaders.)

Mediation meant that the case would never go to trial, so there would be no public vetting. Tagliabue would never have to explain his flawed MTBI committee, or what a rheumatologist was doing heading it, or why the NFL turned a blind eye to the work of independent scientists. Goodell would never have to disclose what he knew about the risk of concussions and when he knew it. The settlement is not an admission of guilt. Moreover, under the terms of the agreement, players who died before 2006 are disqualified from receiving anything. There would be nothing for Mike Webster's family or Terry Long's or Justin Strzelczyk's.

Nor would any funds be provided for future players diagnosed with CTE.

About two hundred families, including some of Luckasevic's clients, will opt out of the settlement. Seau's family will opt out, choosing instead to go after the NFL personally in a suit alleging wrongful death.

Luckasevic and other lawyers will fight to keep the cases alive in an effort to force the NFL to answer for what they did; let the public hear this, over and over again, until it sinks in:

The league lied. They had the evidence and chose to ignore it. They had the evidence at least since 2005, when one unlikely scientist, a man from nowhere who would not go away, who would not back down, found proof.

Nobody talks about any of these matters, or any of Bennet's research, in Enugwu-Ukwu. It's as if that story is unfolding on another planet, or in another century. If anyone here in the village mentions Bennet's work at all, it's "He's a doctor!" and "He lives in America!" Is there anything else?

Right now he's with Oba, dressing him. Armed guards are stationed outside the doors of the village morgue, a concrete hut set back on the edge of the jungle spreading out toward an infinite green. Nobody but Bennet gets in to see Oba.

"To be able to see many points of view," Bennet is saying, alone with his father's corpse. "That is what school does for you, all right." It feels wonderful to have these last moments with his dad, even though he's dead—for Bennet, a mere technicality. "Everything you said was right, Daddy."

There's not a lot of light in here. It's so crude compared to what Bennet has become used to. The table is wooden, a little fan whirs by the window, and red dirt has been tracked in from outside so the old linoleum floor feels gritty.

They did a good job with the embalming, Bennet thinks. No fluids. Everything nice and solid. Excellent preservation. Winny, Uche, and Mie-Mie especially will be happy to know that.

"You were so right, Daddy," he says, again, running a washcloth over his father's cold arms. "I got my education and everything you said was right." He picks up his father's hand, checks the nails for dirt. He wants him to be perfectly groomed for the funeral, and for God.

The robe his sisters provided is white satin. The mahogany casket Mie-Mie bought is top of the line. It's electric. Push a button, and the top pops open! *That is something else.*

"There are many people here to praise you, Daddy, and I am proud to be your son."

He wipes the cloth over his father's face, gently dabbing his eyes and then his lips. He bends over and kisses him.

"I am trying to stay true to myself like you told me," he says. "I am trying to live up to the Omalu name.

"Ka anyï kpe ekpere." Let us pray.

. . .

Up by the gate at the compound, one brown goat with stubby horns looks on, doesn't challenge the rope attaching it to a croton shrub ready to bloom. The gravediggers work up here in tandem. The earth is packed tight as clay, so this will take some time.

As soon as the gravediggers are done it will be time to bury Oba here, next to his mother's grave.

In the meantime, they have a parade. The pallbearers are dressed in colorful red, yellow, and black traditional vestments, and one of them has a horn. Another follows with a drum. They carry the casket and dance with it, around the village, under the billboards and around in the streets, while the family follows. The drumming and the horns create a collective trance.

The paraders stop at the house where Oba was born. The pallbearers put the casket down and the music stops. It is time to open the casket. A pallbearer pushes the button. The top opens with a slow hum, and there is Oba, a small dark head above flowing white satin garments.

"Daddy! Daddy!" Winny cries, collapsing.

"Daddy!" Uche wails.

Theodore and Chizoba come to their sisters' aid.

Mie-Mie holds her mother tight. Ikem stands tall, chanting prayers, and Bennet stands back.

When they close the casket, the drumming starts again, and then the horn. The parade continues through the village and Bennet dances in front of the casket, slaps it with his open hand, kisses it and slaps.

The gravediggers have finished. The hole is deep and red, with perfectly straight sides. Just beyond the grave, forty women in green smocks down the hill have begun setting up their giant iron pots, while teams of wiry men without shoes sharpen knives and a cleaver. The goat has been ushered to the man with the cleaver. Three cows have already been slaughtered. There will be plenty of meat for all.

Standing around the grave, the family is dressed all in white in traditional cotton robes. A hard rain has fallen and so the air feels sharp and the sun stings. The men with their long straps lower Oba's casket into the grave and the priest in gold vestments chants his prayers and rattles his sprinkler of holy water over Oba. Then he steps back, folds his red prayer book, and nods to the men with the shovels to stand back to make way for the wife, who will please come forward now and throw the first fistful of dirt.

All eyes go to Iyom. Tiny and round, a white scarf folded with great flourish on her head, she has her body pressed against the compound wall, pushing against that wall.

"She will not throw dirt," Winny says, standing in front of her mother.

"She must," the priest says.

"She will not," Uche says, and moves next to Winny.

"She must!"

Theodore comes forward. *"She will not."* He goes full-tuba with the proclamation, shouting it, and that's when the fighting starts.

She will not! She must! You promised! You signed! This has nothing to do with the Catholic Church! She must! She must! It's the law! You signed!

"You signed the papers! It's the law!"

"This is bullshit, Father, this is bullshit bullshit bullshit!"

"He will not go to heaven unless she throws the dirt!"

"Who do you think you are?"

"I will leave! I will not bless Oba. He will not go to heaven!"

"Go ahead, leave, you are not welcome here. You are supposed to be a man of God, you use your power to trick people, you must be stopped, you will be stopped!"

"He will not go to heaven if I leave. I will leave if she does not throw dirt this instant!"

Theodore's voice is now one hundred tubas, arms flailing, men nose to nose, Chizoba frozen with his mouth dropped in horror, and Bennet shouting his outrage in rapid-fire bursts, and Winny screaming and Mie-Mie screaming and Uche screaming and their mother crouched, pushing against the wall.

It's an Igbo-style fight, no one backing down, sweat flying, spit spurting, everyone ready for blows, until finally Bennet jumps all at once out of the fray, jumps out of that hot circle of rage, steps to the outskirts, and looks down into the open grave.

He's holding a rose. He looks down at Oba's casket. Oba all alone down there. All the fighting up here.

"Bye-bye, Daddy!" Bennet shouts. And throws the rose.

Everyone watches the flower tumble down into the hole, the first thing to land on the casket. Not dirt—a rose. Not the wife—a son. And so what? The rose on the casket officially and without surrender ends the battle, and the shovelers move in quickly with the dirt.

The music starts. The priest storms off. The gates open and the villagers come rushing in. Families with gifts, a goat or a cow, or cases of beer, brandy, yams, bags of semolina. They will be handed a microphone, and they will shout over the drumming, they will shout in praise of Oba, over the drumming and the horn blowing by the village man who

won't stop for days. Theodore will record the gifts and the
Igbo elders will stand and wave sacred fans and the brandy
and kola nuts won't stop. Some of the mourners bring teams
of dancers, or more drummers, or masquerade shows, and
Theodore will throw money at them in thanks while they per-
form. Ikem and Chizoba will throw money. Winny, Uche, and
Mie-Mie will announce the next group at the top of the hill
and throw money. It goes on like this for four days, constant
parades and dancing and drumming and the horn. Behind the
house, under the tents a band plays Afrobeat funk and hip-
hop tunes, and down the hill there's another band, and across
the road another, the music and parties in pockets. Buckets of
rice and stew and slaw come up constantly from the bottom
of the hill where the cooks work nonstop, and the man with
the cleaver keeps slaughtering.

Bennet floats in and out of the festival. He'll have a brandy
with his brothers, beer with his sisters, and some kola nuts.
He'll throw money, dance with his sisters. Then he'll wave,
slip away, go to his room, and read.

When he gets home to America, he begins composing his
letter to the pope.

ACKNOWLEDGMENTS

Concussion grew out of an article, "Game Brain," that I wrote for Andy Ward in 2009 when he was an editor at *GQ*. He asked me to dramatize a subject that had already been expertly covered by journalists who'd done the heavy lifting of investigative reporting before me, and to whom I am indebted. My thanks to Andy for giving me the opportunity to enter the national conversation, and to Bennet Omalu for allowing me the privilege of unearthing his forgotten piece of the story.

Bennet sat with me over the course of many years recounting the events of his life in Nigeria and in America. He wrote long passages of introspection, some of which appear in these pages, set in italics. Based on these interviews, and hundreds of others with key players in the story, I've re-created scenes as accurately as an informed imagination will allow. My goal was to tell *Bennet's* version of the events leading up to, and the subsequent fallout after, his discovery of CTE. How did this saga play out through his eyes? Bennet gave me permission to document that journey, and we joined forces as honestly as two people could in entering an agreement like that. If there were profits to be made from the product of our work, we would divvy them up, but the main thing was that he would have to give me complete editorial control. He wouldn't get to edit himself. He wouldn't get to read the book until after it was published. He would have to trust me. So Bennet handed over the reins of his legacy to me. I don't know how you thank a person for something that enormous, but I am trying to do that here. Thank you, Bennet, for your fearless willingness to bestow trust.

Thank you to the Omalu family—Theodore, Winny, Uche, Ikem, Chizoba, Mie-Mie, Iyom, and Prema—for opening the doors into their homes and touring me through their memories. Thanks to Julian Bailes and Bob Fitzsimmons for their guidance through the maze, and to the many players and their families, notably Fred and Tia McNeill, who provided an intimate glimpse into what it's like to live with trauma-induced dementia.

I am grateful to Jim Nelson at *GQ* for his early and continued support for telling Bennet's story—and for continuing to champion this kind of long-form journalism—and to the editors who shaped related stories, notably Joel Lovell, Raha Naddaf, Mike Benoist, and Geoff Gagnon; and to researchers Elaine Vitone, Christopher Swetala, Rachel Wilkinson, and Riley Blanton, who dug until they found the treasures.

Elyse Cheney, my agent, ignited the idea of expanding Bennet's story into a book, and she became its ferocious advocate. I am grateful to her for her fearless wisdom and guidance, and to Alex Jacobs and Sam Freilich at the agency.

Here again I come to Andy Ward, now at Random House, for championing the book project along with Susan Kamil, and to Kaela Myers and the others at Random House who made it real, and to Amelia Zalcman for protecting it. I'm thankful to so many of my writer friends who listened and lent courage, namely Wil Hylton, Mike Paterniti, Bill Lychack,

Peter Trachtenberg, Rebecca Skloot, BK, Nancy Mosser Bailey, Kit Ayars, Sally Wiggin, Lynn Cullen, and give special thanks to Jeff Oaks, Geeta Kothari, and Nancy Kirkwood for holding up the fort at the Writing Program while I took leave.

Don Bialostosky, chair of the English Department at the University of Pittsburgh, provided much needed support. My thanks to him and to John Cooper, dean of the Dietrich School of Arts and Sciences, for the patronage.

I'm deeply grateful to all the movie people who committed to telling Bennet's story on-screen: to Giannina Scott for embracing the project with such passion and love, along with Ridley Scott for championing it and the amazing Peter Landesman who pulled off the impossible, to Elizabeth Cantillon, David Crockett, Michael Schaefer, Salvatore Totino, Amal Baggar, Larry Shuman, CAA agent Matthew Snyder, and especially to David Wolthoff for never giving up. My thanks to Will Smith for bringing Bennet to life on-screen with such dignity and grace.

I would like to thank Mark Fainaru-Wada and Steve Fainaru, whose extraordinary book, *League of Denial,* stands as the most comprehensive, encyclopedic account of the history of the National Football League's mishandling of the crisis of traumatic brain injury among players.

A final word of thanks to my giant, supportive family that gives me my footing, notably my husband, Alex; my daughters, Anna and Sasha; and my parents, John and Claire Laskas, whose steady prayers from heaven are duly noted.

AUTHOR'S NOTE

The Bennet Omalu Foundation is a nonprofit organization committed to funding research, finding cures, and providing care for people suffering from traumatic brain injuries and chronic traumatic encephalopathy. Visit thebraintrust foundation.org for information on how to help.

He just wanted a decent book to read ...

Not too much to ask, is it? It was in 1935 when Allen Lane, Managing Director of Bodley Head Publishers, stood on a platform at Exeter railway station looking for something good to read on his journey back to London. His choice was limited to popular magazines and poor-quality paperbacks – the same choice faced every day by the vast majority of readers, few of whom could afford hardbacks. Lane's disappointment and subsequent anger at the range of books generally available led him to found a company – and change the world.

'We believed in the existence in this country of a vast reading public for intelligent books at a low price, and staked everything on it'
Sir Allen Lane, 1902–1970, founder of Penguin Books

The quality paperback had arrived – and not just in bookshops. Lane was adamant that his Penguins should appear in chain stores and tobacconists, and should cost no more than a packet of cigarettes.

Reading habits (and cigarette prices) have changed since 1935, but Penguin still believes in publishing the best books for everybody to enjoy. We still believe that good design costs no more than bad design, and we still believe that quality books published passionately and responsibly make the world a better place.

So wherever you see the little bird – whether it's on a piece of prize-winning literary fiction or a celebrity autobiography, political tour de force or historical masterpiece, a serial-killer thriller, reference book, world classic or a piece of pure escapism – you can bet that it represents the very best that the genre has to offer.

Whatever you like to read – trust Penguin.